1977

GIANTS OF THE FAITH

GIANTS
OF THE FAITH

CONVERSIONS WHICH
CHANGED THE WORLD

John A. O'Brien

THE UNIVERSITY OF NOTRE DAME

HANOVER HOUSE
Garden City, New York

Nihil Obstat: ALOYSIUS J. MEHR, O.S.C.
　　　　　　　 Censor Deputatus
Imprimatur: ✠ LEO A. PURSLEY
　　　　　　　 Bishop of Fort Wayne

Library of Congress Catalog Card Number: 57–12473

TO
Most Reverend Leo A. Pursley, D.D.
Bishop of Fort Wayne
Zealous Shepherd of Souls
With Sentiments of Warm Esteem
The Author Dedicates This Book

Contents

Preface

THE INSPIRATION OF GREAT MEN

When one views from a great distance the vast sweep of the snow-covered Alpine mountain ridge, he sees the lordly Matterhorn and the Jungfrau towering up, high above the others, into the Swiss skies. They dominate the mountain range, give direction to the traveler afar, and print upon his memory a lasting impression. Those peaks gleaming with the eternal snows symbolize for him the glorious summits where earth and heaven meet; their white and silent immensities speak of their brave battle with the elements and their proud victory over the biting teeth of uncounted aeons of time. Like Mount Ararat jutting up above the waters covering the earth, and offering refuge and rest to the dwellers in Noah's ark, these Alpine peaks seem to offer repose to the tired and weary spirit of man.

So, too, when one views the expansive panorama of the nineteen centuries of the Christian era, he sees certain characters towering up above their fellows, dominating with their genius and accomplishments the ages in which they lived. Not infrequently they symbolize the spirit and genius of their generation and offer light and inspiration to all who come after them. To know them intimately is to understand much of their respective eras and to discover the secret of their influence and leadership.

"The history of the world," observed Carlyle, "is but the biography of great men." Certainly it is the most interesting, fascinating, and inspiring part of that history. The imprint of their thought and work is discernible on the subsequent ages. "A man Caesar is born," remarked Emerson, "and for ages after we have a Roman Empire. Christ is born, and millions of minds so grow and cleave to His genius, that He is confounded with virtue and the possible of man. An institution is the lengthened shadow of one man."

When we gaze at the moving panorama of the first century of the Christian era, we see the mighty figure of Paul, Apostle to the Gentiles, towering up above his fellows. Moving up from the apostolic age to that of the Fathers and Doctors of the Church, we find St. Augustine, the ornament of the African Church, looming up above all his contemporaries.

Taking a leap from the ancient to the modern world, we come to the two great figures, Cardinal Newman and Gilbert K. Chesterton, ornaments of the Church of Britain. Among the many notables in the history of the Church in America stand out Orestes Brownson and Isaac Hecker, both of whom have left the imprint of their thought and genius upon their times.

What heightens interest in these leaders is that each is a convert. By the genius of their intellects, aided of course by the grace of God, they worked their way out of the wilderness of contemporary error into the Ark of the Covenant and the Church of the living God: the trysting place of all spiritual and religious truth.

Paul came from Judaism, Augustine from Manichaeism and pagan sensuality; Newman threaded his way back to the Apostolic Church, only to find it identical in doctrine with the Catholic Church of his day. Groping his way through the nebulous fog of Unitarianism, Chesterton arrived at the halfway stage of Anglicanism, only to discover it is but the vestibule to the divinely established temple of truth.

Brownson's pilgrimage was characterized by many detours: freeing himself from the gloomy heritage of Calvinism, he swung to the extreme of Universalism, edged back into Unitarianism, toyed momentarily with the thought of Anglicanism, only to perceive there can be no logical stopping place short of the one universal Church which spans all the centuries of the Christian era. Hecker's journey began in the home atmosphere of Methodism, moved into the latitudinarianism of the New England transcendentalists, only to find the fullness of divine revelation in the historic Mother Church of Christendom.

The most stirring drama in human life is that which is enacted in the inner theater of the soul: the ceaseless and unwearying quest for God and the Church established by Him to lead the pilgrim from earth to heaven. Here are pathos, travail, terror, heartthrob, daring, and high adventure. In comparison with that great enterprise, upon which a soul's destiny depends, all other undertakings are humdrum, prosaic and pedestrian affairs.

Because the method by which each of these giants found his way to the pillar and ground of truth, the Church of the living God, is calculated to offer help and guidance to every truth seeker, we have developed that phase of the life of each with great care and in some detail. The earnest searcher for divine truth will find that many of the difficulties, obscurities, and road blocks which confront him were encountered likewise by these six pilgrims: they turned those road blocks into steppingstones and thus show him that he, too, can accomplish the same feat.

The Almighty stands ready now, as in days gone by, to help each wayfarer find his way, if he will but turn to God in prayer. Prayer is not a one-directional line: reciprocation is of its very essence, for God both listens and replies. Says James Russell Lowell:

> *God is not dumb, that he should speak no more;*
> *If thou hast wanderings in the wilderness*
> *And find'st not Sinai, 'tis thy soul is poor.*

Not only will the reader find in the study of these giants of the faith the sure path to the Church of the living God but also the help and inspiration to live high and noble lives as members of the Mystical Body of Christ. "Precept," observed William Ellery Channing, "is instruction written in the sand. The tide flows over it, and the record is gone. Example is graven on the rock, and the lesson is not soon lost."

With the hope that the stories of these great giants of the faith will provide light and inspiration not only to all truth seekers but also to all men and women eager to live upright and holy lives, we send this book on its way with the humble prayer that the "Giver of every good and perfect gift" will shower His infinitely greater light, blessings, and graces upon all its readers.

Acknowledgments

The author is indebted to the many scholars who have favored him with their thought and suggestions concerning the selection as well as the treatment of the spiritual giants featured in this study, especially Professor Jacques Maritain. He acknowledges the kindness of the following friends who have read the sections of the manuscript within their special fields: Professors Eugene P. Burke, C.S.C., Thomas Barrosse, C.S.C., and Paul McLane, Ph.D., of the University of Notre Dame, Aloys Dirksen, C.PP.S., of St. Charles Seminary, and Dr. Vincent F. Holden, C.S.P. He is grateful to Thomas T. McAvoy, C.S.C., Archivist at Notre Dame, for making the wealth of documentary material on Brownson and Hecker available.

He also wishes to express his profound gratitude to the following publishers and individuals for permission to quote gratis from these books:

Sheed and Ward, Inc. (New York), Hutchinson & Co. (London), and Miss Dorothy Collins for permission to quote from *The Autobiography of G. K. Chesterton*, copyright 1936 by Frances Chesterton, published by Sheed and Ward, Inc., New York.

Sheed and Ward, Inc. (New York), and Miss Dorothy Collins for permission to quote from:

> *The Well and the Shallows*, by G. K. Chesterton, published by Sheed and Ward, Inc., New York.
>
> *Gilbert Keith Chesterton*, by Maisie Ward, copyright 1943, Sheed and Ward, Inc., New York.

John Lane the Bodley Head, Ltd., for permission to quote from:

> *Heretics*, by G. K. Chesterton, published by John Lane the Bodley Head, Ltd., London.

Dodd, Mead & Company (New York) and John Lane the Bodley Head, Ltd., for permission to quote from:

> *Orthodoxy*, by G. K. Chesterton, published by Dodd, Mead & Company (New York), copyright, 1908, by Dodd, Mead & Company; renewal, 1935, by G. K. Chesterton.

Dodd, Mead & Company (New York), Methuen and Co., Ltd. (London), and Miss Dorothy Collins for permission to quote from:

> *Fancies Versus Fads*, by G. K. Chesterton, published by Dodd, Mead & Company, New York.

Faber and Faber, Ltd., and Miss Dorothy Collins for permission to quote from:

Chaucer, by G. K. Chesterton, published by Faber and Faber, Ltd., London.

Miss Dorothy Collins for permission to quote from:
"The Convert," *Collected Poems,* by G. K. Chesterton.

The Macmillan Co. and Miss Dorothy Collins for permission to quote from:
The Catholic Church and Conversion, by G. K. Chesterton, copyright 1926, published by The Macmillan Co., New York.

Doubleday & Company, Inc. (New York), Hodder and Stoughton, Ltd. (London), and Miss Dorothy Collins for permission to quote from:
St. Francis of Assisi, by G. K. Chesterton, copyright 1924 by Doubleday & Company, Inc., New York.

Little, Brown and Co. and Arthur M. Schlesinger, Jr., for permission to quote from:
Orestes A. Brownson, by Arthur M. Schlesinger, Jr., copyright 1939 by Arthur M. Schlesinger, Jr., published by Little, Brown and Co., Boston.

Estate of Hilaire Belloc for permission to quote from two letters written by Hilaire Belloc to G. K. Chesterton.

Estate of Maurice Baring for permission to quote from two letters written by Maurice Baring to G. K. Chesterton.

GIANTS OF THE FAITH

ST. PAUL
Apostle of the Gentiles

I. THE DRAMA ON THE ROAD TO DAMASCUS

Towering above all the Apostles and disciples is the mighty figure of St. Paul, the Apostle of the Gentiles, who with flaming zeal and tireless industry spread the faith of Christ throughout the countries of the Mediterranean world. So inexhaustible was his energy and so matchless his skill in preaching the Gospel to the multitudinous tribes and races which peopled the vast Greco-Roman world that he might well be called the trumpeter of God and the chief herald of the Christian Gospel. For more than nineteen centuries he has stood as the missionary par excellence of the Christian faith, its greatest convert maker, and the model for all seeking to extend Christ's kingdom among the souls of men.

Unlike many of the great orators of the past, who stirred multitudes with their eloquence but left no written record of their soaring utterances, Paul's words and thoughts have come down to us in large measure in his immortal epistles. In addition, his missionary labors and his teaching fill most of the Acts of the Apostles. These pages, along with his fourteen epistles, form almost half of the New Testament, so that he has not inaptly been called the second founder of the Christian faith.

The character, personality, and genius of Paul have long been subjects of absorbing interest and endless research, while his life is one of the most colorful and dramatic of all the missionaries of Christ. His message is of perennial interest and was never more needed than today. A greater knowledge of Paul and a deeper insight into his thought inevitably brings one closer to Christ, in whom the Apostle sought to live. "I live," said Paul, "now, not I; but Christ liveth in me."

With the help of modern research we shall try to bring this many-sided genius to life again, to see the drama that transformed him from an archenemy of Christ into His dauntless champion, to witness his unwearying labors and to hear his eloquent and persuasive discourses to Jews, proselytes, Greeks, Romans, and all the other people whom he sought to win for the Crucified. It is a fascinating story, replete with adventure, pulsing with inspiration, and rich in spiritual values.

"I am a Jew, and I was born at Tarsus in Cilicia." Thus did Paul introduce himself to the Jews rioting against him in Jerusalem. Proud to be a Jew, he was proud too of his native city, to which he refers as "no insignificant city." Tarsus was the capital of Cilicia, a Roman province, lying at the northeast corner of the Mediterranean where Turkey joins the continent of Asia.

Now an obscure Turkish town of 34,000 people, Tarsus was then a flourishing center of trade and commerce, teeming with three hundred thousand inhabitants. The river Cydnus linked it to the port of Rhegna, thus giving it an outlet to the Mediterranean and making it a rival of Athens and Alexandria in trade and culture. Its temples were filled with the idols of Greece and the Orient.

When Paul was a boy in Tarsus, a marble statue of Sardanapalus, the deified founder of the city, stood at one side of the entrance gate. On its pedestal was carved the pagan motto, "Eat, drink, enjoy thyself; the rest is nothing." On the other side stood a statue of Queen Semiramis, the Assyrian version of Astarte and Aphrodite. Paul often had to pass between these two representatives of pagan morality, and as he grew up he came to know of the debaucheries that accompanied their festival worship. Fifty years later, when he had occasion to excoriate those who surrender themselves to the lusts of the flesh, these Eastern orgies came to his mind as he wrote the first chapter of the Epistle to the Romans.

Paul was born at the beginning of the Christian era and was probably a few years younger than Christ. His birth in Tarsus made him technically a Hellenist—a Jew born outside Palestine—but he was a Hebrew in blood, culture, sentiment, and religion. He tells the Philippians that he was "circumcised the eighth day, of the race of

Israel, of the tribe of Benjamin, a Hebrew of Hebrews; as regards the Law, a Pharisee."

The Talmud says that a father's duty toward his son is "to circumcise him, to teach him the law, and to teach him a trade." Paul's father fulfilled this threefold obligation to the letter. He taught his son the trade of tentmaker—a trade common in Cilicia where mountain goats with thick shaggy coats abounded. The natives wove this hair into stiff rough cloth used for tents, carpets, and waterproof cloaks worn by shepherds and caravan leaders.

It is quite probable that the father operated a workshop where such fabrics were woven, and was thus enabled to provide an exceptionally good education for his gifted son. Instead of looking with scorn upon manual labor, after the fashion of the Greeks and Romans, Israel held it in high esteem. Indeed it was customary for her intellectuals, even the Doctors of the Law, to work at a trade: they were artisans or workmen, carpenters like the famous Rabbi Hillel, blacksmiths like Rabbi Isaac, and stewards like Rabbi Oschia.

Paul gloried in his trade and even in the midst of the multitudinous preoccupations of his missionary apostolate earned his living so as not to be a burden to the faithful. He liked to show his hands calloused from the rough work of the loom, exclaiming, "these hands of mine have provided for my needs and those of my companions."

When Paul was circumcised he received a name highly honored, especially in the tribe of Benjamin: the name borne by the first King of Israel, *Saul,* meaning "the desired." It was the custom of Jews settled in Hellenic lands to take also a Greek name, which they used in their relations with pagan society. As *Saulos* in Greek suggests a man who sways on his feet, it would scarcely have been suitable. *Paulos* was preferable: it recalled a glorious name in Roman history and it is not improbable that some ancestor of Paul had received the right to use it from an authentic Paul. "Saul, also called Paul," Luke was to say in speaking of his master.

The two names the boy of Tarsus was to bear symbolized his double spiritual inheritance and his twofold mission: first to the Jews, then to the Gentiles. Though living in a Greek city, the son of the Torah grew up in a Jewish environment, to which he remained ardently faithful. His family belonged to the sect of Pharisees, who prided themselves on "raising the hedge of the Law still higher." At home the family spoke Aramaic, then the common language of

the Jews and the one spoken by Jesus. The family also knew sufficient Hebrew to recite their prayers in the sacred tongue. Paul was
reared according to the pedagogy prescribed by the *Sayings of the
Fathers:* "At five years read the Bible; at ten years study the Mish-
nah, the tradition of the Ancients; at thirteen observe all the precepts." The written Law contained 613 precepts, while the oral Law
comprised a much larger number.

From his earliest youth Paul was trained in the Law, immersed
in the traditions and lore of Israel, and engrossed in the teachings
of the rabbis and Doctors of the Law. Thus Paul grew up an ardent
Israelite, "a Hebrew of Hebrews" he was later to characterize himself, and this intense Jewish training was to leave upon him an indelible imprint. Later on he was to cherish in his mind the words
of Jesus, "Salvation is from the Jews," and no one believed this more
firmly than he. Even after he suffered so much at the hands of his
former co-religionists he refused to disown them and uttered that
marvelous cry of loyalty and attachment: "I could wish to be anathema myself from Christ for the sake of my brethren, who are my
kinsmen according to the flesh; who are Israelites, who have the
adoption of sons, and the glory and the covenants and the legislation
and the worship and the promises."

In spite of all his ardent attachment to Israel and its rich spiritual
legacy, Paul could not escape daily contact with the Hellenic world,
its spectacles, customs, literature, and culture. Outside home he
spoke Greek, a fluent familiar Greek which he had acquired without teachers; it was to stand him in good stead when he began to
proclaim the "good tidings" to the numerous tribes and races in the
vast Hellenic world. Intelligent and quick-witted as he was, Paul
could not remain indifferent to the manifestations of an extremely
civilized society. Though he rejected its pagan morality, Greek
thought and culture were secretly and constantly working upon him
through a subtle form of psychic osmosis.

Though exerted unconsciously, this Hellenic influence was to
leave its stamp indelibly upon the Apostle. It is mirrored in his discourses and letters: they abound with references to Tarsiote life, to
city affairs, commerce, and law. Unlike Jesus, whose allusions were
chiefly to nature, the flowers, birds, oxen, sheep, and the fields, Paul
borrows his comparisons from the wrestling bouts in the arena, the
races and games in the stadium, and the discussions in the market

place. He quotes from such Greek authors as Aratus the Stoic, Menander, and Epimenides.

It was the pervasive influence of Greek culture which was to make Paul conscious that faith is confronted with problems which must be solved by the intellect: it was to orientate him in the domain in which his genius was to find its climactic expression: working out a mighty and enduring rationale of the Christian faith which was to serve the philosophers and theologians of all subsequent ages.

The third influence exercised upon the son of the Torah was the vast Roman Empire, of which his native land was a province. That was the great political reality of his day, and its supranational and universal character made a deep and lasting impression upon him. In the course of eight centuries Rome had grown from a little stone fort on the Palatine to a world empire. Her dominion stretched from the Atlantic on the west to the Euphrates on the east: from the banks of the Danube and the Rhine to the cataracts of the Nile her will was the supreme law.

Gaul, Spain, and Britain as well as the vast oriental empires of Egypt, Assyria, and Parthia, besides numerous minor kingdoms, paid her tribute. The glorious dreams of Alexander the Great were translated into realities when Roman *conquistadori* sat at Antioch, Alexandria, Carthage, Saragossa, Lyons, and York. Rome had now become the greatest empire that the world had ever known, and her eagles had become the one symbol of universal dominion. What Rome had become in the temporal order, that and more, the Apostle came to perceive, the Church of the living God must become in the spiritual order. It must embrace not merely the people of Israel but all the nations of the world, bearing upon its brow the unmistakable mark of God's solicitude for the salvation of all men.

While Paul gloried in his spiritual inheritance from Israel, he exulted likewise in his Roman citizenship. It made him a privileged person; it protected him against despotic officials, who could not inflict upon him severe corporal punishment, such as flagellation, or ignominious torture, such as crucifixion. On many occasions he was to claim its rights and prerogatives. The Apostle saw in Rome's imperial sway not merely an instrument of oppression but a mighty organization, which might under the designs of Providence be used to spread the faith throughout the world. Her famous roads were to become the arteries of the Christian Gospel and thus help to win all men for Christ.

Such then was the threefold world in which Paul grew up: Jewish, Greek, and Roman. Each exercised its distinctive influence upon him, and each is clearly mirrored in his life, discourses, and writings.

At fourteen or fifteen Paul was sent to Jerusalem to continue his studies in the Law and the lore of Israel. To the spiritual fatherland of every believing Jew there came from the Jewish communities of the Diaspora (those outside Palestine) hundreds of students eager to hear the word of the masters in the holy place where the Spirit surely dwelt. None was more ardent or enthusiastic than the boy from Tarsus, whose heart was set upon becoming a scribe, a Doctor of the Law; this profession opened the door to all the positions of honor and prestige in religion, law, letters, and education.

While in Jerusalem he probably resided with his married sister, who had two sons apparently not much younger than Paul. One of these later risked his life to save Paul from assassination. The young boy studied under the illustrious Gamaliel the Elder, the grandson of the famous Hillel. The sole textbook was the Bible in Hebrew, Aramaic, and Greek. The teacher would take the Hebrew texts, word for word, and expatiate upon their significance in the context, singly and in innumerable combinations. It was commonly said that a rabbinical teacher could gather "a bushel of meanings from the angles of every Hebrew letter."

Instead of seeking to substantiate their interpretations by appealing strictly to logic, grammar, unity, and sequence, they appealed chiefly to verbal resemblance: similarities between the subject under discussion and others recorded in the past. They stressed precedent until it groaned and finally collapsed in a welter of absurd refinements and regulations concerning innumerable details of daily life.

To illustrate: An enormous network of specifications governed the maintenance of legal purity. The expert legalist worked out learned and precise answers to such questions as these: With what water must the hands be washed? In what utensils must they be washed? Were they to be washed with one water or with two? How far up on the hands must the first water reach, and how far the second? How were they to be dried?

Concerning the observance of the Sabbath the Pharisees had

erected a mountain of regulations. One violated the Sabbath by carrying a dried fig. "The tailor," they decreed, "shall not go out with his needle near nightfall Friday evening, for he might thus forget and go out carrying the needle on the Sabbath." They solemnly declared it wrong to eat an egg, the greater part of which had issued from the chicken before the second star appeared, because the chicken had broken the Sabbath by laying.

Rabbinical teachers used tradition till it palled beyond human endurance: they multiplied glosses and opinions not only *ad infinitum* but even *ad nauseam*. It is no wonder that Christ's hearers cried out with relief that He taught "as one having authority," and not as the scribes and Pharisees. They were grateful that He explained the meaning of the biblical text in a simple straightforward manner instead of reciting a tiresome list of ancient opinions regarding it.

Instruction was given in the form of rhythmic, cadenced sentences, which were to be memorized word for word, without taking notes. "A good student," says the Talmud, "must be like a staunch cistern, which lets not a single drop of water escape." Thus Paul spent years repeating and droning out sentences, becoming impregnated with the sacred text to his very bones. While he learned much from his Pharisee masters, it is not unlikely that he was also aware of the desiccating influence of such stereotyped and formalistic instruction. Perhaps it was the memory of such teaching that prompted him to write to the Corinthians, "the letter kills, but the spirit gives life."

"I advanced in Judaism," says Paul, "above many of my contemporaries in my nation, showing much more zeal for the traditions of my fathers." He became familiar with every word of the Hebrew and Aramaic texts of the Old Testament, and so thoroughly acquainted with the Greek version that in later years he was able to quote it almost verbatim from memory. In one passage in the Epistle to the Romans, he has no less than eight references in as many lines, and in another he cites texts freely from Osee, Leviticus, Isaias, Joel, Deuteronomy, and the Psalms to demonstrate the justice and power of God. The Old Testament had worked its way not only into his blood stream but even into the very marrow of his bones.

It is not known how long Paul studied in Jerusalem, but it is certain that he left there a confirmed zealot for the detailed observance of the Law. To him it had become God's own revelation of His infinite majesty, power, and righteousness; in it was to be found not only the knowledge of God but salvation as well. When he returned to Tarsus he could see in the snow-covered mountain peaks, in the sparkling waters of the Cydnus, in the stars mirrored in Lake Rhegna, and in the tumultuous waves of the Mediterranean only the visible manifestations of God's invisible attributes—His everlasting power and sovereign dominion over the whole universe.

The period of Paul's life from the end of his studies in Jerusalem to his reappearance there at the stoning of Stephen, commonly placed in the year 36, is shrouded in the same impenetrable obscurity as that which veils the hidden life of Christ at Nazareth. We do not even know if he married, as was the custom of Jewish boys at eighteen. Celibacy was frowned upon by the Hebrews: a rabbinic aphorism declared that God watches until a man is twenty years old to see whether or not he takes a wife, and if he is still single, God curses him. The Talmud permitted the average Israelite to have as many as four wives and even more, though polygamy was not considered appropriate for a Doctor of the Law.

Clement of Alexandria thinks that Paul was married, deducing this from a passage in his Epistle to the Philippians where he speaks of "my loyal comrade." But the great majority of ancient writers—Tertullian, Jerome, Epiphanius, John Chrysostom, and Theodoret—interpret that phrase as referring to one of his male fellow laborers, and hold that Paul never married. This is confirmed by a passage in 1 Corinthians, where he counsels the unmarried and widows to "so remain, even as I." Though there remains the theoretic possibility that when he wrote this he was a widower, having lost his wife perhaps while still a young man, the overwhelming weight of tradition is that he never married.

Immediately after the Ascension the entire Church numbered but one hundred twenty persons in Jerusalem and perhaps a few hundred scattered elsewhere. But ten days later, at Pentecost, three thousand persons were converted by Peter's discourse and their number increased "day by day." Notable progress continued during the five or six years between Christ's death and the stoning of Stephen. This aroused the hostility of the scribes and Pharisees and they launched a vigorous persecution of the Christians.

Stephen, a deacon, was arrested and condemned to be stoned to death. Paul exulted in the condemnation and held the cloaks of some of those who hurled the stones. As they were stoning him, Stephen prayed, "Lord, Jesus, receive my spirit." Then as he fell, he cried out, "Lord, do not lay this sin against them." Not content with that death, Paul continued to vent his hatred of the Christians. "But Saul was harassing the Church," reports Acts, "entering house after house, and dragging out men and women, he committed them to prison."

Breathing threats of vengeance, Paul went to the high priest and secured letters to the synagogues in Damascus, authorizing him to arrest any Christians he might find there and bring them bound to Jerusalem. Armed with letters from the Sanhedrin and accompanied by an escort of armed men, the archenemy of the new religion set out with flaming enthusiasm upon his two-hundred-mile journey. The route traversed the length of Palestine, through Samaria and Galilee as far as Caesarea Philippi, then wound around Mount Hermon and continued on straight across the steppes. That was the track of the caravans in ancient times and it is the bus route of today. For eight days Paul had been tramping through the dust and rubble and was nearing Damascus when suddenly a blinding light from heaven flashed down upon him. Dazzled and bewildered, he fell to the ground.

"Saul, Saul," he heard a voice saying, "why dost thou persecute me?"

"Who art thou, Lord?" he asked.

"I am Jesus," came the reply, "whom thou art persecuting."

"Lord," asked Paul, trembling and astonished, "what wilt thou have me do?"

"Arise and go into the city," replied Jesus, "and it will be told thee what thou must do."

"Now the men who journeyed with him stood speechless," continues the Acts, "hearing indeed the voice, but seeing no one. And Saul arose from the ground, but when his eyes were opened, he could see nothing. And leading him by the hand, they brought him to Damascus. And for three days he could not see, and he ate nothing."

In Damascus there was a disciple named Ananias—thought by some to have been one of our Lord's seventy-two disciples—to whom Jesus appeared.

"Ananias," said Jesus.

"Here I am, Lord," he replied.

"Arise," Jesus ordered, "and go to the street called Straight and ask at the house of Judas for a man of Tarsus named Saul. For behold, he is praying."

Ananias was astonished at this command and told why.

"Lord," he said, "I have heard from many about this man, how much evil he has done to thy saints in Jerusalem. And here too he has authority from the high priests to arrest all who invoke thy name."

"Go," replied Jesus, "for this man is a chosen vessel to me, to carry my name among nations and kings and the children of Israel. For I will show him how much he must suffer for my name."

Accordingly Ananias went to the home of Judas and laid his hands upon Paul.

"Brother Saul," he explained, "the Lord has sent me—Jesus, who appeared to thee on thy journey—that thou mayest recover thy sight and be filled with the Holy Spirit."

"And straightway," reports the Acts, "there fell from Paul's eyes something like scales, and he recovered his sight, and arose and was baptized. And after taking some food, he regained his strength."

Thus occurred an event of such stupendous and far-reaching consequences as to effect the whole future of Christianity. In the history of the origins of Christianity Paul's conversion ranks in importance only second to the resurrection of Christ. It is evident that it impressed the imagination of the apostolic age as forcibly as it astounds ours, for the Book of Acts narrates it not merely once but three times, and on two of those occasions relates it in the words of the Apostle, who recalls it also in his epistles.

The conversion of Paul is all the more astounding because it was so sudden and unexpected, coming like a bolt of lightning out of the clear sky. He always attributed it solely to God and not to any inclination of his own. "The Apostle himself," observes Monsignor Le Camus, "so careful to study himself and to make himself known in the various phases of his religious life, sees no other cause for his conversion than the heavenly manifestation by which he was thrown down. But if he has never said anything of that inner working which would have prepared for his sudden adhesion to Christianity, it is because in his recollections he found nothing."

It is then one of the most striking and amazing transformations in all history. The archenemy of Christ, filled with rancor and hatred, becomes His intrepid Apostle and dauntless champion, consumed with an overwhelming passion to spread His faith to the farthest ends of the earth and to win all the nations of the world for Christ. "At dawn," remarks Isadore O'Brien, O.F.M., "he was the implacable protagonist of circumcision: by dusk he will have taken his first step toward becoming the 'Apostle of the uncircumcised.'" Though the Apostle will have more visions of the Lord and hear His words many times, none of these will be comparable to the appearance of Jesus on the road to Damascus.

What a staggering miracle of grace was that encounter of persecutor and persecuted! Here was exemplified the Christian paradox of loving one's enemy, doing good to those who hate and persecute one and speak all manner of evil against one, as Jesus had counseled in the Sermon on the Mount. No wonder it is that the Apostle penetrated to the heart of the mystery of love in the famous thirteenth chapter of 1 Corinthians and wrote also to the Romans: "Bless those who persecute you . . . Do not avenge yourselves, beloved, but give place to the wrath . . . Be not overcome by evil, but overcome evil with good."

How can we read of that encounter without wonderment, awe, and emotion tinged, must we not admit, with envy, stirring in our hearts? Saul of Tarsus, breathing threats of slaughter, stained with the blood of the first Christian martyr, incandescent with a blazing hatred of Christ and His followers, worse by far than we, had the inconceivable fortune of meeting Jesus personally and being called by his name! Why this singular privilege, this incredible favor? Was it not this staggering miracle which enabled Paul to peer into the mysterious workings of grace and to read the secret designs of Providence, of which he was later to speak so often and with such penetration? What else lay behind his paradoxical and mysterious utterance, "for strength is made perfect in weakness"?

Forever after, he was to be a trumpeter of God's love and the redeeming grace of Christ, which held ajar the gates of eternal life for all who would believe in His name. Yes, that encounter on the road to Damascus was the turning point in the propagation of the faith, for the Light that banished Saul's darkness and the Love that conquered his hatred that memorable day was to shape and fashion the most remarkable witness to His wisdom and love in all history.

Hear him as he proclaims to all the world, "Oh, the depth of the riches of the wisdom and of the knowledge of God. How incomprehensible are his judgments and how unsearchable his ways!" Trumpeting that ecstatic hymn of praise, Paul tramped the highways of the vast Greco-Roman empire, a witness to his Conqueror, proud to be His captive and His slave.

Although Paul owed his conversion directly to the vision and words of Jesus and the accompanying grace, he actually became a Christian through the sacrament of baptism, the common door for all. The impulse of grace was "hard" to resist but not impossible. That is the meaning of Christ's words, "It is *hard* for thee to kick against the goad."

As soon as he recovered his strength Paul joined the disciples in Damascus, and straightway in the synagogues he began to preach that Jesus is the Son of God. All who heard him were amazed.

"Is not this," they asked, "he who used to make havoc in Jerusalem of those who called upon this name, and who has come here for the purpose of taking them in bonds to the chief priests?"

Dumfounded indeed were his listeners as Paul told them that the risen Christ had appeared to him in such theomorphic splendor and glory as to dazzle him, had spoken to him, and now he would die rather than fail to proclaim His divinity. Paul's ministry at this time was a brief one and lasted only "for some days." He withdrew to Arabia, the name then given to the desert area that stretched from the Anti-Lebanon in the north to the Red Sea in the south and the Persian Gulf in the east. The length of his sojourn here is not known: estimates range from a few months to three years.

During this period Paul received a series of revelations from Christ Himself concerning the truths of salvation, and he meditated upon them at length so that he understood them perfectly and could explain them in simple language. The content of these revelations the Apostle termed his "Gospel." "I give you to understand, brethren," he wrote to the Galatians, "that the Gospel which was preached by me is not of man. For I did not receive it from man, nor was I taught it; but I received it by a revelation of Jesus Christ." It was not, of course, a different Gospel from that taught by the other Apostles, but it brought out certain truths with especial force and clarity.

Notable among these, as Fernand Prat, S.J., points out, were the following: equality of all men in the divine plan of redemption; the admission of the Gentiles into the Church on the same footing as the Israelites; the abolition of the Mosaic Law; the liberty which results from it, especially for converts from paganism; justification through faith, independently of the works of the Law; the incorporation of the faithful into Christ by baptism; the union of all in Him— with the communion of saints, which is its corollary; in short, all the properties of the Mystical Body of Christ.

Writing to the Ephesians, Paul tells them of the mystery that was revealed to him. "By revelation," he says, "was made known to me the mystery . . . which in other ages was not known to the sons of men . . . namely, that the Gentiles are joint heirs, and fellow-members of the same body, and joint partakers of the promise in Christ Jesus through the Gospel."

In retiring to a place of solitude such as the Arabian Desert to commune with God, to meditate and pray, Paul was following the example of John the Baptist and of Christ Himself before they began their public ministry. Incidentally this is the example which the Church also follows in preparing candidates for the priesthood and the religious life in general.

When the Apostle completed his novitiate he returned to Damascus and resumed his preaching. To the Jews in the synagogues he boldly proclaimed that Jesus whom they had crucified is the Son of God, that He arose from the dead, and that salvation has come through Him. This was too much for the Jews, and they made a plot to kill him. They were guarding the gates both day and night to prevent his escape, so the disciples took him by night and lowered him in a basket over the city wall.

Paul made his way at once to Jerusalem "to see Peter," whom he knew from revelation to be the head of the Church. On his arrival, he endeavored to join the disciples, but quite understandably they were fearful of him and did not believe that he was a disciple. Barnabas came to his rescue and told them of Paul's miraculous conversion and of his courage in boldly proclaiming the Gospel in the synagogues of Damascus. Whereupon Peter, the head of the Church, James the Less, the Bishop of Jerusalem (the only two Apostles in the city), and the disciples received him into full fellowship and welcomed his participation in their mission.

He spent fifteen days with them, during which time he doubtless conferred at length with Peter. It is easy to picture the chief of the

Apostles taking Paul on walks through the Holy City, to the Cenacle, where Jesus had celebrated the Last Supper and where the Holy Spirit had descended upon them at Pentecost, to the Garden of Gethsemane, to the hill of Calvary and to the Sepulcher from which He had risen on Easter morn. How we would like to have accompanied them and to have listened to their conversation! "And he moved freely among them in Jerusalem," says the Acts, "acting boldly in the name of the Lord."

It was doubtless during this first sojourn in Jerusalem that Paul had the vision which he narrated later on to the Jews. While he was praying in the Temple, he relates, Christ appeared to him. "Make haste and go quickly out of Jerusalem," said Jesus, "for they will not receive thy testimony concerning me . . . Go, for to the Gentiles far away I will send thee."

Christ's words of warning were soon fulfilled. Paul's bold disputes with the Jews, particularly with those who had come to Jerusalem from their homes outside Palestine, stirred their anger and resentment, and they made plans to kill him. When the Christians learned of this they prudently secreted him out of the city. He went first to Caesarea and then returned to Tarsus. There the Apostle remained for some five or six years, winning such converts as he could and waiting until Peter, the head of the whole Church, inaugurated the work of evangelizing the pagan world. This Peter did at Caesarea, where he baptized Cornelius, the centurion of the Italian cohort and the first Gentile to become a Christian.

In the wake of the persecution which saw Stephen stoned to death, many disciples fled from Jerusalem, scattering to Phoenicia, Cyprus, and Antioch. At Antioch their preaching was remarkably fruitful and they received large numbers into the fold. When this good news reached the ears of the Church in Jerusalem, they sent Barnabas to investigate. When he saw the multitude of converts, "he rejoiced and exhorted them all to continue in the Lord with steadfast heart; for he was a good man and full of the Holy Spirit and of faith."

The challenge presented by this great field of missionary work caused Barnabas to recall Paul and his flaming zeal to preach the Gospel to the Gentiles. The head of the Church, Peter, by his reception of Cornelius had evidently decided that the time had come to open wide the door to the Gentiles. Who could bring them in

more effectively than the ardent Tarsiote? Had not Christ designated him as His "chosen vessel" for this precise work? The stage
seemed to be set for Paul's appearance as the missioner par excellence.

So off went Barnabas to Tarsus to summon Paul. Once before, he
had presented Paul to the Church in Jerusalem: now he was to present him to the Church in Antioch—then Peter's own see. We can
imagine the avidity with which Paul accepted the invitation of
Barnabas and hurried back with him to the city where the door was
opening to the vast Gentile world.

"For a whole year," reports the Acts, "they took part in the meetings of the Church and taught a great multitude." It was in Antioch
that the followers of Christ were first called "Christians." As a great
famine was raging in Judea, the Christians at Antioch took up a collection for their needy brethren and chose Barnabas and Paul to
bring their alms to Jerusalem. This was Paul's second visit as a Christian to the Holy City.

They found the Church there in difficult straits: King Agrippa had
launched a fierce persecution of the Christians, James, the brother
of John, had been beheaded, and Peter was in prison. After handing
their alms to James, the brother of the Lord and the Bishop of Jerusalem, they returned to Antioch, taking Mark, the cousin of Barnabas,
with them.

Here Paul is to receive a momentous summons, from none other
than the Holy Spirit Himself, to cast his net out into the mighty deep
to draw into the bark of Peter a draft far more copious than was ever
gathered from the Sea of Galilee.

II. MISSIONARY JOURNEYS AND DEATH

The spotlight of the Acts now shifts from Peter and Jerusalem to
Paul and Antioch, as the stirring drama of Paul's mighty missionary
enterprise begins to unfold. After Barnabas and Paul returned to
Antioch they were together with Simon Niger, Lucius of Cyrene,
Manahen, the foster brother of Herod the tetrarch, and other prophets and teachers. While they were fasting and praying, the Holy
Spirit said to them: "Set apart for me Saul and Barnabas unto the
work to which I have called them."

Thus under the direction of the Holy Spirit, the Apostle, accompanied by Barnabas and Mark, sets forth upon his first missionary journey—the first systematic, all-out effort to win the Gentile world for Christ. They went to Seleucia and from there sailed to Cyprus. This is an island in the northeastern corner of the Mediterranean, about one hundred forty miles long and fifty miles wide. On landing at Salamis, its commercial capital, they preached in the synagogues. Then they slowly crossed the whole island until they reached Paphos, a city on the west coast and the seat of the government.

Here they encountered a Jewish magician, Bar-Jesus, who was also a false prophet. He was staying with Sergius Paulus the proconsul, a man of discernment, who invited Paul and Barnabas to preach their Gospel to him. But the magician tried to thwart their work and to turn the proconsul away from believing in Christ. Inspired by the Holy Spirit, Paul fastened his eyes upon the sorcerer.

"O full of all guile and of all deceit," exclaimed Paul, "son of the devil, enemy of all justice, wilt thou not cease to make crooked the straight ways of the Lord? And now, behold, the hand of the Lord is upon thee, and thou shalt be blind, not seeing the sun for a time."

Instantly there fell a mist and a darkness upon him, so that he had to have someone lead him by the hand. Upon seeing what had happened, the proconsul believed, and was astonished at the Lord's teaching.

Except for his two brief, trembling questions to Jesus, as he lay stricken on the road to Damascus, this is Paul's only direct utterance thus far in the Acts and his first recorded word in his stupendous task of winning the pagan world for Christ. From this point on in the Acts, Saul is always called Paul, and his name is invariably mentioned before that of Barnabas to indicate that he has become the head of the mission previously directed by his associate.

The results of this change of leadership soon become evident. Doubtless concluding that Cyprus—the natural dependency of Syria —and Cilicia would embrace the faith when these two countries became Christian, Paul chose Asia Minor as the field of his apostolate. Accordingly he sailed for Perge in Pamphylia, eight miles above the mouth of the Cestrus. Here Mark, apparently dismayed by the daring project of the Apostle and by the dangers and hardships of the journey, abandoned the expedition and returned to Jerusalem. Paul and Barnabas pushed on across the rough mountains of Pisidia, which were infested by brigands and crossed by frightful precipices. Their destination was the Roman colony in Antioch, not, of course, the great Antioch in Syria, but the country town in Pisidia.

Here Paul preached in the synagogue on the Sabbath day. Luke reproduces the substance of the discourse to show the general pattern he followed in his preaching in the synagogues. Paul sets forth the vocation of Israel, the predictions of the prophets, and their providential fulfillment by the Messias, Jesus of Nazareth, who brought redemption to all by His death upon the cross. The Apostle's preaching attracted such great crowds that the Jews became filled with envy and blasphemously contradicted all that he said.

"It was necessary," declared Paul, "that the word of God should be spoken to you first, but since you reject it and judge yourselves unworthy of eternal life, behold, we now turn to the Gentiles. For so the Lord has commanded us, 'I have set thee for a light to the Gentiles, to be a means of salvation to the very ends of the earth.'"

Upon hearing this, the Gentiles rejoiced and many glorified the word of God and believed. The envious Jews incited some of the prominent people of the city, however, and, stirring up a tumult against the Apostles, had them driven from the district.

Undismayed, the Apostles turned their footsteps toward Iconium, three or four days distant, where they encountered the same hostility from the Jews and the same eager welcome from the Gentiles. They remained a considerable time, preaching the Gospel fearlessly, confirming their preaching with signs and miracles, and winning many Gentile converts. Enraged, the Jews conspired with the rulers to have the Apostles stoned, but they learned of it in time to escape to Lystra, some eighteen miles distant, where they continued their evangelical labors.

Here Paul cured a man lame from birth. Seeing the miracle, many thought Paul and Barnabas were gods and sought to worship them. The Apostles had difficulty in restraining them and in convincing them that they, too, were men, proclaiming the Gospel of the one true God. Soon Jews from Antioch and Iconium arrived, laid snares against the Apostles, and had Paul stoned and dragged out of the town, leaving him for dead. The disciples came, however, and lifted him up and surreptitiously brought him back to Lystra.

The next day Paul and Barnabas went to Derbe, about forty miles

away on the frontier of the province of Galatia. Here they resumed
their preaching and teaching and brought the good tidings to many
people.

The Apostles had now completed their circuit. They deemed it
advisable to retrace their steps in order to visit their neophytes and
to ordain priests in each church founded by them at such great cost.
In addition, they exhorted the faithful to stand steadfast in the face
of opposition, prayed with them and commended them to the Lord.
After completing that mission, they passed through Pisidia and came
to Perge, where they halted to preach the Gospel, perhaps while
awaiting a boat for Attalia, a port twelve miles distant.

Thence they sailed to Antioch in Syria, the city in which they had
received their commission from the Holy Spirit, and from which they
had embarked upon their mission. Upon their return after an absence of at least three years, they were received with transports of
joy and thanksgiving, for God had clearly opened the door of faith
to the Gentiles.

Paul remained at Antioch almost a year, carrying on his missionary
labors. While there the problem of the status of the Gentiles in the
Church became acute: some Judeo-Christians coming from Jerusalem claimed that the Gentiles must undergo circumcision according
to the Mosaic Law. They would thus in effect require the Gentiles
virtually to become Jews before being admitted to baptism and
membership in the Christian fold. Here was a curious carrying over,
perhaps unwittingly, of the old, outmoded concept of Jewish exclu-
siveness, of salvation only through conformity with the Law of Moses.
The rite of circumcision was obnoxious to the Gentiles, and its en-
forcement would constitute a serious road block to many of them.

Against this, Paul and Barnabas protested strenuously; so it was
decided that a meeting should be held at Jerusalem to solve the
problem. They were selected to represent the community of Antioch
and accordingly the two set out for the Holy City. On their way they
passed through Phoenicia and Samaria, spreading the news of their
success with the Gentiles, and causing much rejoicing among the
brethren there and later in Jerusalem, where they were warmly welcomed and acclaimed. After both sides were heard and the question
was thoroughly discussed, Peter announced the decision—a truly admirable one.

"Brethren," he said, "you know that in early days God made choice among us, that through my mouth the Gentiles should hear the word of the gospel and believe. And God, who knows the heart, bore witness by giving them the Holy Spirit just as he did to us; and he made no distinction between us and them, but cleansed their hearts by faith. Why then do you now try to test God by putting on the neck of the disciples a yoke which neither our fathers nor we have been able to bear? But we believe that we are saved through the grace of the Lord Jesus, just as they are."

Upon hearing this, the whole meeting quieted down and listened attentively while Paul and Barnabas told of the great signs and wonders that God had done among the Gentiles through them. Then James, the Bishop of Jerusalem, noted alike for his piety and his attachment to the Mosaic Law, spoke in support of Peter's decision. Accordingly the assembly sent Barnabas and Paul, along with Judas and Silas, to Antioch with the following letter:

"The brethren who are apostles and presbyters send greeting to the brethren of Gentile origin in Antioch and Syria and Cilicia. As we have heard that some of our number have disturbed you with their teaching, unsettling your minds, persons to whom we had given no instruction, we have decided, being assembled together, to select representatives and send them to you with our beloved Barnabas and Paul: men who have pledged their lives for the name of our Lord Jesus Christ. We have therefore sent Judas and Silas, who themselves also by word of mouth will give you the same message. For the Holy Spirit and we have decided to lay no further burden upon you but this indispensable one, that you abstain from things sacrificed to idols and from blood and from what is strangled and from immorality; keep yourselves from these things, and you will get on well. Farewell."

Great indeed was the joy of the Christians of Antioch on receiving this message. Having fulfilled his mission, Judas returned to Jerusalem while Silas remained. Later on Peter came to Antioch. As usual when outside Jerusalem, he did not hesitate to associate freely with the converted Gentiles and to eat with them, though this was, of course, contrary to the Mosaic Law. That, as he had formally announced at Jerusalem, did not bind Gentile converts. Did it still bind converts from Judaism? The question arose when some meddlesome ones arrived from Jerusalem, passing themselves off as emissaries of

James. They scrupulously refrained from such free mingling and dining with Gentile converts.

Rather than disedify or displease these fanatics, Peter, probably in the interest of peace and concord, discontinued his free association with the Gentiles. So great was the influence of his example that Barnabas and many other Jewish Christians followed suit. This separation became noticeable, especially at religious gatherings and at the celebration of the agape or love feast. Thus the Gentile Christians were put in the unpleasant alternative of being deprived of his society or of giving up their lately acquired privilege: freedom from the restrictions of the Mosaic Law as decreed at the Jerusalem assembly.

Quick to perceive the divisive consequences of such a practice, Paul registered a stout protest. "But when I saw," he relates, "that they [the Judaizers] were not walking uprightly according to the truth of the gospel, I said to Cephas before them all: If thou, though a Jew, livest [usually] like the Gentiles and not like the Jews, how is it that thou dost compel [by the force of example] the Gentiles to live like the Jews?"

Paul then presented some other weighty reasons, not for the purpose of convincing Peter, who was perfectly in accord with him in regard to the principle involved, but to convince the Judaizers present. "We know," he said, "that man is not justified by the works of the Law, but by the faith of Jesus Christ. Hence we also believe in Christ Jesus, that we may be justified by the faith of Christ, and not by the works of the Law; because by the works of the Law no man will be justified."

Peter recognized the reasonableness of Paul's contention and graciously agreed that Jewish Christians and Gentile Christians were to suffer no division in the matters of free association and eating, since the Mosaic Law had lost all binding force. The point at issue was not a principle but a procedure—a matter of practical prudence, discretion, and tact. The incident brings out Paul's clear recognition of the authority of Peter as the head of the Church.

By addressing Peter in the presence of all, he served the double purpose of publicly acknowledging Peter as the supreme authority and of getting all the Judaizers to acquiesce, once Peter had spoken. It is difficult to know which of the two is to be the more admired; Paul for his clear insight, or Peter for his willingness in welcoming a critical suggestion and his humility in accepting it when second thought showed it to embody the more prudent and the wiser procedure.

Removed, as we are, by nineteen centuries from the apostolic age, we are inclined to think of the whole dispute as a petty affair, a tempest in a teapot. To the Christians of the first century, however, it was the greatest crisis which confronted the Church since the Crucifixion. The whole future of the Church was at stake. If the Judaizers triumphed, Christianity would remain an obscure Jewish sect and its world-wide mission would have been strangled by the swaddling clothes of Hebrew particularism, rigorism, and exclusivism.

That the decision of Peter both at Jerusalem and at Antioch was in favor of opening wide the door to all nations, without let or hindrance of any kind, is striking evidence that Christ was keeping His promise to be with His Church "all days even unto the consummation of the world." Far from nursing resentment against Paul for his criticism, Peter, writing in the last year of his life to the churches in Asia Minor—Paul's own churches—besought them to pay special heed to the letter which Paul, his "most dear brother," had written to them: the very letter in which Paul tells the Galatians how he "withstood him [Peter] to his face." Here was a lesson in magnanimity which the vicars of Christ's Church and all its members have never forgotten.

Freed from anxiety about the Judaizers, Paul was now eager to resume his missionary work. He was uneasy about the fate of the churches so recently founded; so he decided to revisit them and extend his missionary conquests still further. Barnabas was willing to accompany him but wanted to take Mark along. Recalling how the latter had deserted them in Pamphylia, Paul demurred: a sharp contention arose, with the result that Barnabas and his cousin sailed for Cyprus, while Paul and Silas set off on foot for Asia Minor.

The choice of Silas was a happy one, for, like Paul, Silas was a Roman citizen and was well known for his ardent sympathy for the Gentiles. The disagreement between Paul and Barnabas did not disturb their friendship, as we shall see later, and actually resulted in the launching of two fruitful missions instead of one.

Crossing the Amanus Mountains by the Syrian Gates and skirting the Gulf of Issus, Paul and Silas passed through the whole of rural Cilicia as far as Tarsus. There Paul's converts heard with joy the decision taken at Jerusalem. From Tarsus they journeyed over a picturesque road that ascended from a tropical country abounding in fields of cotton and groves of palm trees to snow-clad mountains from which they descended to the plains of Lycaonia. They stopped at Derbe and Lystra, where they met Timothy, the son of a believing Jewess and a Gentile father.

Paul was so favorably impressed with the piety and character of Timothy, that he prevailed upon the young man to cast his lot with the missioners. Since he had not been circumcised, Paul performed this rite on him, knowing that he would thereby be more readily accepted and listened to by the Jews when he entered their synagogues to preach. At Jerusalem the Apostle had refused to yield to the demand of the Judaizers that Titus, a convert from paganism, and then his assistant, be circumcised. He did this because he refused to recognize the principle for which the Judaizers were contending: that converts from paganism could enter the Church only through the intermediate door of Judaism and that circumcision was necessary for salvation.

Here there was no such principle at stake: it was merely a question of prudence and tact, and since Timothy's mother was Jewish, Paul was willing to make this harmless concession to the Jews so that his young collaborator would not seem to his compatriots an apostate from Judaism. Though the case is somewhat different from the one at Antioch, where Peter withdrew from the Gentiles to conciliate the Jewish Christians, it shows that Paul, too, was willing to make concessions in the hope of winning more of his compatriots for Christ. Like Titus, Timothy was raised to the priesthood and later became an auxiliary bishop under the Apostle.

Passing through Phrygia and the country parts of Galatia, Paul planned to preach in the province of Asia but was forbidden by the Holy Spirit. After entering the province of Mysia they proceeded to Troas. Here one night Paul had a vision: a Macedonian standing and saying, "Come over into Macedonia and help us." Regarding the message as sent by God, Paul and his companions set sail for Europe.

Here a new personage suddenly enters upon the scene. Luke, the author of the Acts, reveals his presence by the brief remark, "So sailing from Troas, *we* ran a straight course to Samothrace." The new companion was to become Paul's active collaborator, his faithful historian and devoted physician, and the author of the third Gospel.

He was a native of Antioch but he had relatives in Macedonia and probably in Philippi itself. It is to this new companion that we are indebted for most of our knowledge of the Apostle's far-flung missionary labors.

Upon their arrival at Philippi they found that the Jews were not numerous enough to possess a synagogue, but had an uncovered oratory about a mile west of the city. Thither they went on the first Sabbath day to preach the Gospel to some women assembled there. One of them, Lydia, was touched by divine grace and asked for baptism. After she and her entire family had embraced the faith she solicited the honor of lodging the Apostles in her house, and insisted so strongly that they could not refuse her. Here the Apostles doubtless celebrated the "divine mysteries," as Holy Mass was called: thus the house of Lydia may be said to be the first Christian church established on the soil of Europe.

Here Paul drove out an evil spirit from a girl who was a soothsayer. She belonged to several proprietors who employed her as a fortuneteller, and thus they received considerable revenue. As a result of Paul's exorcism she was deprived of her gift of divination. Whereupon her angry masters rushed to the lodging of Paul and Silas and dragged them to the market place where the magistrates were officiating. The Apostles were stripped of their clothing, beaten with rods, and cast into prison, where their feet were fastened in stocks.

At midnight when the Apostles were singing their praises to the Lord and the other prisoners were listening to them a great earthquake shook the prison: the doors flew open, and the chains fell from all the prisoners. Seeing the doors wide open, the jailer thought that the inmates had escaped and he was about to kill himself. Paul prevented him, however, and assured him that all had remained. Impressed by this evident miracle, the jailer and his whole family received baptism.

Upon being released the next day, they passed through Amphipolis and Apollonia and came to Thessalonica. As was his custom, Paul preached for three Sabbaths in the synagogue and a considerable number of Jewish proselytes and Gentiles believed and joined Paul and Silas. But the Jews incited a mob and stirred up such an uproar that the Apostles left under the cover of night for Beroea. Here they preached with great success until Jews from Thessalonica stirred up a riot against them. Silas and Timothy remained, with instructions to join Paul later, while the Apostle departed with an escort for Athens.

Standing on the hill of Mars, where the council called the Areopagus held its meetings, Paul delivered a memorable address, especially framed for the inquiring, philosophical minds of the sophisticated Greeks.

"Men of Athens," he said, "I see that in every respect you are extremely religious. For as I was going about and observing objects of your worship, I found also an altar with this inscription: 'To the Unknown God.' What therefore you worship in ignorance, that I proclaim to you. God, who made the world and all that is in it, since he is Lord of heaven and earth, does not dwell in temples built by hands; neither is he served by human hands as though he were in need of anything, since it is he who gives to all men life and breath and all things.

"And from one man he has created the whole human race and made them live all over the face of the earth, determining their appointed times and the boundaries of their lands; that they should seek God, and perhaps grope after him and find him, though he is not far from any one of us. For in him we live and move and have our being, as indeed some of your own poets have said, 'For we are also his offspring.'

"If therefore we are the offspring of God, we ought not to imagine that the Divinity is like to gold or silver or stone, to an image graven by human art and thought. The times of this ignorance God has, it is true, overlooked, but now he calls upon all men everywhere to repent; inasmuch as he has fixed a day on which he will judge the world with justice by a Man whom he has appointed, and whom he has guaranteed to all by raising him from the dead."

When they heard of the resurrection from the dead some began to sneer, while others said, "We will hear thee again on this matter." Apparently this skeptical and fickle people were not ripe for the Gospel, for Paul's preaching seems to have brought in but few. Luke mentions in particular Dionysius the Areopagite, who, according to Dionysius of Corinth, was later the first Bishop of Athens, and also a woman called Damaris, of whom we know nothing but her name.

From Athens Paul proceeded alone to Corinth. Here the Apostle preached in the synagogue every Sabbath until the violent opposition of the Jews denied him entrance; he then withdrew to the adjoining house of a proselyte, Titus Justus. "Do not fear," said Christ in a vision, "but speak and do not keep silence; because I am with thee, and no one shall attack or injure thee, for I have many people in this city."

Accordingly Paul continued his missionary labors without stint for eighteen months: this he was able to do, in spite of the storming protests of the Jews, because of the friendly attitude of the proconsul Gallio. The Apostle won many converts, including Crispus, the president of the synagogue, and his whole household. Finally he decided to go to Jerusalem in fulfillment of a vow, made perhaps in a moment of danger. The two Epistles to the Thessalonians were written during the early months of his sojourn at Corinth.

Bidding farewell to the brethren at Corinth, Paul sailed for Ephesus with two devout Christians, Aquila and Priscilla. As usual he entered the synagogue and proclaimed the good tidings to the Jews. He then went to Caesarea and from there to Jerusalem, where he paid his respects to the brethren. Then he journeyed to Antioch where he remained some weeks.

Here the Apostle decided to launch his third great missionary journey. Since he had assigned Silas to continue the convert apostolate at Corinth and Timothy to direct the missionary work in Greece, he took Titus as his companion. They journeyed through Galatia and Phrygia, strengthening the churches in those countries, and then reached Ephesus.

Here Paul resumed his preaching in the synagogue for three months. At the end of that period he taught daily in a classroom placed at his disposal by a certain Tyrannus. This continued for two years so that the word of the Lord reached both Jews and Greeks throughout all that territory. His ministry was crowned with many miracles and "the name of the Lord Jesus came to be held in high honor." Indeed, so mightily did the word of the Lord spread and prevail that the magicians collected their books, valued at fifty thousand pieces of silver (about nine thousand dollars) and burned them, as an evidence of their renunciation of their superstitious practices.

The marvelous success of Paul's missionary work ruined the sale of small reproductions of the temple of Diana and statuettes of the goddess, which devout pilgrims had been wont to purchase. Whereupon a certain Demetrius, the head of the guild of silversmiths, summoned a group of those craftsmen to protest Paul's preaching. Nevertheless Paul remained at Ephesus about three years, during which time he supported himself by working at his trade. In addition to his frequent preaching and his daily classroom teaching, the tireless missionary found time to write the first Epistle to the Corinthians.

They were much concerned about the miraculous gifts some of them had received, especially the gift of tongues. The imprudent use of this gift, when no one was present to interpret what they said, caused much confusion. Paul wrote to tell them that there were higher and more necessary gifts and a more excellent way to speak, namely by charity. His exposition of this virtue is one of the immortal classics of the world's literature, and the following lines are among the most frequently quoted in any major tongue.

"If I should speak with the tongues of men and of angels, but do not have charity, I have become as sounding brass or a tinkling cymbal. And if I have prophecy and know all mysteries and all knowledge, and if I have all faith so as to remove mountains, yet do not have charity, I am nothing. And if I distribute all my goods to feed the poor, and if I deliver my body to be burned, yet do not have charity, it profits me nothing.

"Charity is patient, is kind; charity does not envy, is not pretentious, is not puffed up, is not ambitious, is not self-seeking, is not provoked; thinks no evil, does not rejoice over wickedness, but rejoices with the truth; bears with all things, believes all things, hopes all things, endures all things.

"Charity never fails, whereas prophecies will disappear, and tongues will cease, and knowledge will be destroyed. For we know in part and we prophesy in part; but when that which is perfect has come, that which is imperfect will be done away with. When I was a child, I spoke as a child, I felt as a child, I thought as a child. Now that I have become a man, I have put away the things of a child. We see now through a mirror in an obscure manner, but then face to face. Now I know in part, but then I shall know even as I have been known. So there abide faith, hope and charity, these three; but the greatest of these is charity."

Old and new fields were now beckoning to the Apostle. After exhorting the brethren to remain steadfast in the faith, Paul set out for Macedonia. Numerous disciples, divided into two groups, accompanied or awaited him at Troas. These were Sopater of Beroea, Aristarchus and Secundus of Thessalonica, Gaius of Derbe, Timothy, Tychicus and Trophimus of Asia, and finally Luke, the author of the Acts. The latter records minutely all the stages of this voyage: Philippi, Troas, Assos, Mitylene, Chios, Samos, Miletus, Cos, Rhodes, Patara, Tyre, Ptolemais, Caesarea and Jerusalem.

Three remarkable facts are worthy of note in passing. At Troas Paul restored to life the young Eutychus, who had fallen from a third-story window while Paul was preaching far into the night. At Caesarea the Holy Spirit, through the prophet Agabus, foretold Paul's arrest but did not dissuade him from going to Jerusalem. At Miletus he delivered before an assembly of the presbyters from Ephesus a memorable discourse, in which he summed up his labors among them and bade them a tearful farewell. Because it mirrors so accurately the Apostle's ceaseless and unwearying solicitude, devotion, and love for all his children in the Lord, it is worth presenting in the summary form in which Luke reports it.

"You know," he began, "in what manner I have lived with you all the time since the first day that I came into the province of Asia, serving the Lord with all humility and with tears and in trials that befell me because of the plots of the Jews; how I have kept back nothing that was for your good, but have declared it to you and taught you in public and from house to house, urging Jews and Gentiles to turn to God in repentance and to believe in our Lord Jesus Christ.

"And now, behold, I am going to Jerusalem, compelled by the Spirit, not knowing what will happen to me there; except that in every city the Holy Spirit warns me, saying that imprisonment and persecution are awaiting me. But I fear none of these, nor do I count my life more precious than myself, if only I may accomplish my course and the ministry that I have received from the Lord Jesus, to bear witness to the gospel of the grace of God.

"And now, behold, I know that you all among whom I went about preaching the kingdom of God, will see my face no longer. Therefore I call you to witness this day that I am innocent of the blood of all; for I have not shrunk from declaring to you the whole counsel of God. Take heed to yourselves and to the whole flock in which the Holy Spirit has placed you as bishops, to rule the Church of God,

which he has purchased with his own blood. I know that after my
departure fierce wolves will get in among you, and will not spare
the flock. And from among your own selves men will rise speaking
perverse things, to draw away the disciples after them. Watch, therefore, and remember that for three years night and day I did not
cease with tears to admonish every one of you."

Then he concludes with the touching farewell: "And now I commend you to God and to the word of his grace, who is able to build
up and to give the inheritance among all the sanctified. I have
coveted no one's silver or gold or apparel. You yourselves know that
these hands of mine have provided for my needs and those of my
companions. In all things I have shown you that by so toiling you
ought to help the weak and remember the word of the Lord Jesus,
that he himself said, 'It is more blessed to give than to receive.'"

When he finished he knelt down and prayed with them. "And
there was much weeping among them all," observes Luke, "and they
fell on Paul's neck and kissed him, being grieved most of all at his
saying that they would no longer see his face. And they escorted
him to the ship."

It is to be noted that Paul, like the true missionary that he was,
was not content to seek to win converts merely by preaching or
teaching "in public": he supplemented those sermons and lectures
by going "from house to house, urging Jews and Gentiles to turn to
God in repentance and to believe in our Lord Jesus Christ." Just as
formerly, when persecuting Christians, he was "entering house after
house, and dragging out men and women," so now he was using the
same effective house-to-house method to win converts. The great
missionary thus shows that the convert apostolate does not permit
the luxury of waiting for people to apply for instruction, but demands that Christ's apostle take the initiative and go "from house
to house" to reach and win them.

While Paul was one of the most forceful and persuasive of all the
heralds of the Christian Gospel, he was even more eminent as a
"shoe-leather Apostle," wearing out his sandals and shoes in the
ceaseless search for souls. For more than thirty years he tramped
over dusty roads, rocky mountain trails, desert wastes, and fields
studded with thistles and briars, throughout the vast Greco-Roman
empire in the feverish quest of the "other sheep." In his three missionary journeys alone, the Apostle covered more than thirteen

thousand miles: neither persecution nor sickness could halt his unwearying and endless journeying. Probably no man in all history sought with greater courage, determination, and persistence to fulfill the Savior's twofold command, "Go! Preach!" than the Apostle of the Gentiles.

After his door-to-door canvassing had recruited a goodly number of interested persons, he would assemble them in a private home for a course of systematic instruction. Here is the beginning of what we today call the inquiry class or the information forum. A detailed study of the Acts shows that Paul made generous and almost constant use of this effective means of instructing catechumens.

He found it as easy to expound the teachings of Christ to a large number as to a single person, and much more interesting and fruitful. Indeed, he was not content to conduct merely one inquiry class of an evening but normally had two: one for beginners and another for the advanced catechumens.

"In the evening," points out the eminent Pauline scholar, Monsignor Joseph Holzner, "Paul had catechumen's instructions for beginners and for those who were advanced; then he preached a sermon and wherever possible, at least on Sundays, he celebrated the Eucharist. He was always starting new classes for converts in private homes under the direction of his helpers." As the neophytes became more numerous, Paul made generous use of assistants—well-instructed lay persons—to teach them under his supervision.

At Ephesus we get a particularly vivid picture of the systematic use the Apostle made of the inquiry class. After three months of preaching and teaching in the synagogue, Paul found that the discussions almost always ended in ugly scenes and bitter words because of the obstinacy and wrath of the Jews. Accordingly he withdrew his neophytes from the synagogue and instructed them in a lecture hall of which Tyrannus, probably a convert, was in charge. From eleven o'clock in the morning until four o'clock in the afternoon the Apostle conducted public inquiry classes for catechumens in various stages of advancement.

Attending these classes were people from all walks of life: storekeepers, merchants, clerks, students, laborers, philosophers, officials, men and women of the upper classes, slaves and freemen. By using simple, clear language and illustrating his points with examples, Paul found it possible to teach all thoroughly and effectively. If he was to "teach all nations" and "preach the Gospel to every creature," he found it necessary as a general rule to give group instruction.

In so doing, he was but following the example of the divine Master, who spoke to large audiences along the roadside, on mountains, in valleys, and along the seashore. Indeed, so thickly did His auditors crowd around Him on the seashore that not infrequently He was obliged to get into a boat and go out some distance, so that he could be seen and heard by all more satisfactorily. Hence the method which not only Paul but also our Blessed Lord used most frequently to instruct people and win converts was the inquiry-class method.

Paul's tireless industry is all the more remarkable in view of his fragile health. Though contemporary or authoritative documents say nothing about Paul's physical appearance, he is depicted in the earliest documents, paintings, and sculptures as short in stature, broadshouldered, somewhat bald, with slightly aquiline nose, closely knit eyebrows, thick, grayish beard, fair complexion, and of a pleasing and affable manner. Despite his unimpressive stature, however, he was unquestionably a man of dignified appearance and bearing, and radiated a magnetism difficult to resist.

When we come to his health we are on even more solid ground. We know that he suffered a serious illness in the year 50, and that from the year 43 he was plagued with an infirmity from which he never succeeded in freeing himself. From his Epistle to the Galatians we learn that while preaching among them he suffered from "a physical infirmity." In his Second Epistle to the Corinthians he says, "And lest the greatness of the revelations should puff me up, there was given me a thorn of the flesh, a messenger of Satan, to buffet me." Though the Apostle never disclosed the precise nature of that affliction, it is generally considered to have been some chronic illness, perhaps malaria, migraine headaches, or acute eye trouble.

After this brief detour let us return to Paul's missionary journey. Upon arriving at Jerusalem, Paul and his companions received a hearty welcome from the Christian community and from James, their bishop. Upon the advice of the elders, Paul entered the Temple with four men, all of whom were fulfilling their Nazarite vow. This vow bound one to serve God for a limited period or for life, to abstain from intoxicating beverages and from shaving one's head. The Apostle was recognized by some Asiatic Jews, who aroused the people by charging that he had brought Gentiles into the Temple.

Whereupon Paul was dragged out of the Temple and severely beaten. Only the intervention of the Roman tribune, Claudius Lysias, saved him from being murdered.

Paul was led in chains to the fortress Antonia. While in prison he was favored with a vision of the Lord, who said to him, "Be steadfast; for just as thou hast borne witness to me in Jerusalem, bear witness in Rome also."

When the tribune learned through Paul's nephew that the Jews had conspired to slay the prisoner, he sent him under a strong escort to Caesarea, which was the residence of the procurator Felix. It was an easy matter for Paul to confound his accusers, but, as he refused by bribery to purchase his liberty, Felix kept him in chains for two years until the arrival of his successor, Festus.

The new governor wished to send the prisoner back to Jerusalem to be tried in the presence of his accusers. Knowing the plans of his enemies to kill him, Paul appealed as a Roman citizen to Caesar. Thenceforth his case could be tried only at Rome. Before his journey to Rome, the Apostle was granted another opportunity of defending himself before a select group comprising King Agrippa II, his sister Bernice, the procurator, tribunes, and the principal men of the city.

Here was a setting of great splendor, an audience of the highest rank. The ranking dignitary was, of course, the King, whose judgment Festus was especially eager to get. Herod Agrippa II, born and educated in Rome, was the cultured patron of Josephus and, having inherited the protectorate of the Temple, was interested in all that concerned the Jewish religion. He was, however, living incestuously with his sister Bernice, who later became the mistress of Vespasian and then of his son Titus. Paul adapts his presentation to his cultured audience: aware of Agrippa's knowledge of the Law, he shows how the Gospel is the fulfillment of the Old Testament and that he had acted as a loyal Jew in becoming an Apostle. His address is a masterpiece of skillful presentation and persuasive reasoning and is worth quoting.

"I think myself fortunate, King Agrippa," begins Paul, "that I am to defend myself today before thee against all the accusations of the Jews, especially as thou art well acquainted with all the Jewish customs and controversies; I beg thee therefore to listen to me with patience.

"My life, then, from my youth up, the early part of which was spent among my own nation and at Jerusalem, all the Jews know; for they have long known me, if only they are willing to give evidence, that according to the strictest sect of our religion I lived a Pharisee. And now for the hope in the promise made by God to our fathers I am standing trial; to which promise our twelve tribes hope to attain as they serve night and day; and it is about this hope, O king, that I am accused by the Jews. Why is it deemed incredible with you if God does raise the dead?

"And I then thought it my duty to do many things contrary to the name of Jesus of Nazareth. And this I did in Jerusalem; and many of the saints I shut up in prison, having received authority from the chief priests to do so; and when they were put to death, I cast my vote against them; and oftentimes in all the synagogues I punished them and tried to force them to blaspheme; and in my extreme rage against them I even pursued them to foreign cities.

"But while I was journeying on this business to Damascus with authority and permission from the chief priests, at midday, O king, I saw on the way a light from heaven brighter than the sunshine round about me and my companions. We all fell to the ground, and I heard a voice saying to me in Hebrew, 'Saul, Saul, why dost thou persecute me? It is hard for thee to kick against the goad.' And I said, 'Who art thou, Lord?' And the Lord said, 'I am Jesus, whom thou art persecuting. But rise and stand upon thy feet; for I have appeared to thee for this purpose, to appoint thee to be a minister and a witness to what thou hast seen, and to the visions thou shalt have of me; delivering thee from the people and from the nations, to whom I am now sending thee, to open their eyes that they may turn from darkness to light and from the dominion of Satan to God; that they may receive forgiveness of sins and an inheritance among those sanctified by faith in me.'

"Therefore, King Agrippa, I was not disobedient to the heavenly vision; but first to the people of Damascus and Jerusalem, and then all over Judea and to the Gentiles, I set about declaring that they should repent and turn to God, doing works befitting their repentance. This is why the Jews seized me in the temple and tried to kill me. But aided to this day by the help of God, I stand here to testify to both high and low, saying nothing beyond what the Prophets and Moses said would come to pass: that the Christ was to suffer, that he first by his resurrection from the dead was to proclaim light to the people and to the Gentiles."

When Paul had finished Festus exclaimed, "Paul, thou art mad; thy great learning is driving thee to madness."

"I am not mad, excellent Festus," replied Paul, "but I speak words of sober truth. For the king knows about these things and to him also I speak without hesitation. For I am sure that none of these things escaped him; for none of them happened in a corner. Dost thou believe the prophets, King Agrippa? I know that thou dost."

"In a short while," said Agrippa, "thou wouldst persuade me to become a Christian."

"I would to God that," remarked Paul, "whether it be long or short, not only thou but also all who hear me today might become such as I am, except for these chains."

Whereupon the King, Festus, Bernice, and the others withdrew and continued to discuss the matter, concluding, "This man has done nothing to deserve death or imprisonment."

"This man," said Agrippa to Festus, "might have been set at liberty, if he had not appealed to Caesar."

Though the Apostle's discourse had evidently made a profound impression upon King Agrippa, perhaps even convincing him of the truth of the Christian religion, it could not remove the barrier to God's grace, which the monarch's immoral conduct had erected. Only Agrippa could remove that road block, and this he was unwilling to do. It offers a capital illustration of the truth that purity of heart and a clean conscience are not less necessary than intellectual conviction in embracing the faith of Christ and thus becoming a member of His Mystical Body.

In the fall of the year 60 Paul, along with other prisoners, was placed under the escort of the centurion Julius aboard a vessel sailing for Myra in Lycia. Accompanying the Apostle were Luke and Aristarchus. As the season was advanced, the voyage was slow and difficult. Skirting the coasts of Syria, Cilicia, and Pamphylia, they landed at Myra in Lycia, where the prisoners were transferred to an Alexandrian vessel bound for Italy.

The winds were persistently adverse, however, and with great difficulty they reached a place in Crete called Fair Havens. Though Paul strongly urged that they spend the winter there, those in charge insisted on venturing on, only to be lashed by a driving tempest.

For fourteen days they drifted aimlessly until the vessel was wrecked on the coast of Malta. After spending the three months of winter there, they continued their journey to Rome, arriving probably late in March.

At Rome Paul was permitted to occupy private lodgings, with a soldier to guard him. He was free to receive visitors and to preach the word of God. He called upon the leading Jews and addressed them; since here, as elsewhere, many refused to accept his message, he welcomed and instructed all who came to him. During this period the Apostle maintained contact with the various churches which he had established.

"And for two full years," reports the Acts, "he remained in his own hired lodging; and he welcomed all who came to him, preaching the kingdom of God and teaching about the Lord Jesus Christ with all boldness and unhindered. Amen." With these words the Book of Acts suddenly and abruptly ends, leaving us to grope our way in the darkness which shrouds the last years of the Apostle's life.

From the pastoral Epistles and from tradition it appears that Paul was finally acquitted. He had long desired to carry the Gospel into Spain and many scholars believe that he fulfilled this desire after being released from prison. The testimony of St. Cyril of Jerusalem, St. Epiphanius, St. Jerome, St. Chrysostom and Theodoret, the witness of the Muratorian fragment and of the *Acta Pauli* confirm the tradition of Paul's journey there.

He appears to have returned eastward by way of Rome, where he wrote the Epistle to the Hebrews, destined for the Jewish Christians of Palestine. Leaving Rome in company with Timothy, he visited Crete, where he founded a church and appointed Titus over it. From Crete the tireless missionary pushed on to Ephesus, where he left Timothy to rule the church. He then journeyed to Macedonia, and there he wrote his First Epistle to Timothy.

Crossing the Aegean again, the Apostle visited Troas, Ephesus, and Miletus and returned to Corinth. From one of these places, perhaps Ephesus, he wrote to Titus, requesting him to join him at Nicopolis in Epirus, across from Italy, where he had decided to spend the winter. It was probably between the spring and autumn of the year 66 that he wrote the two pastorals: the First Epistle to Timothy and the Epistle to Titus.

The following spring Paul was again arrested and imprisoned in

Rome, where he wrote the Second Epistle to Timothy. Reliable information is completely lacking as to the circumstances surrounding his final arrest and transference to Rome. Some scholars think that he was caught in the persecution of the Christians launched by Nero, and convicted under the charge of preaching the Christian faith. His confinement this time was so strict and his prison so difficult of access that one of his disciples, Onesiphorus of Ephesus, who had come to Rome expressly to see him, had great difficulty in finding him.

Nevertheless a few of his devoted friends succeeded in getting into communication with the prisoner, who gratefully records their names. They were Eubulus, Pudens, Linus, Claudia, and some others, whom fear of the tyrant Nero had not paralyzed. Long accustomed to feverish activity, the Apostle chafed in his dungeon like a lion in a cage. He experienced an acute sense of loneliness and to this was added anxiety about the churches suffering persecution. It was in this state of mind that he wrote to Timothy:

"Make haste to come to me shortly; for Demas has deserted me, loving this world, and has gone to Thessalonica, Crescens to Galatia, Titus to Dalmatia. Luke only is with me. Take Mark and bring him with thee, for he is useful to me for the ministry. But Tychicus I have sent to Ephesus. When thou comest, bring with thee the cloak that I left at Troas with Carpus, and the books, especially the parchments."

The Apostle feels certain that he has nothing more to hope for from human sources. "I am already being poured out in sacrifice," he says, "and the time of my deliverance is at hand. I have fought the good fight, I have finished the course, I have kept the faith." He turns now with confidence to the divine Master whose name he has carried afar unto the Gentiles. "For the rest," he continues, "there is laid up for me a crown of justice, which the Lord, the just Judge, will give to me in that day; yet not to me only, but also to those who love his coming . . . The Lord will deliver me for his heavenly kingdom; to whom be the glory forever and ever . . . The Lord Jesus Christ be with thy spirit. Grace be with you. Amen."

After this farewell the curtain falls upon the Apostle, hiding from our view the last days of his earthly pilgrimage. Did he live long enough to receive his cloak and books, and to press to his heart his beloved Timothy? We can't say. All that we know with certainty is that he died by the sword, on the outskirts of Rome, toward the end of Nero's reign.

An ancient and enduring tradition has perpetuated for us the memory of the spot where the Apostle of the Nations baptized the pagan soil of Rome with his blood. It was a lonely valley, about three miles from the walls of Rome and a little east of the Ostian Way. Formerly called *Aquae Salviae,* meaning "healing waters," it goes to-day by the name of Three Fountains, with three churches marking the spot. A small community of Trappists maintains a silent vigil over the hallowed place and jealously guards its sanctuaries.

At the appointed hour, a centurion with a squadron of praetorian guards came to take Paul from his dungeon. Pale, sickly and gaunt from hunger and confinement, the great missionary begins his last journey. His head is bare, his shoulders a bit stooped, and his beard is growing white; but his flashing eyes mirror the power of an invincible will and give him the appearance not of a captive but of a conqueror. A crowd of the idle and the curious, eager for bloody spectacles, follow after the guards. Trailing a little behind is a small silent group of Christians. Luke, the beloved physician, Pudens, Linus, Eubulus, Claudia, and perhaps Mark and Timothy are there.

Passing through the city gate at the foot of the Aventine, they walk a little more than two miles along the road to Ostia, then turn to the left on a crossroad which led to the highway to Ardea. A quarter of an hour later the cadence beaten by the buskins of the guards on the cobblestones dies; they step off the highway into a little valley set in a framework of low, wooded hills—the place of execution.

The prisoner is first stripped, then bound to the stake. His emaciated and worn body receives the last of its many scourgings, but this is the most ruthless of all, for he is now an outcast of society. His bleeding body bends forward to welcome the sword. The blade flashes for a moment in the sun; there is a thud, and the Apostle's head falls bleeding to the ground. Paul the missionary is now the martyr, and the one burning desire of his life is fulfilled: he is with his Lord and Master, Jesus Christ.

The disciples gathered up reverently the mortal remains and bore them along the Ostian Way about three quarters of a mile in the direction of Rome, and buried them in a cemetery belonging to a Christian family. Over the grave they reared a little structure on which they carved the simple epitaph: *Paul, Apostle, Martyr.* After his victory the Emperor Constantine built a basilica over Paul's tomb. Over it today rises the majestic Basilica of St. Paul outside the walls, and in the center, around Paul's tomb are sculptured his own words, which fittingly epitomize his whole life: "For to me to live is Christ and to die is gain."

"About the same time," observes Fernand Prat, "on the other side of the Tiber, at the foot of the Vatican hill, the chief of the Apostles, Peter, was crucified, head downward." At the Council of Jerusalem the two great Apostles, in a famous act of communion and of brotherhood, had divided the world between them: now they were united in death and in glory. With tender reverence and love Rome has always linked together the two mighty champions of the faith, in life and in death illustrious witnesses for Christ, whose relics she has guarded with jealous and ceaseless care.

On June 29, A.D. 258, when the persecution under Valerian threatened the Christian tombs with profanation, the faithful gathered up the sacred remains and deposited them together in a catacomb on the Appian Way. It was the date of this transference which determined in the Latin Church their feast day—June 29. The year commonly assigned for their martyrdom is A.D. 67—a date forever sacred to the Christian world.

III. A PRICELESS LEGACY

When the praetorian soldier flashed his sword in the Roman sunlight and severed the head from its bruised and bleeding body, he doubtless thought that he had blotted out forever the name and memory of the man who had been foolish enough to preach the Gospel of a crucified Christ. Little did he dream that long after the mighty Roman Empire had fallen into dust, and after nineteen centuries of tumultuous history had swept away all the thrones, dynasties, and kingdoms of Europe and Asia, the name of that condemned criminal would be enshrined in the memory of the Christian world, and the grubby parchments which he had left behind him at Troas would be treasured among the most precious spiritual possessions of mankind.

From those parchments have streamed currents of thought, which have brought light to the blind, hope to the despondent, strength to the weak, and have changed the lives of countless millions. They have been a cloud by day and a pillar of fire by night to the groping footsteps of men in all the intervening ages. Even more than his ceaseless journeying by land and sea they have brought Christ, His faith, and His love to the minds and hearts of men and extended His kingdom throughout a world of whose vastness even Paul never dreamed. Indeed, Paul was never more alive than he is today— thanks to his immortal epistles.

Since unfortunately the epistles are not much more than a hermetically sealed box for many people, let us see if we can break that box open and let the readers glimpse the beauty and grandeur of its contents. Let us get a close-up of these documents, examine their style, structure, form, and order, see how they were composed, glance at some of the principal doctrines they develop, and appraise the precious legacy of truth they bequeath to us.

While the Acts provides a partial history of Paul's missionary work and sets the stage for some of his discourses, it does not supply us with a satisfactory or adequate record of his teaching or his thought. For this we must turn to his letters. It was his unsurpassed zeal in spreading the faith and his paternal affection for the numerous churches which he established that prompted the Apostle to write the fourteen canonical epistles. It is certain, however, that he wrote other epistles which have not come down to us. In 1 Corinthians mention is made of a previous letter, and in Colossians he refers to a letter directed to the Laodiceans, and in Philippians he seems to hint at other letters to the community at Philippi: all have been lost.

After preaching in a community and establishing a congregation the Apostle, in his solicitude for their continued growth and welfare, would sometimes write them letters. Hence they were written to confirm, or complete, or prepare for, or even to take the place of his personal ministrations. Misunderstandings and abuses had to be corrected, questions answered, and difficulties solved. With the exception of the Epistle to the Romans, they were composed to meet particular needs or circumstances, either of communities or individuals. They were written with authority, however, and were intended to be read publicly. It is a tribute to the genius of the author that writings so produced should transcend merely local needs and interests and constitute a heritage of universal interest and perennial value.

All the epistles, even those addressed to Romans and Hebrews, were written in Greek. This was not the Greek of the classical writers, such as Demosthenes and Plato, but the Hellenist dialect commonly used by the masses. Though Paul was a master of this idiom, and could on occasion speak it with eloquence and grace, he did not strive after literary elegance or polished diction in his letters.

Conscious of the power of truth to win the assent of the mind, he scorned the use of meretricious adornment as a cosmetic make-up unworthy of the Gospel. Christ, he points out, sent him "to preach the gospel not with wisdom of words lest the cross of Christ be made void." Indeed, he gives us his own evaluation of himself as a writer when he declares, "Even though I be rude in speech, yet am I not so in knowledge; but in every way we have made ourselves clear to you."

To Paul the word was merely a means to an end: the communication of thought. At times he is so possessed with the thought that it flows from his gifted mind like water under such pressure that it bursts the dike of language seeking to contain it. Not infrequently it is so tempestuous and many-faceted that it breaks through the outward envelope of words and shoots out in many directions like sparks from an anvil.

This explains the anacolutha, digressions, parenthetic thoughts, ellipses, pleonasms, and other irregularities, which render at times a strictly literal translation difficult. Occasionally he indulges in Hebraisms, and in his eagerness to overtake his own thought at times violates strict grammatical construction.

In spite of such structural defects and irregularities, the epistles grip one with the power and genius of their thought and at times rise to a soaring eloquence. They abound in picturesque expressions and metaphors, questions and exclamations, climaxes, antitheses, and many other figures of speech. The Apostle's intellectual brilliance and depth of feeling impart to his language loftiness, amazing power, and at times a lyrical beauty. St. Jerome remarked that Paul's words struck him like peals of thunder.

How were the epistles composed? The Apostle generally dictated his letters to an amanuensis and then, by way of authentication and signature, wrote the final salutation with his own hand. Thus at the end of the Second Epistle to the Thessalonians the Apostle says: "I, Paul, greet you with my own hand. This is the mark in every letter.

Thus I write." Perhaps the Epistle to Philemon, which is only about a page in length, because of its intimate and personal character and its unusual brevity, was written by Paul himself.

The epistles were written on papyri, a material made from strips of the stalk of the Egyptian papyrus plant. Thin vertical strips about a yard long and a few inches wide were joined lengthwise and then reinforced by another layer of strips placed crosswise. When compressed together the two layers formed a sheet of "paper," the word being derived from "papyrus." The writing was done with ink and reeds or sharpened goose quills. In consequence, the physical act of writing letters like those of Paul was a slow, tedious, and tiring labor which is difficult for us even to imagine in this day of rapid dictation to stenographers and dictaphones.

Various references in ancient manuscripts indicate that it took about an hour to write seventy-two words. Hence it is probable that the scribe could not always keep pace with the dictation of the Apostle, in whose active mind fresh ideas and images raced with lightning-like velocity. This would explain the broken structure of sentences, the thoughts left dangling in mid-air, the piling up of parentheses and the other irregularities of composition, which render certain passages difficult to understand.

The scribe wrote crouched on the ground, holding the paper on a tablet in his left hand: ordinarily he could not work more than two or three hours at a stretch. As Paul worked by day to earn a living, when he was not teaching or preaching, he was probably able to devote only the hours of the evening or the night to his letters. Hence it is estimated that the writing of the Epistle to the Romans, comprising 7101 words, must have kept Paul and his scribe busy for about forty-nine days, working two hours each night, or thirty-two days, working three hours a night. These facts give one an idea of the enormous amount of thought, work, time, and pains the Apostle spent in the effort to communicate his ideas and sentiments to his spiritual children dispersed so widely throughout the countries of the Mediterranean world.

The order of the Pauline epistles in our modern Bibles is practically the same as that prevailing in the latter part of the fourth century, as witnessed by the Council of Laodicea and by St. Augustine. The arrangement does not follow the chronological order. In the first place are the epistles addressed to the communities, ranked according to the length of their contents and the relative dignity of the churches.

Thus we have Romans, 1 and 2 Corinthians, Galatians, Ephesians, Philippians, Colossians, and 1 and 2 Thessalonians. In the second place are the epistles addressed to individuals: 1 and 2 Timothy, Titus, and Philemon. The Epistle to the Hebrews is in the last place because it was the last epistle to be admitted into the canon by the universal Church.

Paul's epistles have the same threefold external form or structure common to ancient letters: an introduction, the body of the letter, and the conclusion. The introduction ordinarily contains the name of the writer and the name of one or more associates, the name of the church or person to whom the letter is addressed, the greeting, and occasionally a benediction. In the body of the Pauline epistles dogmatic truths are developed and demonstrated, and then practical exhortations for religious life are given. The conclusion includes personal messages, greetings to individuals or from individuals, and final blessings.

Although in writing the epistles Paul did not intend to present a systematic exposition of the whole of the Christian faith, a *Summa Theologica* like that of St. Thomas Aquinas, he treats so many doctrines and their application to daily life that the epistles constitute a veritable storehouse of theology. From the earliest centuries the Fathers and Doctors of the Church have drawn upon them for their sermons and their writings. St. John Chrysostom (344–407), who is considered the ablest commentator on the Apostle, compares these letters to inexhaustible mines of precious metals, and to unfailing springs which flow the richer the more we draw from them.

Although it is impossible to treat or even to enumerate all these doctrines, it may be well to point out the central and pivotal thoughts which recur in these letters. They are the following:

1. All men, whether Jews or Gentiles, have been redeemed by Jesus Christ the Son of God through His passion and death upon the cross. Writing to the Galatians, Paul said: "God sent his Son, born of a woman, born under the Law, that he might redeem those who were under the Law, that we might receive the adoption of sons." To Timothy he wrote urging that prayers, intercessions, and thanksgivings be made for all men. "This," he said, "is good and agreeable in the sight of God our Savior, who *wishes all men to be*

saved and to come to the knowledge of the truth. For there is one God, and one Mediator between God and men, himself man, Christ Jesus, *who gave himself a ransom for all."*

In the Epistle to the Ephesians he said: "Christ also loved us and delivered himself up for us as an *offering and a sacrifice* to God." To the Romans he declared: "But God commends his charity towards us, because when as yet we were sinners, *Christ died for us. Much more now that we are justified by his blood, shall we be saved* through him."

2. The source of all grace, and of the justification and salvation of all mankind from Adam to the last man that shall live, is Jesus Christ. Writing to the Galatians, Paul said: "You are all the children of God through faith in Christ Jesus. For all you who have been baptized into Christ, have put on Christ. There is neither Jew nor Greek; there is neither slave nor freeman; there is neither male nor female. For you are all one in Christ Jesus." To the Romans he wrote: "For if by the offense of the one the many died, much more has the *grace of God,* and the gift in the grace of the one man Jesus Christ, abounded unto the *many . . .* For just as by the disobedience of the one man the many were constituted sinners, so also by the obedience of the one the *many will be constituted just."*

3. The purpose of the Mosaic Law was to lead to Christ the Savior, and hence with the death of the Redeemer it ceased to have meaning, utility, or purpose, and was abrogated. There were no longer valid grounds for distinguishing between the Israelite and the Gentile. To the Romans, Paul wrote: "For Christ is the consummation of the Law, unto justice for *everyone who believes . . .* For there is no distinction between Jew and Greek, for there is the same Lord of all, rich toward all who call upon him." To the Galatians he declared: "For I through the Law have *died to the Law* that I may *live to God."*

4. All the faithful are intimately united with Christ, forming with Him one mystical body of which He is the head and we are the members. In his Epistle to the Ephesians, Paul writes: "I therefore, the prisoner in the Lord, exhort you to walk in a manner worthy of the calling with which you were called, with all humility and meekness, with patience, bearing with one another in love, careful to preserve the unity of the Spirit in the bond of peace: *one body and one Spirit,* even as you were called in one hope of your calling; one Lord,

one faith, one Baptism; one God and Father of all, who is above all, and throughout all, and *in us all.*"

A few verses later the Apostle declared that a diversity of graces has been bestowed upon different members "for building up the body of Christ, until we all attain to the unity of the faith and of the deep knowledge of the Son of God, to perfect manhood, to the mature measure of the fullness of Christ . . . We are to practice the truth in love, and so grow up in all things *in him who is the head, Christ.* For *from him the whole body* (being closely joined and knit together through every joint of the system according to the functioning in due measure of each single part) *derives its increase* to the building up of itself in love."

Developing this same beautiful and profound truth in the First Epistle to the Corinthians, he says: "For as the body is one and has many members, and all the members of the body, *many as they are, form one body, so also is it with Christ.*" Equally explicit is Paul in writing to the Colossians: "He [Christ] is the *head of his body, the Church* . . . I rejoice now in the sufferings I bear for your sake; and what is lacking of the sufferings of Christ I fill up in my flesh for *his body, which is the Church.*"

Indeed this truth was first revealed to Paul when, as he was hurrying along the road to Damascus to seize Christians, imprison and persecute them, Christ appeared to him and said, "Saul, Saul, why dost thou persecute *me?*" Thus did the frightful realization break in upon Paul that the members of the Church are so joined with Christ, their head, as to constitute one body, and in persecuting that *Church* Paul was in reality persecuting *Christ* Himself.

Thus it is evident that Jesus Christ, the Son of God made man and the Redeemer of all mankind, is the center of all Paul's teachings and the cornerstone of his whole theological edifice. More than that, Christ was the center of his very being. Christ permeated the thoughts of his mind, throbbed in all the emotions of his heart, and reigned in every act of his will. Paul lived for Christ, labored for Christ, died for Christ.

Christ was the *alpha* and the *omega* of Paul's being, the axis around which his whole universe revolved, the be-all and the end-all of his very existence. "For to me to live is Christ," exclaimed Paul, "and to die is gain." And again he cries ecstatically, "It is now no longer I that live, but Christ lives in me." What other man that ever lived could say that with equal truth? Truly Paul was a Christ-intoxicated man if there ever was one. No wonder it is that in his letters the name *Savior* occurs over 300 times, *Jesus* more than 240 times, and the name of *Christ* over 400 times.

So much then for a general panorama view of the epistles. Let us now present a few selected passages which have become classics in the literature of all languages. They are worthy not only of repeated perusal but also of being committed to memory so that we can the better assimilate their thought content, bring it into our blood stream and weave it into the marrow of our bones. Carrying these beautiful selections in our minds means that even in our solitude we shall have the company of one of the greatest geniuses and holiest men that ever lived.

In his Epistle to the Romans, Paul presents a penetrating and memorable analysis of the two forces—the flesh with its lusts and the spirit with its aspirations—which war within the citadel of the human soul, struggling for the ascendancy. In depicting so vividly this inner struggle, Paul is writing the autobiography not so much of himself as of the whole human race.

"For we know that the Law is spiritual but I am carnal, sold into the power of sin. For I do not understand what I do, for it is not what I wish that I do, but what I hate, that I do. But if I do what I do not wish, I admit that the Law is good. Now therefore it is no longer I who do it, but the sin that dwells in me. For I know that in me, that is, in my flesh, no good dwells, because to wish is within my power, but I do not find the strength to accomplish what is good. For I do not the good that I wish, but the evil that I do not wish, that I perform.

"Now if I do what I do not wish, it is no longer I who do it, but the sin that dwells in me. Therefore, when I wish to do good I discover this law, namely, that evil is at hand for me. For I am delighted with the law of God according to the inner man, but I see another law in my members, warring against the law of my mind and making me prisoner to the law of sin that is in my members. Unhappy man that I am! Who will deliver me from the body of this death? The grace of God through Jesus Christ our Lord."

Where is the individual who has not felt himself compelled at times to cry out with the Apostle, "I do not the good that I wish, but the evil that I do not wish, that I perform"? It mirrors the tear-drenched experience of mankind from the time of Adam, and alas! it shall continue to reflect that sad experience until the crack of doom. Listen to Ovid as he cries out, *"Video meliora proboque, Deteriora sequor"*—I see and approve the better things but I do the worse.

Paul not only lays bare the anarchy within the human soul but also points to the power, which, if invoked, will unfailingly turn the tide of battle in our favor: "the grace of God through Jesus Christ our Lord." When the psychologist will have written his last line after probing the deepest and most persistent conflict in human nature, it will be found that he has but spun out in scientific language the truth laid bare by Paul in simple words and with transparent lucidity.

At the summit of Paul's vision stands Jesus Christ: the goal of all his striving and the object of all his love. To imprint this vision of Christ upon all his followers he exhausted all his efforts: words flowed from him in torrents when he sought to hymn his praise and love for the Incarnate God, Christ Jesus, who drew Paul from the darkness into the light. Listen to the Apostle as he seeks to mirror that burning love, kindle it in the hearts of his followers, and have them manifest it also to one another. Writing to the Philippians, he says:

"For to me to live is Christ and to die is gain . . . If, therefore, there is any comfort in Christ, any encouragement from charity, any fellowship in the Spirit, any feelings of mercy, fill up my joy by thinking alike, having the same charity, with one soul and one mind. Do nothing out of contentiousness or out of vainglory, but in humility let each one regard the others as his superiors, each one looking not to his own interests but to those of others.

"Have this mind in you which was also in Christ Jesus, who though he was by nature God, did not consider being equal to God a thing to be clung to, but emptied himself, taking the nature of a slave and being made like unto men. And appearing in the form of man, he humbled himself, becoming obedient to death, even to death on a cross. Therefore God also has exalted him and has bestowed upon him the name that is above every name, so that at the name of Jesus every knee should bend of those in heaven, on earth and under the earth, and every tongue should confess that the Lord Jesus Christ is in the glory of God the Father."

Like the good shepherd that he was, Paul never failed to warn his spiritual children against the dangers threatening their faith and virtue. In a beautiful passage in the Epistle to the Ephesians he bids them to put on the complete armor of God's soldier, to fight effectively against the forces of wickedness.

"Brethren," he says, "be strengthened in the Lord and in the might of his power. Put on the armor of God, that you may be able to stand against the wiles of the devil. For our wrestling is not against flesh and blood, but against the Principalities and the Powers, against the world-rulers of this darkness, against the spiritual forces of wickedness on high. Therefore take up the armor of God, that you may be able to resist in the evil day, and stand in all things perfect.

"Stand, therefore, having girded your loins with truth, and having put on the breastplate of justice, and having your feet shod with the readiness of the gospel of peace, in all things taking up the shield of faith, with which you may be able to quench all the fiery darts of the most wicked one. And take unto you the helmet of salvation and the sword of the spirit, that is, the word of God.

"With all prayer and supplication pray at all times in the Spirit, and therein be vigilant in all perseverance and supplication for all the saints—and for me, that when I open my mouth, utterance may be granted to me fearlessly to make known the mystery of the gospel, for which I am an ambassador in chains; so that therein I may dare to speak as I ought . . . Peace be to the brethren, and love with faith, from God the Father and the Lord Jesus Christ. Grace be with all those who have a love unfailing for our Lord Jesus Christ. Amen."

In a memorable passage in the First Epistle to the Corinthians, Paul describes the lot of the Apostles, making capital use of antitheses. "Let a man so account us," he says, "as servants of Christ and stewards of the mysteries of God . . . God has set forth us the apostles last of all, as men doomed to death, seeing that we have been made a spectacle to the world, and to angels, and to men. We are fools for Christ, but you are wise in Christ! We are weak, but you are strong! You are honored, but we are without honor!

"To this very hour we hunger and thirst, and we are naked and buffeted, and have no fixed abode. And we toil, working with our own hands. We are reviled and we bless, we are persecuted and we bear with it, we are maligned and we entreat, we have become as the refuse of this world, the offscouring of all, even until now!

"I write these things not to put you to shame, but to admonish you as my dearest children. For although you have ten thousand tutors in Christ, yet you have not many fathers. For in Christ Jesus, through the gospel, did I beget you. Therefore, I beg you, be imitators of me, as I am of Christ. For this very reason I have sent to you Timothy, who is my dearest son and faithful in the Lord. He will remind you of my ways, which are in Christ Jesus, even as I teach everywhere in every church."

The Apostle reaches heights of soaring eloquence in describing for the Romans the unfaltering love of Christ—his favorite theme. Notice the effective use he makes of questions and exclamations, so that the letter seems not so much a written document as the actual voice of Paul, pleading and exhorting.

"Now we know," he says, "that for those who love God all things work together unto good . . . If God is for us, who is against us? He who has not spared even his own Son but has delivered him for us all, how can he fail to grant us also all things with him? Who shall make accusation against the elect of God? It is God who justifies! Who shall condemn? It is Christ Jesus who died; yes, and rose again, he who is at the right hand of God, who also intercedes for us!

"Who shall separate us from the love of Christ? Shall tribulation, or distress, or persecution, or hunger, or nakedness, or danger, or the sword? . . . But in all these things we overcome because of him who has loved us. For I am sure that neither death, nor life, nor angels, nor principalities, nor things present, nor things to come, nor powers, nor height, nor depth, nor any other creature will be able to separate us from the love of God, which is in Christ Jesus our Lord."

While Paul was languishing as a prisoner in Rome he thought of the numerous churches he had established and of the shepherds he had placed over them. He wanted to infuse into them his own quenchless zeal for souls. While he addresses his words specifically to Timothy, they apply to all who have the care of souls. Notice how the quick staccato thrust of the Apostle mirrors his own feverish, restless zeal.

"I charge thee," he writes, "in the sight of God and Christ Jesus, who will judge the living and the dead by his coming and by his kingdom, preach the word, be urgent in season, out of season; reprove, entreat, rebuke with all patience and teaching. For there will come a time when they will not endure the sound doctrine; but having itching ears, will heap up to themselves teachers according to their own lusts, and they will turn away their hearing from the truth and turn aside rather to fables. But do thou be watchful in all things, bear with tribulation patiently, work as a preacher of the gospel, fulfill thy ministry."

The force and cogency of Paul's words were greatly increased by the compelling power of his own example. His followers saw the Apostle practice what he preached: this gave his words an eloquence which no literary craftsmanship or oratorical skill could impart. Burning with love for his crucified Lord and Savior Jesus Christ, Paul could not fail to transmit something of that warmth and devotion to his listeners and his readers. Hence it is against that background that the epistles are always to be read. To get the most out of their perusal, one should have at his side, at least on the first reading, a commentary on the epistles.* This will enable him to understand the occasional passage where the structure is somewhat involved or the meaning is not immediately apparent.

So much for the epistles. Now for a brief close-up and appraisal of the man behind them: Paul, the teacher, preacher, Apostle, writer, missionary, and martyr who became "all things" for Christ, even unto death.

It must be acknowledged at the outset that Paul had two distinct advantages over his fellow Apostles. Firstly, with the exception of a few, his letters have come down to us, thus giving us an authentic and far-reaching glimpse of both his thought and work. It is not unlikely that some of the other Apostles wrote letters to their flocks, which did not enjoy the good fortune to survive.

Secondly, he had in Luke an able biographer and apologist: the "beloved physician" not only sketched his extensive missionary labors but also defended him from the criticism of his detractors. The missionary labors of most of the other Apostles had no historian to record them: we are left with blank pages instead of with sheets crammed full with the moving story of their zeal, resourcefulness, sacrifices, and deaths. Hence it is only fair to acknowledge that one

---

* A Commentary on the New Testament, William H. Sadlier, Inc., N.Y. Written by the group of scholars who prepared the Confraternity Edition of the New Testament, this volume is of great helpfulness for the general reader. More voluminous and detailed is The Epistles of St. Paul, by C. J. Callan, O.P., Joseph F. Wagner, Inc., N.Y., which will appeal particularly to the student. Both are excellent and will repay careful reading and study.

reason why Paul looms up so large in the history of the infant Church is because we know so much about him.

The Apostle displayed real genius in framing a plan for the propagation of the faith and in devising means to put that plan into effective operation. It was his policy to concentrate, after the manner of a general, on strategic centers, organize them thoroughly, and use them as a base for further operations. He made it a practice to revisit the scenes of his former labors and, when prevented from doing so, he maintained contact by letter or by carefully chosen lieutenants.

Paul saw in the dispersion of Israel a providential preparation for the spread of the Gospel, and he capitalized on it to the maximum. He used the synagogues of the Hellenistic world as a sounding board to reach not only his kinsmen according to the flesh but also that considerable fringe of the Gentile world which had been attracted to the religion of Yahweh. When the Jews refused to accept his message he turned increasingly to the Gentiles and showed how the Gospel met their deepest needs.

His success in entering into their minds, glimpsing the hunger in their hearts, and in stripping the practice of the faith from its nonessential, Judaic elements, obnoxious to them, is a tribute to his genius. To him is due the lion's share of the credit for thus freeing the infant Church from the strangling swaddling clothes of Jewish exclusivism. In this important enterprise he both took the initiative and pushed it through to a successful culmination. In so doing he rescued the Church from the greatest peril it faced in the whole first century.

In the choice of collaborators Paul exercised great discernment. Loyalty to him and the use of his methods of evangelizing were required of all those in close association. When Barnabas failed to share Paul's judgment concerning the use of the former's cousin Mark, the Apostle let both of them withdraw on a mission of their own. Apollo and other talented speakers must have thought it strange when they saw the persuasive words of human eloquence set aside in order that the Christian thing might stand forth for what it was, a "demonstration of the Spirit and of power, that your faith might rest not on the wisdom of men but on the power of God."

Whatever may have been the natural talents of Timothy, Titus, Silas, and Luke, they developed under Paul's tutelage and inspiring leadership into lieutenants of very high caliber: they became able to extend the master's work and, when necessary, to administer in his place. The fact that some of these co-workers, if not all, were the converts of other men, casts an interesting side light upon Paul's strong sense of unity with the other Apostles.

Indeed, it is a mistake, commonly made by those who remember only the brief disagreement of Peter and Paul at Antioch on a matter of procedure, to picture the latter as conducting his missionary work with little or no consultation with the Apostles at Jerusalem, and even as purposely holding aloof from them. Early in his apostolate Paul went to Jerusalem expressly to see Peter and the others, and to be welcomed by them into the body of the Apostles. Back again he went from the missions, bearing alms for the brethren ravished by famine. Thither, too, he went to secure an authoritative solution of the problem as to how Gentiles were to be received into the Church.

He tells the Corinthians that the Gospel he is preaching is the same Gospel as that preached by the other Apostles. "Whether then it is I or they," he says, "so we preach, and so you have believed." How edifying and inspiring it is to see him leave his missions to go to Jerusalem to submit the Gospel he is preaching to the Gentiles in order to secure from the authorities in the Holy City their hearty approval. "I went up," he tells the Galatians, "in consequence of a revelation, and I conferred with them on the Gospel which I preach among the Gentiles, but separately with men of authority; lest perhaps I should be running, or had run in vain." Note, too, that he did this in compliance with a revelation from God. In short, no Apostle in his preaching stressed the necessity of unity more than Paul and none put his preaching into practice more unmistakably than he.

Paul displayed a singular genius in touching the hearts of men and in winning them for Christ. Aside entirely from his penetrating insight into the Gentile mind and character and his skill in the presentation of the Gospel to them, the Apostle radiated a sympathy, compassion, and love which rarely failed to warm the hearts of his hearers. Acknowledging his own infirmity and weakness, he set before them the example of Jesus and His burning love with compelling appeal primarily because he, too, experienced that love and he wished to share it with others. It was because he himself was so deeply moved that he was able to move others. What warmth of affection there is in his discourses, cropping out in such frequent phrases as "my dear children," "our glory and joy," and "my brethren, beloved and longed for, my joy and my crown."

Cardinal Newman singled out Paul's sympathy as the gift which particularly distinguished him. In a beautiful passage he says: "To him specially was it given to preach to the world, who knew the world: he subdued the heart, who understood the heart. It was his sympathy which was his means of influence: it was his affectionateness which was his title and instrument of empire." It was in virtue of this gift of sympathy that Paul was able to spread about his person an aura of fragrance and to draw the hearts of his hearers to him as by a sort of magnetic attraction.

How few are the men who can say with the Apostle: "For, free though I was to all, unto all I have made myself a slave that I might gain the more converts. And I have become to the Jews a Jew that I might gain the Jews; to those under the Law, as one under the Law (though not myself under the Law), that I might gain those under the Law; to those without the Law, as one without the Law (though I am not without the law of God, but am under the law of Christ), that I might gain those without the Law. To the weak I became weak, that I might gain the weak. I became all things to all men, that I might save all."

It was because Paul had such a passionate love of Jesus and such warm affection for men that he not only had enthusiasm himself for the spread of the Gospel but also radiated it to his disciples and converts. In its etymological sense, enthusiasm means "God within one"; in this sense Paul was full of enthusiasm because he was filled with God: Christ permeated every atom of his being. It was this enthusiasm which endowed his physique with a stamina which has amazed all subsequent generations.

No mountain was too rugged or stubborn for him to climb, no field too studded with thorns and briars for him to traverse, no sea too storm-ridden for him to sail in order to bring Christ and His Gospel to darkened intellects and famished hearts. It was this flaming enthusiasm which drove Paul on his continuous journeying and kept him forever on fire to win the world for Christ. Transmitting this enthusiasm to his disciples, he bound them to him with hoops of love stronger than iron or steel.

See him as he blazes a new and triumphal highway for the Gospel, starting at Jerusalem and ending at the limits of the Western world. Planning his conquest of the world for Christ, he establishes spiritual citadels at such strategic points as Tarsus, Antioch of Pisidia, Ephesus, Alexandria of Troas, Philippi, Thessalonica and Corinth. He plants the banner of his Master throughout the Roman provinces of Syria, Cilicia, Galatia, Asia, Macedonia, Achaia, and Illyricum: it waved in triumph from the desert of Damascus to the Adriatic Sea.

He enlarges the beachhead of Peter in Rome and then pushes on to Spain, where the Pillars of Hercules mark the confines of the then known world. The conquests of Alexander pale into insignificance before the achievements of this daring and resolute soldier who raised aloft the cross of Christ in the countries of the vast Mediterranean world from Palestine to the Strait of Gibraltar. Back of that mighty conquest was a divine enthusiasm springing from the love of God and of souls; this was the divine spark which kindled Paul's dream of conquest and supplied him with the power to make that dream come true.

No writer of prose or poetry has hymned the virtue of fraternal charity more eloquently than Paul or practiced it more assiduously than he. The unsurpassed classic on this topic is his soaring passage in the First Epistle to the Corinthians: "If I should speak with the tongues of men and of angels, but do not have charity, I have become as sounding brass or a tinkling cymbal."

To Paul, Christian altruism owes its noblest expression: "Do nothing out of contentiousness or out of vainglory, but in humility let each one regard the others as his superiors, each one looking not to his own interests but to those of others." To the Apostle, Christian humanism owes its motto: "For the rest, brethren, whatever things are true, whatever honorable, whatever just, whatever holy, whatever lovable, whatever of good repute, if there be any virtue, if anything worthy of praise, think upon these things."

These lofty and noble sentiments flowed spontaneously from the Apostle's profound appreciation of the Christian mystery. His penetrating intellect worked by intuition, and he perceived more clearly than others the universal efficacy of the Redemption. If salvation is for all men, and if in Christ there is neither Jew nor Gentile, bond nor free, it is because the power that works salvation is not the Law of Moses but faith in Him who "was delivered up for our sins, and rose again for our justification."

In consequence of these amazingly clear perceptions, Paul stressed the primacy of the life of grace over mere external observances with a vigor and clarity unsurpassed by any of the Twelve. Though Christians were emancipated from the Mosaic Law, they were not free from the law of the Spirit. It was the death of Christ which emancipated men from the tyranny of sin and the grave and enables them to live a new life in union with the Risen Christ. By virtue of that union the Christian renders willing and joyous service, inspired and borne on by the Holy Spirit. The "slaves of Christ" are the only persons who are truly free, for "where the Spirit of the Lord is, there is freedom."

How is it that Paul had such a luminous perception of these profound truths? Why was he able to become the foremost exponent of the Christian faith to the Gentile world and the greatest theologian of all time? These questions become all the more acute when it is recalled that the Apostle spent a total of but fifteen days with the Apostles at Jerusalem before beginning his intensive missionary work, and indeed had done some preaching even before that. The unmistakable answer is: he was favored with a series of divine revelations in which these great truths were made clear to him.

"For I give you to understand, brethren," he wrote to the Galatians, "that the gospel which was preached by me is not of men. For I did not receive it from man, nor was I taught it; but I received it by a revelation of Jesus Christ." A few lines later he explained that after his conversion "without taking counsel with flesh and blood, and without going up to Jerusalem to those who were appointed apostles before me, I retired into Arabia." During that period of prayer, meditation, and preparation for his apostolate, God doubtless furthered his growth in knowledge of the divine mysteries by additional revelations.

At various intervals in his ministry the Apostle alluded to the supernatural source of some of his teachings. Thus in explaining the Holy Eucharist to the Corinthians, he said: "For I myself have received from the Lord (what I also delivered to you)." In a later letter he wrote them more about the revelations with which God favored him.

"If I must boast," he wrote, "it is not indeed expedient to do so—but I will come to visions and revelations of the Lord. I know a man in Christ who fourteen years ago—whether in the body I do not know, or out of the body I do not know, God knows—such a one was caught up to the third heaven. And I know such a man—whether in the body or out of the body I do not know, God knows—that he was caught up into paradise and heard secret words that man may not repeat . . . And lest the greatness of the revelations should puff me up, there was given me a thorn for the flesh, a messenger of Satan, to buffet me."

In addition to this series of revelations, Paul received others directing him where to preach and where not to evangelize. In an address to the presbyters of the Church assembled at Miletus, he said: "And now, behold, I am going to Jerusalem, compelled by the Spirit, not knowing what will happen to me there; except that in every city the Holy Spirit warns me, saying that imprisonment and persecution are awaiting me." Besides this extraordinary source, Paul had, of course, the primitive Christian catechesis—the oral catechetical instruction of catechumens—upon which all the members of the Church drew: this was common source material for the four Evangelists as well as for Paul. The Church was a going concern for nine years before a single word of the New Testament was written. Indeed, the rhythms of the primitive catechesis echo and re-echo throughout his epistles. Added to this common fund of information, however, were the numerous direct divine revelations to Paul: these alone explain both his amazing understanding of the Christian religion and his pre-eminence as a theologian in the Apostolic Church.

What was the title which Paul preferred above all others? It was "slave of Christ Jesus." That was what he sought always to be. From that memorable day when his eyes were opened after the blinding experience on the road to Damascus he had eyes only for Jesus. From that day onward indomitable faith in a crucified Savior was the dynamo that charged his energies, the star that guided him on his far journeys, and the wings that lifted him to the sunlit heavens and enabled him to bring back some of its light to dispel our darkness. A consuming love for Jesus, a fierce passion to live in Him and for Him, and a ceaseless craving to be His slave in life and death were the forces which animated his whole being and inspired all his thoughts and deeds. "If any man does not love our Lord Jesus Christ," he said, "let him be anathema." With Dante, Paul, too, could say of Christ's all-embracing love, "I saw ingathered, bound by love in one volume, the scattered leaves of all the universe."

"To think so magnificently of Jesus," remarks D. J. O'Herlihy, "to be wise with that wisdom which is none other than Jesus and Him crucified, to be urged on by an enthusiasm and a personal love for Jesus that still burns and inflames across the centuries: all this was granted to Paul, so much so that the phrase 'in Christ Jesus' occurs as a refrain in his writings and recapitulates all his thoughts. Old age did not wither nor custom stale the beautiful relationship."

The genius of the great Apostle has captured the imagination and provoked the admiration of scholars of all schools of theological thought and of all religious faiths. "St. Paul," says Professor Henry L. Goudge of Oxford University, "was the first theologian of the Christian Church. Every branch of theology owes a debt to him, not only doctrinal theology but moral, pastoral and ascetical also. He is our greatest teacher about the Church, the Ministry and the Sacraments; he is the Apostle of faith, the faith which lays hold upon the living Christ."

Similar is the appraisal of Professor Heinrich of Berlin University. "Of all the Christians of the first generations," he says, "St. Paul is by far the most conspicuous, in very truth a man of genius. When Jesus and the faith of His first disciples had won their victory over this man—their greatest adversary—then Christianity triumphed as it never did before or since."

Igino Giordani of the Vatican Library concludes his great work on the Apostle by saying: "Paul is the example of a perfect teacher. He is essential in substance, uncompromising in dogma, and pleasing in secondary matters. He is varied in exposition and always confirms his words by his own life. The power and efficacy of his words lie in the fact that his listeners always saw them lived out in Paul. Paul was burning with love for Christ and from Paul they understood who Christ was."

Professor Edgar J. Goodspeed, a prominent American scriptural scholar, describes Paul as "a man of vision, power and conviction, dealing with people very much like ourselves, but dealing with their problems and weaknesses with such extraordinary patience, penetration and understanding that what he said to them can still guide and instruct us, and teach our generation the lessons of faith, tolerance, love and courage it still greatly needs to learn."

In France the greatest authority on St. Paul was the late Fernand Prat, S.J. "Humanly speaking," he says, "nothing is lacking to the glory of St. Paul. He has left behind him a literary heritage which places him in the first rank of writers and which is a priceless treasure for Christian theology . . . No one has ever extolled brotherly love with more eloquence because no one better understood and practiced it."

Giuseppe Ricciotti, one of the leading scriptural scholars of Italy, remarks: "Today Christianity in large measure means Paul, just as human civilization in our era signifies in large measure Christianity. The truly civilized man, consciously or unconsciously, is today to some extent a disciple of Paul."

St. Jerome, the greatest biblical scholar of the early Church, paid high tribute to St. Paul and singled out his benignity as unexcelled. "Perhaps unexampled in history," he says, "Paul, that heart of fire, so ardent in his aspirations, so terrible to his adversaries, so uncompromising toward error, has for his friends, collaborators, and spiritual children infinite consideration and regard."

No writer in any language, however, has commented on the work and genius of Paul with greater penetration or beauty than St. John Chrysostom, the "golden-tongued orator" among the Fathers of the Greek Church. In a discourse on the Apostle he reaches heights of soaring eloquence and lyrical beauty. "Would that it were now given me," he says, "to throw myself round the body of Paul, and be riveted to the tomb, and to see the dust of that body that 'filled up that which was lacking' after Christ, that bore 'the marks' that sowed the Gospel everywhere. Yea, the dust of that body through which he ran to and fro everywhere! The dust of that body through which Christ spoke, and the Light shone forth more brilliant than any lightning!"

It is difficult to do justice in appraising Paul because, like Leonardo da Vinci, he was such a versatile genius and such a many-faceted soul. In each facet he mirrored, like a prism, his divine model, Christ Jesus, whose image was forever before his rapt and admiring gaze. He was an ascetic like Alphonsus Liguori, but he was also a shepherd of souls like Philip Neri; he was a mystic like John of the Cross, but he was also an objective thinker like Thomas Aquinas. Like Francis Xavier he opened up a vast new world to Christianity, but like Carlo Borromeo he was a peerless organizer and practical administrator.

To the lambs of the flock and to repentant sinners he could speak with the gentleness, compassion, and affection of the Beloved Disciple John, but to the breeders of dissension and strife he could speak with the indignation and wrath of Christ as He drove the money-changers out of the Temple. With the weak and the lowly he could walk with the humility of Francis of Assisi, but when principle was at stake he could be as firm as Ignatius Loyola and as intransigent as John the Baptist before the incestuous Herod.

All these myriad qualities blended in Paul in a perfect synthesis, like a seven-branch candlestick which throws out but a single light; from the candle that was Paul there likewise radiated but one flame: that from the Christ who dwelt within him. "Paul," points out Igino Giordani, "is one of the most complete men in recorded history, in whose formation, grace and nature, Judaism and Christianity combined to make of him a universal person." What other man could say with him, "I became all things to all men, that I might save all"?

To appreciate the colossal influence of Paul upon the whole Christian movement one has to recall, not only the large portion of the New Testament filled by his fourteen epistles and the seventeen chapters of the Acts reporting his sermons and his missionary labors, but also the influence exercised by his writings and his activities upon his two disciples, Mark and Luke, the authors of the second and third Gospels. The Gospel of John and the Apocalypse likewise reflect the influence of Paul's theological thought and writings. Without Paul what a slender volume the New Testament would be!

The most important of all the qualities in Paul's complex character was his holiness. The measure of sanctity is conformity to the will of God in all things and perfect conformity spells perfect holiness. To achieve such perfect conformity that he would live Christ and dwell in Him and he in Christ was the obsessing passion of the Apostle's life. Paul was therefore one of the holiest men that ever lived. Indeed, that eminent biblical scholar and profound student of St. Paul, Cuthbert Lattey, S.J., does not hesitate to say: "That St. Paul was one of the greatest saints in the world's history goes without saying: possibly indeed the greatest after our Lord (who was holy with the infinite holiness of the Godhead) and our Lady."

The judgment of eminent scholars, the witness of Holy Scripture, and the testimony of history confirm the conclusion that Paul is one of the greatest saints—possibly *the* greatest—in all Christendom and indeed one of the greatest men that ever lived. As Jesus Christ our Savior may justly be called the untarnished mirror of the infinite and eternal Godhead, so Paul may not unjustly be termed the authentic mirror of Christ, whose Apostle, slave, and martyr he was. Genius that he was in so many fields, the quality which above all others commends him to us is his Christlikeness. That is why he serves as an admirable model for all Christians: he leads them into the likeness of Christ. "Be imitators of me," he said to the Corinthians, "as I am of Christ."

While Christians in general are willing to give ready assent to the conclusion of scholars concerning Paul's unique greatness and holiness, they do not put that belief sufficiently into practice nor on a scale commensurate with his eminence. They do not read his stirring epistles or study his life or meditate upon his labors and sacrifices sufficiently to make the Apostle live in their minds, capture their imaginations, chasten their hearts, and nourish their souls. This is the great need today. To help meet that need there should be in all parishes devotions to St. Paul, as there are to St. Francis of Assisi, St. Anthony of Padua, St. Joseph, St. Jude, and St. Theresa, the Little Flower.

The writings of Paul should be read and studied in schools, colleges, and seminaries; they should be explained from the pulpit. His life and deeds should be woven into the minds of Christians until their hearts throb in union with his, until he dwells within them as Christ dwelt within him. No age needs him more than our own. At a time when the edifice of the infant Church was threatening to collapse under the blows of the synagogue his stooped shoulders held it aloft and freed it from danger. Not less swift or effective will be his intercession in this age of unprecedented crisis.

No individual who invokes his aid will be left unanswered. As the Apostle interceded with Philemon on behalf of his runaway slave Onesimus, and begged the owner to forgive him and to receive him no longer as a slave but "as a brother most dear," so will he intercede with the divine Master for whom he poured out his life. Pray daily to the great Apostle. Spend at least a few minutes each day in reading the Acts or the epistles. Study, too, and meditate upon that still greater book, his heroic and holy life, in which his love for "Christ and Him crucified" lights up every page. Then that love will burn in your heart, make you too the slave of Christ Jesus, and enable you to say with the great St. Paul, "It is no longer I that live, but Christ lives in me."

ST. AUGUSTINE
Greatest of the Fathers

I. THE QUEST FOR DIVINE TRUTH

Foremost among the Fathers of the Church is St. Augustine, Bishop of Hippo and Doctor of the Universal Church. Orator, littérateur, psychologist, philosopher, and theologian, he has left the imprint of his many-faceted genius upon Christian life and thought as has no other prelate or scholar of the early Church. Similar to the place of St. Paul among the Apostles is that of St. Augustine among the Fathers: pre-eminent among them in depth of scholarship and in lasting influence. Indeed, his *Confessions* has been a best seller in every age and has been more widely read than all the writings of the other Fathers and Doctors of the Church combined.

St. Augustine has been regarded by some, points out Christopher Dawson, as the inaugurator of a new era and the first medieval man, and by others as the heir of the old classical culture and one of the last representatives of antiquity. Though there is an element of truth in both these views, he is essentially a man of his own age. Marking a turning point in history, that age saw the fall of Rome, the passing of that great empire which had dominated the fortunes of the world for more than five centuries, and the laying of the foundations of a new world. To a greater degree than any emperor, soldier, or statesman, Augustine was a builder of the bridge which was to lead from the old world to the new.

When Augustine was a boy Julian the Apostate made a last desperate attempt to wrest the Roman Empire from Christ and restore it to the heathen gods. When he had reached full manhood Augustine witnessed the action of Theodosius the Great in binding together for better or for worse the fortunes of Christianity and the empire, of bishop and emperor. In old age he saw the division between east Rome and west Rome, and thus the birth of the West. Alaric and the Teutonic tribes were destroying the western empire and building their own kingdoms on its ruins. Finally, as he lay on his deathbed, Augustine learned that the Vandals, representatives of the new world coming into being, were besieging his episcopal city.

Thus was Augustine a man of the transitional period. "He stood," remarks Karl Adam, "with watchful eye upon the threshold of a new epoch, in which paganism was overcome by Christianity, the empire by the barbarians, and when the first outlines of the west that was to be were beginning to be traced upon the sky of history."

The transitional period of history in which Augustine lived enabled him to serve as a link between two worlds and thus invests his life with especial interest; but even more it is his character, personality, sentiments, and thought which have held the interest of mankind for fifteen centuries. However much he may owe to the spirit of the dying ancient world, he is in all essentials a modern man, modern above all in his interest in the phenomena of the inward life. These have not changed since Augustine's day, and hence his vivid and detailed description of these phenomena give to much of his writing a perennial freshness and charm.

Born at Tagaste, a small town of Numidia in North Africa, on November 13, 354, Aurelius Augustine was the son of a Christian mother, Monica, and a pagan father, Patricius. Of this union several children were born: St. Augustine speaks of his brother Navigius, who left a family behind him, and of a sister who died a dedicated virgin. Shortly after birth Augustine was enrolled as a catechumen, the sign of the cross was made over him and the salt of the catechumens was placed on his mouth, but he was not baptized.

It was the custom of many Christian parents to postpone baptism until early adulthood so that the guilt attaching to the sins of youth might not be made greater and more dangerous by following upon baptism. In his later years Augustine deplored this unfortunate custom. Comparing the reasoning underlying this practice to that of a sick man who wished to be made sicker in order that he might more quickly be healed, he suggested that his sick soul might better have been healed in the beginning by the waters of baptism.

As a boy Augustine grew up speaking Punic, the native language of the region, and early acquired a good grounding in Latin. He learned some Greek, but never acquired any great facility in it. Monica instructed him in the Christian religion and taught him to pray. While still a little boy he became dangerously ill and begged to be baptized. Monica got everything ready, but when the illness soon subsided baptism was deferred.

In force during Augustine's childhood was the "Discipline of the Secret," by which many of the fundamental doctrines of the Christian religion were withheld from catechumens to prevent their desecration at the hands of pagans. Special care was taken not to publicize the articles of the Creed. Moreover, catechumens were not admitted to the most solemn parts of the Mass and only during the weeks immediately preceding their baptism were they permitted to learn the Creed. Hence it is easy to understand why Augustine's knowledge of Christianity was so fragmentary and inadequate.

This meager instruction was supplemented, however, by the edifying example of Monica's deeply spiritual life, in which prayer was ever prominent. This early Christian training left three great ideas deeply engraven upon his mind: a divine Providence, the future life with terrible sanctions, and, above all, Christ the Savior. "From my tenderest infancy," recalls Augustine, "I had in a manner sucked with my mother's milk that name of my Savior, Thy Son; I kept it in the recesses of my heart; and all that presented itself to me without that Divine Name, though it might be elegant, well-written, and even replete with truth, did not altogether carry me away."

Augustine excelled in his studies at the school in his native town, though he admits that his preference at that age was for games and play. Finishing the local school at twelve, Augustine was sent to Madaura, some twenty miles to the south, to continue his studies. Thus at a tender age he was withdrawn from the pious influence of his mother.

"Madaura," points out Vernon Bourke, "was a center of pagan culture and learning: the dominant religion was that of the ancient Roman gods, fused somewhat with the cults of peculiarly African deities." One of its most celebrated sons was Lucius Apuleius, a distinguished rhetorician of the second century A.D., in whose literary traditions the citizens gloried. In its schools Augustine learned the rules of Latin grammar and composition from the diligent reading of the classic models of Roman prose and poetry. For the most part these classics dealt with the stories of the ancient pagan gods.

It is doubtful if there was a Catholic church in the town, and it seems certain that Augustine made no progress either religiously or morally while there. There were many celebrations in honor of the various gods and goddesses: some were the degrading rites of Bacchus, others were orgies in which men roamed the streets in drunken revels, assaulting and robbing people, and pretending that they were obeying the gods within them. It was impossible for the young student to avoid seeing some of these lewd and licentious spectacles.

Augustine's four years of study in Madaura yielded two contrasting results. The first was the development of a set of pseudo-ideals and a code of conduct fundamentally pagan and morally bad. The second was the acquisition of a wide knowledge of Cicero, Varro, Sallust, Horace, Ovid, Persius, Terence, and Catullus. Above all, he became familiar with the works of Vergil. Thus he developed a feeling for the niceties of Latin grammar and construction, which was to prove of such advantage to him in his subsequent literary labors.

When Augustine returned to Tagaste in his sixteenth year Patricius noticed that his son was come to man's estate, and he told Monica that they might soon look forward to some grandchildren. In that sun-scorched land virile development is precocious, and Augustine had inherited from his father a passionate nature. When Monica learned that he could no longer remain under the care of the women of the household she counseled him to guard against sins of the flesh and, in particular, never to defile a married woman. To this last injunction Augustine remained unfalteringly obedient.

It was not without reason that Monica was alarmed at her son's arrival at this dangerous period. Prevailing pagan customs encouraged the throwing off of restraint and countenanced indulgences sadly at variance with the Christian code. In addition, there was the example of Patricius, whose infidelities she had endured to prevent worse consequences and in the hope of winning him ultimately to the Christian faith and its way of life. Neither could she fail to perceive that much of his ardor and passion had found lodgment in her son. She could only hope and pray that Augustine would survive the onslaught of puberty with no serious damage to his character.

Conscious of the marked talent of their son and proud of his success in the schools of Tagaste and Madaura, the parents were determined that he should continue his education: they wished to send him to Carthage so he could become a lawyer and ultimately secure an important government position. Unfortunately, however, it required several months to collect the necessary funds, and Augustine had to spend the year in an idleness which proved fatal to his virtue. Roaming the streets at night with pagan companions, he yielded to the seductions which abounded on every side.

Describing his conduct at this period in the *Confessions,* he would seem almost to exaggerate his immoralities: "Behold, with what companions I traveled the ways of Babylon, wallowing in its mire, as if in cinnamon and precious ointments. And in its bowels, to which I clung ever more tenaciously, my invisible enemy walked roughshod over me, and seduced me because I was very willing to be seduced."

In the late autumn of 370, in the beginning of his seventeenth year, Augustine enrolled in the rhetoric schools of Carthage. It was through the generosity of Romanianus, a wealthy citizen of Tagaste, that Augustine was enabled to continue his education. This generous man continued for many years to take a special interest in the career of his gifted protégé, and provided him with a home and funds. Carthage teemed with pagan amusement, attractions and seductions of every variety. Even the worship of the pagan deities was accompanied by lewd ceremonies, obscene dances, and lascivious spectacles.

Augustine responded to the challenge of his more advanced studies with earnestness and relish, but his motives were vanity and ambition. Soon the intoxication of his literary success, the licentiousness of the students, and the seductions of the city brought about his moral downfall.

"I came to Carthage," he relates, "and a frying-pan full of unholy loves crackled around me. I was not yet in love, but I loved love itself. Because my want was hidden deep within me, I hated myself for wanting little. I sought something to love, loving love itself; I hated security and a life which had no dangers. . . . To love and to be loved was sweet to me, sweeter still if I enjoyed my beloved corporeally. So, I polluted the spring of friendship with the filth of concupiscence and I darkened its brightness with the fire of lust. Though I was foul and immoral, I eagerly endeavored, in my consummate vanity, to appear elegant and urbane. Thus, I rushed headlong into the love in which I desired to be enveloped."

It was not long before the seventeen-year-old student acquired a permanent mistress, and in the second year of his residence in Carthage a son was born to them. They called the boy Adeodatus, meaning the Gift of God. Augustine was devoted to this son, who seems to have inherited many of his father's talents. The name of the girl is unknown, but she remained faithful to Augustine and won his ardent love in return.

For fifteen years he remained in the thralldom of this alliance. Today it would be called a "common-law marriage," but Augustine always chafed and squirmed under the consciousness that he was living in sin. Why he did not marry her is not clear. The speculation is that she was from a lower station in life, for Monica seems never to have suggested that they should marry. For fifteen years he lived with her almost without interruption until 385, when Monica persuaded him to cast her off.

"One woman only," he writes, "to whom I was faithful, although experience showed me how great is the difference between the bond of legal marriage entered into for the purpose of propagating life, and a contract of illicit love of which children are born that are undesired, but who, once born, command our affection." Nevertheless it was this alliance which doubtless saved the young man from worse groveling in the filth of promiscuous lasciviousness. "However inadequately," remarks Papini, "the well-springs of Augustine's iniquity were closed, and he was right in naming the innocent fruit of his sinning, the Gift of God."

Patricius died in 371, too soon to see his grandson, but not before he embraced the Christian faith—thanks to Monica's example and to her fervent and unceasing prayers. Though the first object of her heart's desire was granted, Monica had a long wait for the second—the conversion of her wayward son. Despite his father's death, Augustine was able to continue his studies in Carthage owing to the generous aid of Romanianus. Indeed the passing of Patricius seems to have meant little to Augustine, for he passes over the event with brevity, and with none of the tenderness which characterizes all his references to his mother.

In 373 Augustine read Cicero's *Hortensius*, a dialogue in praise of philosophic wisdom. It stirred him deeply and instilled in him a love of philosophy, which remained with him through life. Henceforth he regarded rhetoric merely as a profession, while his heart was in philosophy.

It was at this time that Augustine came in contact with some Manichaeans, followers of Mani, a Persian who had founded a new creed in the middle of the previous century. It flattered the intellect by maintaining that no doctrine should be accepted on faith. It taught the agreeable doctrine that in man, as in the universe, two principles are struggling for dominance. One is good, the other is evil. If perchance the evil principle becomes dominant in one, there is nothing for him to do but observe the interesting psychological struggle going on within. Hence when a Manichaean fell into sin, he could simply claim that his better nature had been overcome by the forces of evil.

As the problem of evil was already pressing upon Augustine, who had been struggling to reconcile his wayward conduct with his ideals of virtue, he found in Manichaeism a convenient solution: he was not responsible for his evil actions. The clouding of his ethical insight and the weakening of his will, resulting from his loose living, made him especially susceptible to this sophistry. A good conscience and a pure heart would have been proof against it, and in later years none recognized this more clearly than Augustine himself. "I sought with pride," he says, "what only humility could make me find. Fool that I was, I left the nest, imagining myself able to fly; and I fell to the ground."

Indeed he came to view the bondage in which his intellect was held by the Manichaean heresy as comparable to the concubinage in which his will was enthralled. "What," he asks, "could have induced me for nearly nine years, despising the religion which had been instilled into me by my parents, to follow those men and to listen to them eagerly, if not their assertion that we are frightened by superstition and allow faith to come before reason?" In his own person, observes M. H. Allies, the future doctor was to give the lie to all subsequent skeptics who boast, with the Manichaeans, that faith debases the intellect while unbelief ennobles it.

His long captivity in Manichaeism, painful and humiliating though it was, served to sharpen his perception of a truth, important alike for psychology and for religion: the reciprocal influence of conduct and belief. He came to recognize vice as the factor chiefly responsible for obscuring the light which enlightens every man coming into this world. He had painful recollections of the treacherous hold which sensuality had upon his will and its darkening effect upon his ethical insight. "Give me chastity, O God," he would cry, but then perceiving the abandonment of the sensual pleasure it would entail, he would add, "But not yet." The attachment to vice caused the prayer to die stillborn. The *yet* was a long time coming: he was shipwrecked not only in morals but also in faith. Heresy darkened his intellect as vice padlocked his will: a double thralldom.

After three years of study in Carthage, Augustine returned to Tagaste and established a school of rhetoric. The urbane young professor captivated his pupils, but not his mother. Her joy at seeing her son was tempered with grief over his loss of faith and the deplorable change in his way of life. It seems that he brought Adeodatus and his mother with him, and this added to Monica's displeasure. Like the devoted mother that she was, however, she continued to pray for the son for whom she had already wept many tears.

She was consoled by a vision in which she saw herself standing on a wooden rule while a youth in resplendent garments approached her. When he inquired about the cause of her grief, she replied that she had lost her son. Whereupon the youth comforted her, saying, "Wherever Monica is, there also Augustine will be." Then in her dream Monica perceived her son was standing at her side.

Monica construed this to mean that her son would eventually return to the Catholic faith and be saved. She told Augustine about this, and besought him to return to her home. But he argued that the dream could indicate that she would adopt his views and become a Manichaean. "No, no," said Monica, "he did not say, 'Where he is, there shall you be,' but 'Where you, Monica, are, there shall he be.'" This, Augustine realized, was the true interpretation. He was secretly dismayed to note that his sophistry was no match for his mother's staunch faith.

Being a woman of action as well as of prayer, the solicitous mother sought to enlist the aid of a bishop.

"Speak to my son," she said, "correct his heretical views, and bring him back to his holy faith."

"No," he replied, "Augustine is not properly disposed for instruction. When I was a young man, I too was infected with Manichaeism, but further study showed me its fallacies."

Thus he implied that further study by Augustine would likewise cure him of his error. Not satisfied with such a vague assurance, Monica tearfully begged for more definite action.

"Leave me," said the prelate somewhat abruptly, "and continue to live as you have been living. It is not possible that the son of so many prayers and tears should perish."

This prophetic utterance, which became justly celebrated, has spared the prelate from the condemnation he deserved for his cautious restraint, indeed so ultra-cautious that one is tempted to call it by another name. In fact, one cannot but think, if the bishop had heeded the mother's tearful plea and summoned Augustine forthwith, explained the fallacy of Manichaeism, and given him a thorough course of desperately needed instruction in the faith and in Christian morals, that Augustine would not have lingered for so many years in error and corruption. To make up for the bishop's inaction Monica continued to weep and to pray. Though young enough to have remarried, she consecrated her widowhood to holy chastity, prayers, fasting, and the doing of good works.

Augustine conducted his school in Tagaste for little more than a year. Among his pupils was Alypius, only slightly younger than his teacher, who remained closely attached to his master through the years. Augustine had formed a close friendship with another young man with whom he had gone to school when they were children. Though this young friend, whose name is not disclosed, was a Christian, Augustine persuaded him to become a Manichaean. Some months later he fell sick and appeared to be dying; he was baptized while unconscious and he immediately recovered.

When Augustine began to jest about this cleansing of an unconscious soul, the youth abruptly stopped him. Augustine was greatly taken back by this change in his friend. A few days later the youth suffered a relapse and died. Augustine's grief knew no bounds. Death seemed to have struck at everything he cherished. The bottom seemed to have fallen out of his life. Ardent in his friendships and loves, Augustine was no less intense in his griefs.

"By this sorrow," he says, "my heart was enveloped in darkness, and everything that I gazed upon was death. My birthplace was torture to me and my home a wondrous unhappiness. The things we had known and enjoyed together became, in his absence, the source of crucifying pain to me. My eyes sought him everywhere, but I did not find him. I hated all things, because they did not possess him;

nor could they say to me: 'Look, he is coming!' as they did when he was alive but absent. . . . O madness, ignorant of the manly love that is fitting to men! O foolish man, that I was then, suffering immoderately from the events of human life. Thus I stormed, gasped, cried, and was troubled. There was no rest for me, nor advice. For I carried about my wounded and bloodstained soul, which was unwilling to be so moved by me, and I could find no place to rest it."

This overwhelming grief is cited by Augustine in the *Confessions* as his reason for leaving home and going to Carthage. But in another account of the matter, where Augustine writes with less emotion, he mentions that Tagaste had little to offer him as a teacher, whereas Carthage was the greatest city in Africa. Thither he went to seek his fortune. He looked forward to the gaining of wealth and fame and probably to a position in the provincial government, for which rhetoric was the open-sesame.

In the autumn of 374 Augustine conducted his first classes in Carthage. Romanianus seems to have provided him with living quarters in the vicinity of the Forum and the Street of the Bankers. For eight years Augustine taught here. Among his pupils were the two sons of Romanianus, a gifted student named Nebridius, and later his devoted friend Alypius came to join them.

Augustine read widely and profoundly in classical literature, and much of the learning in the *City of God* is traceable to the studies of this period. He settled down to a quiet life with Adeodatus and the child's mother and gradually lost interest in the sensual allurements of Carthage. He took a keen interest in astrology and magic, which played such large roles in the life of the average citizen and even in the affairs of the government. Entering a poetic tournament, Augustine carried off the prize, and the proconsul Vindicianus publicly crowned the young author.

Following the publication of this poem, his first published work, Augustine wrote a work, *On the Beautiful and the Fitting*, published in 380, and dedicated to Hierius, a famous orator then living in Rome. Augustine now began a serious study of Manichaeism, with the result that disenchantment with this system of coarse, material dualism speedily set in. He found their so-called science could not stand close scrutiny and they were unable to answer his questions. They told him, however, that their great scholar, Faustus, Bishop of Milevis, would soon be coming to Carthage and that he had all the answers.

In Augustine's twenty-ninth year the celebrated Faustus came to Carthage, but his arrival brought only disappointment and disillusionment to the young inquirer. Augustine discovered that Faustus was an utter stranger to all scientific knowledge, a mere babbler in words.

"When he came," relates Augustine, "I found him a charming man, delightful in his speech, who babbled very sweetly about just the same things of which the others were accustomed to speak. But of what value to my thirst was this most attractive bearer of precious draughts? My ears were already cloyed with such things. They did not seem better to me because they were better said; nor were they true because eloquently spoken; nor was the soul wise because the face was agreeable and the speech elegant. They, who had continually promised him to me, were not good judges of these things; to them he appeared prudent and wise, because he delighted them as a speaker."

Augustine noted too the sharp contrast between the immorality of the Manichaeans and their affectation of virtue; he was appalled by the feebleness of their arguments in controversy with Catholic scholars. The spell was broken. Though Augustine did not immediately sever his formal connection with the sect—he was never a member, only an auditor—he now rejected their doctrines. His thralldom had lasted nine years.

Once again Augustine felt the urge to move his school. This time his heart was set on Rome, the heart of the empire, and a city fabulous to any resident of the provinces. Here would be greater opportunities for professional success and honor: he had hopes of equaling the fame of other African orators who had won renown in the imperial city. The news of Augustine's decision was anything but pleasing to Monica. Having lost her son spiritually to the Manichaeans, she was now in danger of losing all contact with him in far-off Rome. This meant she would have to abandon all hope of influencing him by her exemplary life to return to Christ.

A strong-minded and resolute woman, she went to him and implored him not to leave her. Since his mind was set on it, however, she offered to go with him. Apparently Augustine agreed to this proposal, for they went together to Carthage, the point of embarkation.

On a hill near the harbor was a chapel dedicated to St. Cyprian. Augustine persuaded his mother to rest there overnight, telling her that he had to go down to the port to bid good-by to a friend.

That night in the autumn of 383 Augustine quietly slipped aboard a vessel and sailed for Rome, dreaming of honor and fame in the great city of the Caesars, and little thinking of the weeping mother he had left behind. Deceived, deserted, and heartbroken, Monica returned to Tagaste, but she did not cease to pray for her wayward son. Abandoned, too, were Adeodatus and his mother. It is not even clear that he arranged for their support: he says nothing about it. Left behind also were his pupils and Romanianus, his kindly patron, to whom he had not even said good-by.

What a strange action on the part of one who, in spite of his other faults, had never been lacking in ardor and love for his friends! How can it be explained? The best explanation is that he was sick at heart, disillusioned in his adopted religion, overwhelmed by mental and moral difficulties for which he could find no answer. Life in Carthage had become a weary treadmill, with little hope of his achieving any of his eager goals. Many of his pupils had proved to be unruly hooligans.

He wanted to cut the moorings of the past and start afresh in the big city where he had a rendezvous with destiny. When he had made good he would return in triumph and make his old friends proud of him. How often this impulse and plan have stirred the heart and kindled the brain of impetuous and headstrong youth?

Arriving in Rome with letters from Faustus and other African friends, Augustine was hospitably received into the home of a Manichaean friend who, like himself, was not a member but only an auditor. Hardly had he settled there when he was stricken with a raging fever—probably malaria—that threatened his life. His long entanglement in Manichaeism had, however, destroyed his faith in the efficacy of the sacraments so that he had no wish to be baptized. As he wrote later, he was "going to hell, and carrying all his sins with him."

From afar, however, Monica was watching over her son. Though unaware of his illness, she knew with the sure intuition of a mother's heart that his soul was feverish and sore. She redoubled her prayers for him; she besought the intercession of the saints; she gave alms to the poor; she attended Mass daily and went to church a second time each day to hear a sermon or to pray. It was only his mother's pleading tears and ceaseless prayers, Augustine later declared, that saved him from a twofold death: physical and spiritual.

For the time being, only the flesh was saved, but silently, slowly, and painfully another cure was being wrought by the mysterious action of grace. Augustine now began his classes in rhetoric; there is a tradition in Rome that his school was on one of the streets between the Caelian and Aventine hills in the quarter inhabited by Africans —the Via Capo d'Africa, which still exists. Though the Roman pupils did not misbehave like the ones in Carthage, they had another habit not less disconcerting to the impecunious Augustine: when time for payment had just about arrived they would leave in a body for the classroom of another teacher!

It is interesting to note that during these months Augustine might have made the acquaintance of Jerome, the great scriptural scholar and the future saint, who was living nearby on the Aventine in the house of the famous Marcella. There he was directing a group of pious matrons and maidens along the path of monastic sanctity. Besides serving as secretary to Pope Damasus I, Jerome was also preparing the Vulgate version of the New Testament.

Augustine the Manichaean was scarcely in a position, however, to approach either of these great souls. Later on he would dispute with Jerome by letter, but they never met, or if they did, neither recognized the other. These two towering giants of the Western Church, Fathers and Doctors, remarks G. Papini, "may have jostled each other in some narrow Roman lane, but never, either then or afterward, did they exchange a word" of greeting.

In view of the students' habit of dodging their payments, Augustine's school was not a financial success. Before the year was out he learned that the prefect of Rome had received a request from Milan for a municipal teacher of rhetoric. Augustine applied for the post and, after demonstrating his ability as a speaker before Symmachus, the Roman prefect, received the appointment. As Augustine traveled to Milan in the dignified luxury of the imperial transport, he may well have been wondering if he was not at last arriving. Yes, he was to keep his rendezvous with destiny in Milan, but it was a destiny of which the ambitious young professor little dreamed.

From the autumn of 384 to that of 386 Augustine taught rhetoric in Milan, and his brilliant lectures won him a wide circle of friends and admirers. Alypius came to join him, and later came Romanianus, who brought Adeodatus and his mother with him; even more important was the arrival of Monica and her son Navigius. The saintly mother was favored with extraordinary visions. While crossing the Mediterranean she calmed the sailors who were frightened by a violent gale, assuring them that God had revealed to her that she would reach her destination.

Naturally she rejoiced to find that Augustine was no longer actively interested in Manichaeism, and she assured him "that before she departed from this life she would see him a full-fledged Catholic." Evodius, another Tagastean, joined Augustine's circle. A minor government official, he decided upon being baptized a Catholic to devote himself to the service of the Church. Like Alypius, he was to play a key part in the future life of Augustine.

The foremost citizen of Milan at that time was its able, scholarly, and saintly bishop. In him secular learning and spiritual culture were marvelously blended, and were made to serve both the empire and the Church. This extraordinary man had been civil governor of the provinces of Liguria and Aemilia, with headquarters at Milan. In 374 a meeting of Christians, Arian and Catholic, was held in the Basilica of Milan for the purpose of choosing a successor to the deceased bishop. Fearing disorders because of the bitter feeling between the two factions, Ambrose attended the meeting in his capacity of governor. To his immense surprise he was nominated by popular acclaim for the episcopal office.

Though he belonged to a noted Christian family, he was still only a catechumen. The choice was approved by Pope Damasus and Emperor Valentinian, and so Ambrose was baptized, ordained a priest, and consecrated a bishop within a few days. When Augustine came to know him eleven years later Ambrose had become one of the most famous bishops in the Western Church: an able administrator, an eloquent speaker, and a foremost interpreter of Holy Scripture.

The bishop received Augustine in a kind and paternal manner but with a certain reserve: Augustine was not yet a catechumen and doubtless his reputation as a loose-living Manichaean had preceded him. Ambrose was outspoken, however, in his praise of Monica and congratulated him on having so holy a mother. Augustine came often to hear the bishop preach and called repeatedly at his home, where anyone was always free to enter. Augustine would have liked to discuss with the learned churchman some of the philosophical problems with which his mind was seething. But he invariably found the bishop either busy with many callers or so intent upon his reading that Augustine hesitated to intrude, and after a while he would regretfully withdraw in silence.

What a pity that he did not muster up enough courage to lay bare his troubled mind and unquiet heart to the great prelate! What a pity, too, that Ambrose did not know the quality of that intellect, then struggling for the light, that was later to illuminate such vast areas of philosophy and theology with its unrivaled genius. Doubtless Augustine's exile would have been greatly shortened. As it was, however, that period of groping uncertainty was to last for three more years.

His search for truth led him through various fields. At first he was attracted by the philosophy of the academies, with its pessimistic skepticism. Then Neoplatonic philosophy inspired him with genuine enthusiasm. No sooner had he read certain works of Plato and more especially of Plotinus than the hope of finding the truth rose within him. The Neoplatonic intellectualized world of ideas replaced the materialism of Manichaeism; here he found the admonition to seek for truth outside the material world, and from created things he learned to recognize the invisible God. In helping Augustine to form a concept of spirit, Neoplatonism enabled him to bridge the gap between Manichaean materialism and the Christian understanding of a purely immaterial substance.

Furthermore, these Neoplatonic concepts aided him in arriving at the solution of the problem of evil, long a thorn in his side. As a Manichaean he had conceived evil as a real substance, existing in opposition to the good. "Such a real positive evil," as Vernon Bourke points out, "would either demand a real cause or it would have to be the eternal reason for its own existence." Plotinus suggested that evil was not a substance but was simply non-being: a lack of absolute goodness necessarily present in an imperfect world. This was all that Augustine needed to decide that evil, in the cosmic sense, was not a substance but simply the privation of good. Only God, he concluded, is absolute Goodness; the lack of goodness in created things is merely the reflection of the imperfection of the universe.

These Neoplatonic concepts served Augustine as a bridge over which he crossed safely into the spiritual realm. He now began to read the New Testament again and particularly St. Paul, and the difficulties and contradictions, which he had previously experienced, no longer arose. The same spiritual wisdom which he had eagerly perceived in Plotinus he now found in much greater measure in the New Testament. From the scholarly sermons of Ambrose he had learned the basic principles for the interpretation of Scripture.

Now he began to grasp a truth of far-reaching consequence: to be wise it is not sufficient merely to know the truth, but it is necessary to live justly and virtuously. This he learned not from Plato but from the teachings of Jesus as recorded in the Scriptures. "Plato," he says, "gave me knowledge of the true God, Jesus Christ showed me the way." Though he was now sufficiently advanced to understand the intellectual message of Christianity, he was unfortunately not yet ready to put its moral precepts into practice. The obstacle was not in the intellect but in the will and in his uncircumcised heart.

Believing that a proper marriage would help her son over this road block, Monica was largely instrumental in having him become engaged to a girl of his own social rank. The girl was two years younger than the marriageable age and, as Augustine puts it, "because she was pleasing, I waited." Much to the vexation of Monica, who lived in the same house, Augustine was still living with Adeodatus' mother. Now that he had become formally engaged to another, Augustine was forced reluctantly and regretfully to terminate his association with his paramour and send her back to Africa. That it was anything but a callous or coldhearted dismissal is evident from his *Confessions*.

"The woman with whom I was accustomed to sleep," he writes, "was torn from my side, since she was an impediment to my marriage. My heart, which clung to her, was cut and wounded and bleeding. She returned to Africa, vowing to God that she would never know any other man, and leaving with me my natural son."

This development leaves unanswered a number of questions, the chief of which is this: Why did not Augustine marry the woman with whom he had lived so many years, the mother of his son, who was almost his wife? Despite his passionate nature, he had always remained faithful to her, and he reciprocated her deep and unwavering love. Was it simply her lack of social rank and of a dowry that made her unacceptable in Monica's eyes as a suitable wife for her son? Such factors seem paltry and unworthy of serious consideration by a Christian mother, especially in view of the claims the girl had upon Augustine after giving him the best years of her life. Why the separation from her young son, who must have been as dear to his mother's heart as was Augustine himself?

These are questions which have never been answered and probably never will be. One would like to think that her sacrifice and her vow of perpetual chastity helped to win the grace of the latter virtue for the man she loved so much but would see no more. On this note of self-surrender and immolation this nameless woman fades from the picture, and one can't suppress the hope that she was reunited with Augustine and her son in Paradise.

The banishing of his first and only woman companion did not catapult Augustine into the high state of virtue and chastity for which Monica had hoped. Long habits are not easily broken, and Augustine had not as yet the habit of prayer or the grace of the sacraments to help him. The heritage of his father, still hot in his veins, and the momentum of fifteen years proved too much for Augustine's frail resolve, if indeed he had made any at all. He could not endure the prospect of two years of celibacy and soon took a mistress. He frankly confesses that he regarded existence without a female companion as impossible: such seemed to him no better than a term of punishment.

In not a few geniuses the gadfly of prurience and the urgency of sex seem more than normally clamorous and exigent, and Augustine seems undoubtedly to have been numbered among them. "Augustine," observes G. Papini, "was made up of sex and a brain, both at white heat and each at war with the other. He would never be saved until sex had been vanquished by the power of the soul."

"I sighed and longed," he says, "to be delivered but was kept fast bound, not with exterior chains but with my own iron will. The Enemy held my will, and of it he made a chain with which he had fettered me fast; for from a perverse will was created wicked desire or lust, and the serving this lust produced custom, and custom not resisted produced a kind of necessity, with which, as with links fastened one to another, I was kept close shackled in this cruel slavery. I had no excuse as I pretended formerly when I delayed to serve Thee, because I had not yet certainly discovered Thy truth: now I knew it, yet I was still fettered. . . .

"I had nothing now to reply to Thee when Thou saidst to me,

'Rise, thou that sleepest, and rise up from the dead, and Christ shall
enlighten thee' . . . I had nothing, I say, at all to reply, being now
convinced by Thy faith, except lazy and drowsy words, 'Presently,
by and by; let me alone a little while longer'; but this 'presently'
did not presently come; these delays had no bounds, and this 'little
while' stretched out to a long time."

As his words indicate, it had now become painfully clear to Augustine that the road block to his attainment of the divine truth and
wisdom he so earnestly sought was not intellectual but moral. Here
was a clear challenge to all the latent powers of his character and
will: the effort to respond to that challenge shook him to the very
foundations of his being. Seeking help to meet this challenge, he
went not to a philosopher but to a saintly old priest, Simplicianus.
The choice was excellent. The elderly priest would give him advice,
not engage in fruitless dialectics as a younger one might do. Learning of the young professor's high regard for Neoplatonism, he told
him of the conversion of the noted Platonic scholar, Victorinus, whom
he had counseled and guided.

Intent upon attacking Christianity, Victorinus began to read the
New Testament and other Christian works and became convinced
of the truth of the Christian religion. He confided to Simplicianus
that he had read himself into the Church.

"I shall believe that," replied Simplicianus, "when I see you worshiping in the Church and receiving the sacraments and not till
then."

It was just the jolt needed to awaken the philosopher to a twofold truth of supreme importance: the Church is not merely a philosophical or theological system but a living organism of which Christ
is the head; one is united with it only by baptism and profession of
faith. In the presence of a vast throng, Victorinus made that profession, showing that he had the courage of his convictions.

The story made a tremendous impression upon Augustine, who
perceived the parallel between his situation and that of Victorinus.
"I burned," he says, "with the desire to do likewise." He may well
have wondered, too, at the "chance" which brought him to the very
person who had filled the role of adviser to Victorinus under strik-
ingly similar circumstances. His admiration for the convert grew all
the more when he learned that his decision cost him his teaching
position because of the hostility of the apostate emperor, Julian. Why

should not he follow this courageous philosopher's example? The force of long habit bound his will, however, and he justified his procrastination by murmuring, "Soon, in a little while, I shall make up my mind, but not right now." How similar it was to his oft-repeated half prayer, "Give me chastity, O God, but not yet!"

Augustine continued to read the Scriptures, especially the Pauline epistles, attended Mass frequently and listened with ever increasing pleasure and admiration to the sermons of Ambrose. He was visited by Pontitian, a fellow African and a devout Christian, who held an important post at the imperial court. Finding a copy of St. Paul's epistles on the table, he turned the conversation to the life of St. Anthony of Egypt and of the marvelous development of monasticism in the Eastern Church. He related that when he was at Trèves, during the emperor's residence there, he went for an afternoon walk with three other court officials.

Walking two by two through the gardens near the city walls, Pontitian and his companion became separated from the other two: the latter had discovered a hut in which some monks were living, and there they found a copy of the *Life of St. Anthony,* which they began to read. They were so fascinated by what they read that they decided to renounce their worldly careers and dedicate themselves to the service of God. The story stirred Augustine deeply: it challenged him in much the same way as had the Victorinus incident. Describing the effect of the story upon him, Augustine says:

"While his words were being spoken, Thou, O Lord, didst twist me round upon myself, taking me by the scruff of my neck and placing me right in front of myself, so that I might unwillingly observe myself. Thou didst place me before my own face, that I might see how ugly I was, how distorted and sordid, how stained and full of sores. And I saw, and was horrified; I could find nowhere to flee from myself."

In his former half desires of conversion he had been wont to beg of God the grace of continence, but he was at the same time somewhat afraid of being heard too soon. "In the first dawning of my youth," he says, "I had begged of Thee chastity, but by halves, miserable wretch that I am; and I said, 'Give me chastity, but not yet'; for I was afraid lest Thou shouldst hear me too soon, and heal me of the disease which I rather wished to have satisfied than extinguished."

When Pontitian departed he doubtless little dreamed that his story had fanned the professor's troubled mind to a white heat of spiritual fever. The malady had reached a crisis.

"Having said his say and finished his visit," relates Augustine, "he went away, and I returned into myself. What thought did not come into my head? With what cogent reasons did I not scourge my soul, that it might be one with me, who was striving to go after Thee? It was refractory; it refused, and did not excuse itself. Every argument was answered and overcome: a mute fear alone remained, which dreaded, like death, being restrained from the force of a habit which led to death."

Alypius noticed how deeply moved was his friend. His staring eyes, the unnatural color of his face, the excited tone of his voice, and his whole appearance betrayed the intense struggle going on within him. Prudently Alypius remained silent while Augustine blurted out partly incoherent questions.

"What are we suffering?" he exclaimed. "What is it? What did you hear? The unlearned rise up and force their way into heaven, and we, with all our learning but no heart, see, do we not roll about in flesh and blood? Because they have preceded us, are we ashamed to follow? Or is it that we are not ashamed of not even following?"

Thus distraught, Augustine burst out into the garden. Not wishing to leave him alone when he was so disturbed, Alypius followed him, and they sat down in a spot as far from the house as possible. No other one can describe as well or as exactly as Augustine the thoughts which crowded his mind and the emotions which flooded his soul as he went through the crisis which changed his life.

"Thither I was drawn," he says, "by my mental agitation. There no man would impede that burning struggle in which I was fighting against myself, until it should end in the way Thou didst know, though I did not know it. Only I was out of myself for my good, and I was dying a living death, conscious of my wickedness, unconscious of the good I was to reach in a short time. I turned, therefore, into the garden, and Alypius followed closely after me. Nor did his company make my secret not mine; for would he ever forsake me in this frame of mind? We sat down as far from the house as possible.

"I was groaning in spirit, and was burning with indignation at my not accepting Thy pleasure, and making a compact with Thee, my God, for which acceptance all my bones were crying, and were sending to heaven the voice of praise. There was no getting there by ship or chariot or foot of man as quickly as I by one step had gone from the house into that place where we were sitting. For not only the going thither, but also the getting there, was nothing else than the will to go. This will should be strong and genuine, not a half-hearted will, which is irresolute and struggling, now with the wish to rise, now with the wish to fall. . . .

"Thus was I sick and in anguish, reproaching myself with more than usual severity, turning and re-turning in my chain, until its last snap should be broken; for, slight as it was, still it bound me. And Thou, O Lord, just Mercy, wert speaking to my secret heart, putting before me motives of fear and shame, lest I should again yield, and that small and frail link which remained should not be broken, and should grow strong to bind me afresh. For I said to myself, 'Let it be now, let it be now.' And so I went on, contenting myself with words.

"I was already doing and not doing; neither did I fall back into my former ways, but I was standing still in near proximity to them, and taking my time. And again I tried, and was well-nigh success-ful, and had almost reached the mark and held it in my grasp; and still I fell short of it, and neither reached nor held it, hesitating to die to death and to live to life. I inclined rather to follow the worse course, which was familiar, than the better, which was unfamiliar; and as to that particular moment of time when I was to become dif-ferent, the nearer it approached the more it struck me with horror. Only it did not vanish into the background, nor disappear, but was pending."

Waxing fierce was the conflict within him: lust was beckoning him in the familiar direction; chastity was inviting him to a new life of continence and honor. His erstwhile mistresses tugged at his gar-ment of flesh and softly murmured, "Wilt thou send us away? And from this time forth shall we be with thee no more? Wilt thou be unable to do such and such a thing for evermore?" As he recognizes the sordid indecencies suggested by the words, "such and such a thing," he recoils with shame and horror.

"Let Thy mercy," he cries out, "preserve the soul of Thy servant from them. What pollution and what shame! And I heard them with much less than half an ear, not contradicting me openly before my face, but, as it were, murmuring behind my back, and disappearing like a runaway thief to induce me to look round. Still they delayed me in my desire to tear myself away from them, and to go where I was called, because the strong force of habit said to me, 'Dost thou think to do without these things?'"

Turning his face in the direction of chastity, he sees a still more alluring and inspiring sight. "In the direction in which I turned my face," he says, "and whither I was fearing to pass, the pure glory of chastity, with her serene and holy mirth, was disclosed to me. With honest words of encouragement she bade me come and not doubt, and held out her fair hands, full to overflowing with the examples of the good, to receive and embrace me. In them were crowds of boys and girls, and young people, and people of all ages; there were sober widows and aged virgins; and in no one of them was that same chastity sterile, but she was the fruitful mother of sons of joy by Thee, O Lord, her spouse."

Chastity smiled at him in admonishment and asked, "Canst thou not do what these have done? Or indeed can they do it of themselves, and not rather in the Lord their God? The Lord their God gave me to them; what art thou doing and not doing? Cast thyself upon Him with confidence; He will receive and heal thee."

Filled with great confusion because he still heard the whispered enticements of his former mistresses, Augustine hesitated in suspense.

"Turn a deaf ear on earth," counseled chastity, "to those unclean members of thine, that they be mortified. They speak to thee of delights but they are not as the law of the Lord thy God."

A flood of tears welled up in Augustine's eyes. Feeling that solitude was more suitable for the shedding of tears, he left Alypius and threw himself down under a fig tree to give full vent to his anguish.

"And Thou, O Lord," he cried, "how long? How long, O Lord, wilt Thou be angry unto the end? Be not mindful of our former iniquities." Feeling that it was these which held him captive, he continued to cry, "How long? How long? Is it to be tomorrow and tomorrow? Why not now? Why not this very hour put an end to shame?"

The climax was at hand. God was to answer his pitiful cry in a striking and dramatic manner. "I was saying these things," he says, "and weeping in the bitterest sorrow of heart; and all at once I heard a voice, like the voice of a boy or a girl, I know not which, coming from the next house, repeating over and over again in a musical tone, 'Take and read; take and read.' Composing myself instantly, I began most earnestly to ponder whether there was any game whatever in which children were wont to sing similar words, nor could I remember ever to have heard them before.

"The violence of my tears being checked, I rose, interpreting them in no other way than to mean that this was a divine intimation to me to open the Scriptures and to read what first came in my way. For I had heard that Anthony was admonished by a chance reading of the Gospel, as if the words, 'Go, sell all that thou hast and give to the poor, and thou shalt have treasure in heaven: and come and follow me,' had been said to him, and that by this sign he had been at once converted to Thee.

"Thus minded, I returned to the place where Alypius was sitting, for I had put down the book of Epistles in coming away. I took it up, opened it, and read in silence the first chapter which met my eyes: 'Not in rioting and drunkenness, not in chambering and impurities, not in contention and envy, but put ye on the Lord Jesus Christ, and make not provision for the flesh in its concupiscences.' I would not read on, nor was there any need that I should. For I had no sooner read to the end of the sentence than a light as if of security being infused into my heart, all the darkness of doubt was dissipated."

Alypius frequently looked to Augustine for guidance, and now he asked to see what his friend and master had read. Upon being shown the passage, he read it and the words immediately following, "Now him that is weak in faith, take unto you." This he understood to apply to his own weak faith. Without any of the prolonged struggle which had characterized Augustine's conversion, he was then and there strengthened in his Christian faith.

"Then," concludes Augustine, "we went in to my mother with our story, which rejoiced her. We told her how it had happened, and her joy was triumphant. She praised Thee, 'who art powerful to do more than we ask or can understand,' because she saw Thou hadst given her more in my regard than she had been wont to ask Thee for by her sighs and tears. For Thou hadst so converted me to Thee that I sought neither for a wife nor for anything else in this world, holding that rule of faith which Thou hadst revealed to her so many years before that I should hold. 'And Thou didst turn her weeping into joy' much more abundantly than she had desired, and concerning the relations due to my sin much more tenderly and chastely than she had demanded."

Overjoyed indeed was Monica that her prayers had been answered in such a bountiful manner. Her only hope and prayer had been that Augustine might come to live honorably and chastely in Christian marriage; now she learned that he had decided to refrain even from wedlock that he might devote himself, body, mind and soul, to Christ. In this decision she saw the fulfillment of her dream that Augustine would stand beside her on the rule of faith, and thus be united with her both in belief and practice. It was a fulfillment more overwhelming than she had even dreamed: her prayers and tears over the years had been answered as only God could answer them.

This memorable scene, which took place toward the end of the summer of 386, was the climax of Augustine's conversion to the Catholic faith. In the agony of the garden, somewhat akin to the ordeal of Christ in Gethsemane, the soul of Augustine had survived the crisis of its illness: he had made an irrevocable decision to renounce the lusts of the past, to put off the old Adam and to put on the new, to become a baptized Christian, and to strive diligently and earnestly to achieve his salvation. Though the climax came with dramatic suddenness and with overwhelming feeling and convulsive emotion, the conversion had been a long time in building up the forces which were finally to be released in such mighty torrents: the storm had long been brewing.

Augustine's moral conversion had been preceded by an intellectual one. What made his suffering so acute during the period preceding the agony in the garden was the consciousness that he knew full well what was right for him to do but still he was doing the opposite. With St. Paul he could cry out, "The good which I will, I do not; but the evil which I will not, that I do."

In the emancipation of his will from the tyranny of lust there are clearly discernible the following influences: the cumulative force of Ambrose's sermons, the wise advice of Simplicianus, the stories about Victorinus and the friends of Pontitian, and above all the unceasing prayers, tears, sacrifices, and example of Monica, which opened the floodgates of God's mercy and grace. The weak flabby velleities of Augustine were transformed into mighty muscular volitions, so that

Augustine actually did what he wanted to do instead of the opposite: the rider had at last bridled the runaway horse and had it under control.

Augustine's conversion has many elements of kinship with that of St. Paul. Both came with dramatic suddenness; both were characterized by convulsive paroxysms; both effected transformations which were as decisive as they were startling; both resulted in giving to the Church apostles destined to win vast multitudes for Christ. The blinding flash on the road to Damascus was destined to light up the skies of the whole Mediterranean world: the paroxysm of emotion which convulsed the soul of the weeping prodigal in the garden of Milan was destined to have its repercussions in the hearts of men and women in all the succeeding centuries. The former was pulled by God's grace from the ranks of the enemy to be a leader of His forces: the latter was lifted up out of the mire of lust to shed the fragrance of his chastity upon the whole Church and to stand as a symbol of the redemption. Both were miracles of divine grace, which blessed the universal Church with harvests of souls ever increasing in number and in sanctity.

II. THE SINNER BECOMES A SAINT

The die was now cast, and never again was Augustine to turn back, cost what it may. Henceforth he was to face only toward the light and let the shadows flee behind him. His constant prayer was for strength to subdue his passions, purify his affections, disentangle his wayward heart from the inordinate love of creatures, and fit himself for a new life in Christ. "I will plant my feet firmly," he says, "on the ground where my parents placed me."

The memorable scene in the garden at Milan took place in September 386, when Augustine was thirty-two. Only twenty days of class remained before the beginning of the Vintage vacation. For sometime Augustine had been bothered with a chest ailment, so he decided to finish the term and then discontinue the school. He wanted to retire to some quiet place to study, pray, and prepare himself for baptism. Learning of his plans, his friend Verecundus, a grammarian of Milan, offered his country villa at Cassiciacum as a retreat for Augustine and his friends.

Thither in October Augustine repaired. With him were at least eight others: Monica, Adeodatus, his brother Navigius; two cousins, Lastidianus and Rusticus; two pupils, Licentius, the son of Romanianus, and Trygetius; and his devoted companion Alypius. The group settled down to a quiet but active community life, dividing their time between work in the fields, study, prayer, and spiritual conferences. Monica must have been kept busy preparing meals for nine people and acting as mother to all of them.

The quiet and serenity of the semi-monastic life at Cassiciacum realized a dream long cherished by Augustine. Here he sought by austere penance and the strictest watch over his heart and senses to achieve that self-mastery for which he had long been yearning. Often had he cried, "Our heart has been made for Thee, O God, and it shall never rest until it rests in Thee." Now he was desperately anxious to prepare himself for the grace of leading a new life in Christ and becoming in Him a new creature.

"Too late," he prayed, "have I loved Thee, O Beauty ever ancient and ever new, too late have I loved Thee! Thou wast with me, and I was not with Thee; I was abroad, running after those beauties which Thou hast made; those things which could have no being but in Thee kept me far from Thee. Thou hast called, Thou hast cried out, and hast pierced my deafness. Thou hast enlightened, Thou hast shone forth, and my blindness is dispelled. I have tasted Thee, and am hungry for Thee. Thou hast touched me, and I am afire with the desire of Thy embraces."

The substance of many of the conferences and conversations which took place during the seven months spent at this hermitage was embodied by Augustine in his three dialogues, *Against the Academicians, Of the Happy Life,* and *Of Order.* They constitute his earliest extant works and afford a splendid vista of his maturing Christian thought, life, and aspirations during the period of his noviitiate. Here one sees clearly the crystallization of the objective to which he was to devote much of his thought: providing the authority of faith with the support of reason.

Toward the beginning of Lent in 387, Augustine and his little community returned to Milan to prepare for the reception of baptism. At that time it was customary for candidates to spend the period of Lent in mortification and prayer. In addition, they followed a course of instruction under the guidance of the bishop. On Easter eve, April 24, 387, Augustine, his fifteen-year-old son Adeodatus, and Alypius were immersed in water and baptized in the name of the Most Holy Trinity: at the Mass which followed they made their first Holy Communion and probably received the sacrament of confirmation at the same time. How great must have been the joy and exultation of this little trinity of friends as they received their Eucharistic Lord into their hearts! How thin and unsubstantial must all the pleasures of the past have seemed to Augustine in comparison with the ecstasy of this union with his incarnate Lord! It must have been to him as a foretaste of heaven.

It was on this hallowed occasion that Augustine heard the singing of the heart-warming hymns which Ambrose had introduced into the Western Church only the preceding year. "How I wept," says Augustine, "on hearing those hymns and canticles that filled Thy Church with their sweetness, and how deeply did those voices stir me. They caressed my ear, they carried truth to my heart and roused it with loving piety, while my tears flowed freely to my infinite consoling."

With deep devotion Augustine joined in singing the *Deus Creator Omnium,* the last verse of which must especially have stirred him. "In the pure of heart let faith with its cooling breath temper the hot vapours of sleep. Freed from all impure thoughts, let the inmost dreams of our heart be of Thee. Let not the peaceful rest of man be troubled by the snares of a scheming enemy." What prayer could have been more congruous for Augustine, who was often tormented by the memories and dreams of a sensual past?

Stripped of the worldly ambition which had brought him to Italy, Augustine decided to return to Africa and live as a lay monk in his home town, Tagaste. Alypius was eager to follow his master's lead. They were accompanied by Evodius, who had recently been living in Augustine's household. A former officer in the Roman Army and later a government official, Evodius had become a Christian before Augustine; he brought to the Augustinian circle an excellent knowledge of philosophy and a devout disposition. The dialogue on *Freedom of Choice* embodies some of his conversations with Augustine.

During the early summer of 387 the group left Milan and journeyed to Ostia, the port of Rome, where they waited for a boat to return to Africa. While here, Monica was stricken with a fever, and she had a presentiment that her end was near. She felt that her work was done and that Augustine's conversion constituted her *nunc dimittis:* beside her husband in Tagaste a grave awaited her.

Five days before her fatal illness she and Augustine were standing at a window which looked out over the garden of their house at Ostia. Tired from the journey, they looked forward to returning to their homeland. Around the ancestral home in Tagaste were clustered the nostalgic memories of Augustine's childhood and youth: around such scenes memory weaves a garland of flowers that never fade, flowers which distill a fragrance that seems to come from another world. Standing there, mother and son had a heart-to-heart talk in the presence of divine Truth. Their tête-à-tête is recalled with a simple tenderness and a delicacy of feeling which have stirred readers throughout the centuries.

"As the day approached," recalls Augustine, "on which she (Monica) was to bid farewell to this life, which day, O Lord, Thou didst know, though we knew it not, it happened by the secret workings of Thy providence (as I believe) that she and I were standing alone at a window which looked on to the garden of the house inhabited by us. Here, by the mouth of the Tiber, after a toilsome journey, we were resting apart from the crowd, with a view to continuing it by sea.

"We were discoursing together alone very sweetly and, forgetting the past in our desire to grasp the future, were asking each other in the presence of the unvarying truth, which Thou art, what that eternal life of the saints would be which eye has not seen, ear has not heard, nor heart of man has imagined. But yet we grasped with the mouth of our heart after those heavenly streams of Thy fountain, the fountain of life, of which Thou art the source, in order that, drawing hence what strength we were able, we might in some way or other form a picture of this ineffable mystery. . . .

"When, in our conversation, we had reached that point at which pleasure of the senses, however great, and corporeal light, however dazzling, seemed for the exceeding joy of eternal life to be unworthy not only of comparison, but even of mention, we raised our hearts to God in still more burning love, and viewed successively all corporeal things, and heaven itself, whence sun, moon and stars shine upon the earth. And still we rose higher by our secret contemplation, by our praise and admiration of Thy works. Then we came to consider our own minds, and passed them by, that we might attain the region of unfailing plenty, where Thou feedest Israel for ever on the food of truth.

"There life is wisdom, by whom all these things are made, and by whom all past and future things are. Wisdom itself is not made, but is now what it was, and will be the same for ever; or rather, past and future time do not exist in it, but being alone, because it is eternal. For past and future time have no place in that which is eternal. In the vehemence of our desires after wisdom, we grasped it for one moment with our whole heart; and then sighed as that foretaste of the Spirit left us, and we were forced to return to the distraction of human words, which have both beginning and end. What is like to Thy Word, O Lord, which remains in itself without decay and renovates all things?

"We were saying then: Let the tumult of the flesh cease. Let images of earth and waters and air be hushed. Hushed be also the poles of heaven, yea, the very soul, and by not thinking on self may she surmount self. Hushed be all dreams and imaginary revelations. Let every tongue and sign and whatever is merely transitory, be hushed, because all these things say to him who has ears to hear, 'We made not ourselves, but He made us who abideth for ever.' Then, having said this, they, too, should be hushed, because they raised their ear to Him who made them.

"Let Him alone speak, not by them but by Himself, that we may hear His voice, not through tongue or flesh, nor by angel's voice, nor sound of thunder, nor in the dark riddle of a similitude. Let us hear Him, whom we love in these things, without them. Thus, we are straining ourselves and in swift thought are touching on that eternal wisdom which abideth over all. Could this be continued on, and other visions of kind far unlike be withdrawn, and this one ravish and absorb and wrap up its beholder amid these inward joys, so that life might be ever like that one moment of understanding which now we sighed after; were not this 'Enter into the joy of thy Lord?' And when is this to be? Will it be when we all rise again, but, are not all transformed?

"So we were talking, and if not exactly in this way and in these words, Thou, O God, knowest that on the day when we held this conversation, the world with all its pleasures seemed to us, as we spoke, a thing of no account. Then she said, 'As for me, my son, nothing in this life delights me. I know not what more I can still do, or why I am left here, as I have no further hope from this world. There was one thing which made me desirous of dwelling here on earth a little longer, which was, that I might see you a Catholic Christian before I died. My God has abundantly granted my request in letting me see you even despise earthly happiness and become His servant. What am I doing here?'"

A few days later Monica was stricken with a fatal illness and lost consciousness. Augustine and his brother hastened to her side. "Where have I been?" she asked, upon reviving. Then seeing the sorrowful faces of her two sons, she asked, "Will you bury your mother here?" Navigius replied that he would not have her die on a journey but only in her own country. When she heard this, she gave him an anxious look as if to deprecate his caring for such things.

Turning to Augustine, she said, "You hear what he says." Then addressing both, she continued, "Lay this body anywhere; let it not be a care for you. This only I ask of you that you would remember me at the Lord's altar wherever you may be." After having explained this, her last wish, she fell into silence and the fever became more intense.

"But, O invisible Good," reflects Augustine, "I, pondering on the gifts productive of admirable fruits which Thou puttest into the hearts of Thy faithful, rejoiced and gave Thee thanks. For I recalled to mind how extremely anxious she had always been about her grave, which she had prepared for herself by the side of her husband's body. Inasmuch as they had lived together in great harmony, she had a further wish in addition to her former happiness—for the human mind does not easily grasp divine things—and she hoped its fulfillment might come to the knowledge of men.

"She desired that, after her wanderings beyond the sea, it might be given to her to be buried in the same earth as her husband. I know not at what moment this empty desire by the fullness of Thy goodness began to decline in her heart, and I rejoiced in wonder at what she now told me, although at that conversation of ours at the window, when she said, 'What have I to do here?' she seemed not to be desirous of dying in her own country. I also heard afterwards that, during our stay at Ostia, she was talking one day with motherly kindness to some friends of mine about contempt of this life and the happiness of death.

"I myself was not present. In admiration of the strength of soul which Thou hadst given to her, they asked her whether she did not dread leaving her body so far from her native town. Her reply was, 'Nothing is far to God; nor is it to be feared lest at the end of the world He should not recognize whence He has to raise me up.' In the ninth day, therefore, of her illness, in the fifty-sixth year of her age, that devout and holy soul was released from her body.

"I closed her eyes. Grief took possession of my very soul, and poured itself out in tears, so that my eyes with the violence of my sorrow wept themselves dry, and I suffered greatly from this anguish of sadness. When she breathed forth her last breath, my son, Adeodatus, began to weep, but he was silenced by us. In this way, too, force was put upon the childishness which was hidden in my own heart, and it was checked and repressed. Nor did we deem it fitting to celebrate that death with murmuring, tears and groans, this being the ordinary way of showing grief for a certain destitution, or sort of total extinction, which men attribute to the dead. But she neither died unhappily nor was hers a death at all. This was firmly impressed on our minds both by the unerring example of her conduct and by her genuine faith."

Augustine's strong and fervent faith helps him to bear the loss of the best and dearest friend he had upon this earth. "When the body was removed," he continues, "we returned tearless to our home; for I did not weep even during the prayers we prayed to Thee, as the Sacrifice of our redemption was offered for her when the corpse was placed by the grave before it was lowered, according to the usual rite, but all day long I suffered great anguish of heart, and in my agitation I asked Thee as best I could to calm my grief, yet Thou didst not, impressing, I believe, upon my memory by this one instance how strong is the bond of all habit, even upon a soul which now feeds upon no deceiving word."

During the funeral Mass and the interment at the cemetery, Augustine had restrained his tears lest his weeping be misconstrued as implying that she was lost to him forever and thus would disedify the faithful. With characteristic frankness he tells us, however, that on the night after the funeral, alone with his grief, he was overwhelmed with a sense of loss. The consciousness that in this life he would never again see his mother, never converse with her again, never press his lips to her cheek, released a flood of tears that wet his pillow.

"And now, Lord," he says, "in writing I confess it unto Thee. Read it, who will, and let him judge me as he will, and if he finds sin therein that I wept for my mother and for such a mother, let him not deride me, but rather if he be of large charity, let him weep himself for my sins and ask pardon of Christ for me."

Though Augustine was justly proud of the saintly life of his mother, he was not unaware that she was human and, like all humans, subject to sin. He reflects beautifully the tradition and practice of the early Church in beseeching God to look with mercy upon her transgressions, and in asking the prayers of all for the repose of her soul.

"Therefore, O God of my heart, my glory and my life, putting aside just now her good actions, for which I give Thee joyful thanks, I beg Thy mercy for the sins of my mother. Hear me through the redemption which was shown on the Cross for the healing of our wounds, and may He who sitteth on Thy right hand be our Mediator. I know that her life was merciful, and that she forgave her enemies from her heart; do Thou forgive her now her debts, if she contracted any during the course of so many years after the salutary waters of baptism. Forgive her, O Lord, forgive her, I beseech Thee, and enter not into judgment with her. Let Thy judgment praise Thy mercy, because Thy words are true, and Thou hast promised mercy to the merciful. Thou gavest them power to be this. Thou wilt have mercy on the man who inspires Thy compassion, and wilt show mercy when Thou art merciful.

"I believe Thou hast already done what I am now asking, but do Thou commend, O Lord, the voluntary offering of my lips. For as the day of her death was at hand, she did not give a thought to having her body magnificently laid out or embalmed; nor did she crave for a choice monument, nor wish to be buried in her family tomb. These were not the recommendations which she gave to us. She desired only to be commemorated at Thy altar, which she had served without a single day's intermission."

Monica knew that from the altar "the Holy Victim is dispensed, by whom the handwriting which was against us has been blotted out. By that Victim the enemy was conquered who keeps an account of our transgressions, and who, seeking something wherewith to reproach us, finds nothing against Him whose victory is ours. Who will give Him back His innocent blood? Who will restore to Him the price which He paid for us, that His enemy shall thus have power to take us away from Him? Thy handmaid enchained her soul to His sacrament of our redemption by the bond of faith.

"Let no one withdraw her from Thy protecting arm. May the lion and the dragon not interpose main force or artifice in her path. Neither will she answer and say that she has no debt, lest she be convicted by the wily accuser, and fall a prey to him; but she will answer that her debts were forgiven her by Him to whom none may restore that which He, all innocent of debt, gave for us."

Augustine's closing words read like a prayer that springs from the depths of his soul. "May she rest, then, in peace, with the husband before and after whom she never had any, whom she obeyed with patience, bringing forth fruit unto Thee, that she might win him also unto Thee. And inspire, O Lord my God, inspire Thy servants, my brethren, Thy sons, my masters, whom with voice, and heart, and pen I serve, that so many as read these *Confessions* may at Thy altar remember Monica, Thy handmaid, with Patricius, her some time husband, by whose bodies Thou broughtest me into this life, how I know not. May they with devout affection remember my parents in this transitory light, my brethren under Thee our Father in our Catholic mother, and my fellow citizens in that eternal Jerusalem which Thy pilgrim people sigheth after from their exodus unto their return. That so my mother's last request of me, through my *Confessions* more than through my prayers, be, through the prayers of many, more abundantly fulfilled to her."

The scene at Ostia is depicted in the art and literature of all nations: not a little of its fame is due to the touching tenderness with which Augustine has recorded it. Indeed it seems to have been written not so much with ink as with his tears and blood. In all literature it remains unsurpassed in beauty, delicacy, and tenderness: it is unique, too, in that it mirrors a religious experience shared so profoundly by two great saints, so closely related in the flesh and in the spirit.

The death of Monica changed Augustine's plans for an early return to Africa. He remained about a year in Rome, familiarizing himself with the liturgy, teachings, and life of the Church at its very center. He wrote the important treatise on *Freedom of Choice*

wherein he records his conversations with Evodius on the origin of
evil. He followed this with a refutation of Manichaeism, entitled *On
the Morals of the Catholic Church and of the Manichaeans.*

Having decided that some form of semi-monastic life was most
suitable for him and his friends, Augustine sailed for Africa in the
autumn of 388, and after a short sojourn at Carthage, returned to
his native Tagaste. He and his friends withdrew to his estate, where
they led a common life in poverty, prayer, study, and the reading
of Holy Scripture. This community life, in which all things were
held in common and were distributed according to the individual's
needs, was the basis for the monastic system which Augustine later
sketched and which prompted its members to call themselves Au-
gustinians. During these three years of retirement Augustine wrote
On the Book of Genesis, Against the Manichaeans, On the Teacher
and *On the True Religion.*

Adeodatus, who was with his father all this time, had developed
into a youth of extraordinary talent. Augustine had many serious
talks with him, and out of these grew the dialogue, *On the Teacher.*
To the immense grief of the father, Adeodatus died while quite
young, about 389 or 390, thus ending almost in its inception what
promised to be an unusually brilliant career.

The fame of the convert, who was now distinguishing himself by
his holiness as he had already distinguished himself by his learning,
spread far and wide and brought him many invitations to a more
active ministry. He shrank from these, preferring to devote himself
to a life of prayer, penance and study. He had no thought of entering the priesthood and, through fear of being elevated to the episcopacy, remained away from cities in which the see was vacant.

Summoned to Hippo by a friend perplexed over a spiritual problem, Augustine was praying in a church when people suddenly surrounded him. They cheered and begged Valerius, the bishop, to
raise him to the priesthood. They needed a priest who could preach
to them in their native Punic, which Valerius, a Greek, was unable
to do; indeed he was further handicapped by a lack of fluency in
Latin. Despite Augustine's earnest protests, he was obliged to yield
to their insistent pleading, and was ordained in 391. This obliged
him to move to Hippo, where, in a house adjoining the church, he
established a sort of monastery, modeled on his household at Tagaste. Here he lived with Alypius, Evodius and Possidius—all of

whom were to achieve sainthood—"according to the rule of the holy Apostles."

His priestly ministry of five years was most fruitful. In spite of the deplorable custom which in Africa reserved preaching to bishops, Valerius authorized him to preach on any and all occasions. This he did with great effect: nearly four hundred sermons have come down to us, though some were not written by him but were taken down by others as he delivered them. He combated heresy, especially Manichaeism, with prodigious success. So humiliated was Fortunatus, one of its chief exponents, by defeat in a public debate with Augustine that he fled from Hippo.

Augustine abolished the abuse of holding banquets in the chapels of the martyrs and the custom of family fights as a form of public amusement. In October 393, he took part in the Plenary Council of Carthage, presided over by Aurelius, Bishop of Carthage, and at the request of the bishops he delivered a discourse, which in its completed form was subsequently published under the title, *On Faith and Symbol*. Augustine generally preached in Latin, but when among people who understood only Punic he spoke in their native tongue.

Weakened by age, Valerius secured the permission of Aurelius, Primate of Africa, to have Augustine as his coadjutor. Accordingly in 395, at the age of forty-one, Augustine was consecrated bishop as coadjutor to Valerius, and succeeded him in the see of Hippo soon after: an office he was to occupy for thirty-four years. He established community life in the episcopal residence, requiring all the priests, deacons and subdeacons who lived with him to observe religious poverty. "The regular mode of life," said Pope Paschal II, "recognized in the early Church as instituted by the Apostles was earnestly adopted by the blessed Augustine, who provided it with new regulations."

Augustine's residence at Hippo soon became a sort of monastic seminary from which went forth zealous and holy priests; some founded monasteries in many parts of Africa while others became bishops in neighboring sees. No less than ten of his close friends and disciples, including Alypius, are mentioned by Possidius as achieving the episcopal dignity. He also founded a community of religious women, of whom his sister was the first abbess. His letter to this community, outlining the general ascetical principles of the religious

life, along with two of his sermons on this subject, constitutes the
so-called Rule of St. Augustine: the basis of the constitutions of many
canons regular, friars, and nuns. It is no wonder that Augustine
earned the titles of patriarch of the religious and renovator of the
clerical life of Africa.

Augustine became noted for his devotion to the poor: he used the
revenues of his church in relieving their needs, and he sometimes
melted down parts of the sacred vessels to redeem captives. He got
his flock to establish the custom of clothing all the poor of each parish once a year: neither did he hesitate to contract considerable
debts to relieve their pressing needs. Even greater, however, was his
zeal for the spiritual welfare of his flock.

"I do not wish," he said to his people, "to be saved without you.
What shall I desire? What shall I say? Why am I a bishop? Why
am I in the world? Only to live in Jesus Christ: but to live in Him
with you. This is my passion, my honor, my glory, my joy and my
riches." In those ardent words one catches an echo of St. Paul, whom
Augustine read so frequently and admired so much.

The measure of a man's influence is often found in his capacity
for friendship. Something of the secret of Augustine's great influence
upon those with whom he came in contact is to be traced to his generous capacity for friendship and to the warmth of his affection. This
was one of the most significant traits in Augustine's character. "What
was it," he asks, "that gave me pleasure, save to love and to be
loved?" Love, human or divine, was the axis upon which his world
revolved. He was a great lover, and when he learned to love God
the ardor of his love suffused his life, works, and writings, and its
flame has reached undimmed across the arching vault of nineteen
centuries.

To win souls Augustine was willing to meet with infidels and often
invited them to his table. He generally refused, however, to dine
with Christians whose conduct was a public scandal: indeed he did
not hesitate to subject them to canonical penance and to the cen-
sures of the Church. He was fearless in combating injustice and
iniquity, but he never forgot charity, meekness, and good manners.
He made it a rule never to dine out in his own city, lest invitations
should become so frequent as to interfere with his work and become
a source of distraction.

His letters are of particular interest because they reveal not only his own mind but also the customs of the day. In one of his letters to Januarius he remarks that they do well who communicate daily, provided it be done worthily and with the humility of Zaccheus when he received Christ under his roof: but they also are to be commended who sometimes imitate the humble centurion and set apart Saturdays and Sundays or other days to receive, in order to do so with greater fervor.

In a letter to Ecdicia he explains the duties of a wife toward her husband: he advises her not to wear black clothes since this gives him offense, and suggests that she might be humble in mind while wearing gay dress if he prefers her to wear such. He informs her she ought, in all things reasonable, to agree with her husband as to the manner of educating their son, and leave to him the chief care of it. In similar manner he impresses upon husbands the respect, affection and consideration which they owe to their wives.

A good example of Augustine's modesty and humility occurs in his discussion with St. Jerome over the interpretation of a text of Galatians. Due to the miscarriage of a letter, the great biblical scholar, who was somewhat easily provoked, felt himself publicly attacked. "I entreat you again and again," wrote Augustine, "to correct me confidently when you perceive me to stand in need of it; for though the office of a bishop be greater than that of a priest, yet in many things Augustine is inferior to Jerome."

Indeed Augustine was distressed at the violence with which the controversy between St. Jerome and Rufinus was carried on. He was apprehensive of the subtle influence of vainglory in such disputes, in which men cling to an opinion, as he says, "not because it is true, but because it is their own, and they dispute not for the truth but for victory."

A true shepherd of souls, Augustine was ceaseless in defending truth and in combating error. During his long reign as Bishop of Hippo he was obliged to wage unremitting warfare not only against the Manichaeans but also against the Donatists and the Pelagians. The Donatists held that the Catholic Church, by having communion with sinners, had ceased to be the Church of Christ, this being confined within the limits of their sect, and that no sacraments can be validly administered by those not in the true Church. Exceedingly numerous in Africa, they carried their fury to the greatest excesses, murdering Catholics and committing all sorts of violence.

With great learning, patience, and eloquence Augustine refuted their errors: this he did in his numerous sermons and in his writings. This so infuriated the heretics that they publicly declared that whoever would kill Augustine would be doing a service to their religion and would be rewarded by God. In 405 Augustine was obliged to invoke the civil power to restrain the Donatists around Hippo because of the outrages they were perpetrating: in the same year the Emperor Honorius published severe laws against them. In 411 at Carthage a great conference was held between the two parties, and this marked the beginning of the decline of the heresy.

Scarcely had this subsided, however, when the Pelagian heresy began. Pelagius denied the doctrine of original sin and taught that baptism was a title of admission to heaven, and that grace was not necessary for salvation. In 411 he came to Africa with his friend Caelestius to spread his heresy: this brought about its condemnation by a synod at Carthage. Augustine was asked by the tribune Marcellinus to write a treatise refuting its errors. This he did without naming the author of the heresy, hoping thus more easily to win him: he even praised Pelagius by name. "As I hear," he wrote, "he is a holy man, well exercised in Christian virtue: a good man and worthy of praise."

Pelagius was obdurate, however, and persisted in his errors. Augustine then prepared his famous work, *On Nature and Grace,* containing a detailed, complete, and carefully reasoned refutation of this subtle and dangerous heresy. Indeed to him the Church is indebted as the chief instrument of God in the overthrow of this heresy.

The third heresy that Augustine was called upon to combat was Arianism. Concerned chiefly with the doctrine of the Holy Trinity, this widespread heresy denied the divinity of Christ and held that He was merely a superior creature. It was brought to Africa by Maximinus, an Arian bishop, in 428. Though Augustine was then seventy-four, he promptly challenged the heretic to a public debate. Maximinus accepted, but at the end of the first day, to the amazement of all who had expected the discussion to continue for several days, he fled overnight to Carthage. After writing a record of the day's discussion, the venerable bishop then wrote a refutation of the heresy, entitled *Against Maximinus the Heretic.*

The thirty-five-year period of his reign as Bishop of Hippo was one of intense intellectual activity in which the man was overshadowed by the thinker, the writer, the mystic. There were no more of the romantic or dramatic adventures that had characterized his earlier years: he had found the object of his long quest, divine truth, and he was now engrossed in defending and propagating it. While he took part in ecclesiastical councils and engaged heretics in public debate, he spent most of his time in preaching to his flock, meditating upon the eternal verities, writing his numerous books, protecting the weak, helping the needy, and praying in his cell with a devotion that grew ever greater. As the years went by, he became ever increasingly a mouth that proclaimed divine truth and a pen that committed it to imperishable script.

From the inexhaustible fountain of his mighty genius there flowed an endless stream of letters, homilies, pamphlets, and books. He has left us more than a hundred works, some little more than pamphlets and others quite lengthy, like the *City of God*, which fills a volume. They constitute a vast encyclopedia of Catholic thought: psychology, philosophy, moral and dogmatic theology, ascetical and mystical theology, biblical exegesis, education and literature. "Their mission it was," observes Papini, "to strengthen the piety and theology of the Church even unto our own day, and they will live on in the hearts of all lovers of God so long as a single Christian shall remain on earth."

In the early summer of 426 Bishop Severus of Milevis, a lifelong friend of Augustine and one of the original monks in the monastery of Hippo, died. The bishop had told his priests of his choice of one of them as his successor but had neglected to inform the people. In North Africa in those days the people had a good deal to say in the selection of a new bishop, though as a rule they appear to have been quite willing to respect the wishes of a dying prelate. Because of the failure of the bishop to publicize his choice, much confusion and misunderstanding arose at Milevis. Upon the arrival of Augustine the trouble subsided and the candidate designated by Severus was duly installed.

To obviate such possible confusion Augustine determined to designate his successor publicly. On September 26, 426, before a great assembly of the priests and faithful in the Church of Peace in Hippo, Augustine appeared before them with secretaries who recorded the whole proceedings. The venerable prelate told of his coming to

Hippo as a young man, reminded them that he had grown old in the service of the diocese, and mentioned that not many more years were left to him. He told them of the difficulties he had recently witnessed at Milevis and which he wished to avoid here. "I wish to designate," he solemnly declared, "as my successor, the priest Eraclius!"

With shouts of acclaim they hailed his announcement. "Thanks be to God! Christ be praised!" they cried in joyous acceptance of his selection. "O Christ, hear us! Long life to Augustine!" rang out repeatedly in the cathedral.

For years Augustine had planned to go over his numerous works and revise them to reflect the changes in his thought. As far back as 412 he had written to Marcellinus, "I desire, if God permits me, to compile and point out all those things which displease me in my works, in a special treatise, so that men will see I am not one of those people who try to defend everything they have written." No less than fifteen years had elapsed before Augustine found time for this laborious task. This he did in 427, publishing his *Retractions*. The work shows clearly the progress of his thought and is invaluable in clearing up problems of authenticity and chronology as well as disclosing his final views on the many subjects which he had treated. Because few great philosophers have shown such foresight, their followers are often left in the dark as to their final beliefs and convictions.

The closing years of Augustine's life were saddened by the collapse of Roman rule in Africa. Count Boniface, the representative at Carthage of the Roman Empire, was at odds with the Empress Placidia. When he refused to go to Rome to try to justify his attitude she sent an army of Goths against him. Whereupon Boniface invited Genseric and his Vandals to come to his defense. When he saw how formidable was the ally he had brought into the country, he realized they were a potential enemy whose one thought was to plunder, burn, and massacre. Augustine urged him to make peace with the Empress and resist the invading Vandals. This Boniface tried to do, but it was too late. Genseric and his horde of eight thousand Vandals and Alani were already masters of the country.

They laid waste the whole of North Africa, pillaging and burning towns and cities, torturing and murdering the inhabitants. "They spared," wrote Possidius, "neither sex nor age, not even the priests and ministers of God, nor the ornaments, sacred vessels and build-ings of the Church." Only three cities still remained in the hands of the Romans: Carthage, Cirta, and Hippo. Boniface and several bishops fled to Hippo, and Genseric laid siege to the town. The siege lasted fourteen months and finally Hippo was destroyed by fire.

In the third month of the siege Augustine was stricken with a fever, and from the first moments of his illness knew that it was the summons of God. He often spoke of the joy of St. Ambrose in his last moments, and of the words of Christ to a certain bishop in a vision mentioned by St. Cyprian: "You are afraid to suffer here, and unwilling to go hence: what shall I do with you?" Different indeed was the attitude of Augustine. "What love of Christ can that be," he wrote, "to fear lest He, whom you say you love, shall come? Brethren, are we not ashamed to say we love, when we add that we are afraid lest He come?"

On the wall facing his bed he had hung a copy of the penitential psalms. These he recited with tears. While he lay there, a sick man came to him and told him he had been directed in a dream to go to Bishop Augustine to be cured by the imposition of his hands. Hum-ble about his power of intercession, Augustine at first demurred; but when the sick man renewed his plea, he placed his hand upon his head, and the man was cured. "I know," recalls Possidius, "both when he was priest and when he was a bishop, he poured out supplications to our Lord, and the evil spirits departed from them."

In the last days of his illness, despite the waning strength of his body, his mind was absorbed in prayer and meditation. On the threshold of eternity he wanted to be alone with God to deepen that mystical union he had sought so earnestly to form. His great heart went out in torrents of love, and his eyes were moist with tears as he repeated the name he loved most of all in life: "Jesus! Jesus! Jesus!" On the evening of August 28, 430, in the seventy-sixth year of his life, in the presence of a number of bishops and other mem-bers of his household who were praying at his bedside, his heart ceased its beating and his great soul soared upwards to the God whom he had served with such tireless zeal and unswerving love for more than forty years.

"We being present," says Possidius, "the Sacrifice was offered to God for his recommendation, and so he was buried . . . He had made no will, for this poor man of God had nothing to leave." No money or property indeed, but he left a treasure beyond all price, which thieves cannot steal, nor Vandals destroy, nor time itself erode: the legacy of a reformation which gives hope to all sinners and of thoughts which will forever quicken the hearts and illumine the minds of men. Augustine is among those luminous souls, of whom Browning says:

> . . . Through such souls alone,
> God, stooping, shows sufficient of His light
> For us in the dark to rise by. And I rise.

One of the most prolific geniuses that the world has ever known, Augustine is admired not only for the number of his works but also for the variety of their topics, which cover virtually the whole realm of philosophic and religious thought. To traverse that vast ocean is, however, beyond our scope: we shall content ourselves with pointing out a few of the mighty Ararats which jut up into the sky of human thought and after the lapse of fourteen centuries still constitute landmarks for men to travel by.

Augustine is among the few geniuses who speak to both intellect and heart, and to the one as convincingly as to the other. Among the great theologians he is pre-eminently the psychologist. Time and again he makes psychological observation the preliminary and the basis of metaphysics. Indeed he does not hesitate to apply his psychological method to the profound mysteries of the divine life, and to interpret the inner life of the Trinity after the analogy of the human soul. It is this habit of plumbing the realities of the inner life which invests so many of his investigations with a concrete and lucid quality and gives them a warmth, freshness, and universal appeal.

To that extent his theology may be said to be a theology of experience. This does not mean, however, that sacred things and divine truth have no existence for him except as objects of experience or facts of consciousness. A firm believer in absolute truth and in absolutely valid knowledge, he brings these things into relation with himself, and they are for him living and fruitful only through that relation.

In this respect Augustine and St. Thomas Aquinas stand poles apart. To the latter, the subject thinking is completely subordinate to the object thought, to the sublime reality of revealed truth, and the function of the theologian is simply to receive and interpret that truth in silent reverence. He must prescind from all subjective feelings or considerations, either personal or cultural and, in the inviolable security of the mind's cloistered sanctuary, expound the truth in itself, the word of God in itself, in all its pristine purity and integrity. The only tinge of emotion discernible in the thinking of St. Thomas is that of a rapt, single-minded devotion to the revealed word of God.

Thus St. Thomas stands in the rarified atmosphere of the lofty mountain peak, far above the noises of the world below, peering through the telescope of his mighty intellect at the realities of the spiritual universe, oblivious of all else: Augustine looks through the same telescope, but he hears at the same time the voices of his own heart echoing the cries of all humanity, and he is stirred not only by the starry heavens above but also by the voice within his breast.

It is the utter exclusion of all subjectivity which gives to the thought and writing of St. Thomas, the Angelic Doctor, its absolute validity, Alpine stability, and timeless permanence; but that very objectivity gives it at the same time a certain cold, aloof, rigid, and impersonal quality which is in sharp contrast to the quickening and kindling quality that characterizes virtually all that Augustine wrote. It is for this reason that Augustine is so near to the modern man, nearer than any of the great scholastics: that, too, is why he is so much alive and so widely read today. Indeed most readers of his *Confessions* think of him as a contemporary, their next-door neighbor, even their alter ego.

One misses the distinctive genius of Augustine if he thinks of him as a cold, dispassionate intellect searching for the great truths which give meaning and purpose to human life: he searched for them intensely and passionately, struggling for the ultimate meaning of life and wrestling with God. He searched for divine wisdom with his heart as well as with his mind. His constant endeavor was "but to *love* and seek and pursue and clasp and never let go Wisdom herself, wherever I found her. . . . O Truth, Truth, how did the inmost *marrow* of my soul sigh for thee!"

His search has an intensely practical purpose and it springs from the depths of his personal life and experience. To him truth and happiness are fused into an inseparable unity. In finding truth he would find God, in finding God he would find the divine and invisible source of all reality, who alone could give repose to his restless heart and peace to his troubled soul: this spells happiness for him.

To him the mystery of being lies not without but within his own soul. "Go not out!" he says. "Turn inwards into yourself! Truth dwells within, in the inward man." That, too, is where he found God. "I, Lord, went wandering like a strayed sheep seeking Thee with anxious reasoning without, whilst Thou wast within me . . . I went around the streets of the city of this world, and I found Thee not, because in vain I sought without for Thee who wast within myself." What an undertone of deep emotion is audible in these words!

Augustine's writings show how greatly he was influenced by St. Paul, and nowhere else is this influence more pronounced than in his treatment of the supremacy of love. The Apostle's glorious canticle on love, in the thirteenth chapter of his First Epistle to the Corinthians, burned its way into his heart and mind, and became the leitmotiv of much of his mystical and ascetical writing. Time and again he echoes the refrain of St. Paul: "Now the end of the commandment is charity. . . . Love therefore is the fulfilling of the law." Augustine embodied this doctrine in one of his most widely quoted utterances, "Love and do what you will."

The line of reasoning back of this injunction is simple enough: the individual who truly loves God will offend neither Him nor his neighbor, for by offending the latter he also offends God. To Augustine love is the highest, ultimate and deepest reality of all, for God is love. It provides the Christian with motive power and it alone invests his deeds with merit: it is the unfailing mark and the distinguishing characteristic of the true Christian. "Anyone," he points out, "may sign himself with the sign of the cross, may say 'Amen' and sing 'Alleluia,' may present himself for baptism, visit churches and help to build them. The only thing which distinguishes the children of God from the children of the devil is love."

The measure of morality and the criterion of true sanctity are found in the conformity of the will of the individual to the will of God. But this inward surrender and complete dedication of the will to God is brought about only by love. Therefore love becomes the practical index of holiness, the measuring rod of moral character and the thermometer of the blessed life. "To live happily," he says, "is not only to live according to reason, for that would be to live

according to a human standard. To live happily is to live according
to the mind of God."

Probably no one since St. Paul and the Beloved Disciple John had
a deeper appreciation of the virtue of love or a more contagious enthusiasm for it than this bishop of the glowing heart. That is why
the artists of the Church frequently depict him with a flaming heart.
Something of that flame was caught by Dante, who closes his *Divine Comedy* with the line mirroring so perfectly the mind of Augustine; "It is love that moves the sun in the heavens and all the
stars."

The writings of the other Fathers are largely *pièces de circon-
stance,* treating certain heresies and dangers threatening the peace
and unity of their flock, rather than general treatises on Christian
philosophy. But while Augustine has written no formal *Summa* like
that of St. Thomas Aquinas, his writings nevertheless mirror all
the important problems of Christian life and philosophy with a comprehensiveness which surpasses any other writer of the early Church.
His systematic treatise on *The Trinity* alone comprises fifteen volumes and occupied him over a period of nearly thirty years. Not
until one begins to traverse the writings of this genius does he realize
something of the sweep and expanse, the grandeur and the penetration of a mind which has influenced Christian thought more profoundly than any writer since St. Paul.

What is generally regarded as his most important work is *The City
of God.* It is a masterly vindication of the Christian Church, which
is conceived in the form of a new social and civic order rising from
the crumbling ruins of the Roman Empire. It is the first contribution
to the philosophy of history and warrants us in calling Augustine
the founder of this branch of knowledge. While his other works are
of interest, especially to philosophers and theologians, this, like his
Confessions, belongs to general literature and appeals to every soul.
The *Confessions* mirrors a theology which has been fused in the cru-
cible of an individual life, and narrate the history of God's actions
upon the individual, while *The City of God* is theology framed in
the history of humanity, and describes the action of God upon the
world at large.

The fundamental concept of the Church as a world-wide empire,
co-terminous with humanity, was a daring conception at that time
when most of the Church's life and history had to be gleaned from

the catacombs from which she was just emerging. Only one who understood something of the power of the Crucified could have the courage and the daring to picture the infant Church, leaving her swaddling clothes in the dark caves under the hills of Rome, as the mighty institution which was destined to hammer out on the anvil of history the dominant civilization of the world.

While Augustine is called Doctor of Grace, because of his refutation of Pelagianism and his exposition of the subtle influence of God on the human soul, he might well be termed Doctor of the Church for his matchless exposition of its corporate divine life and its essential unity. It was his City of God, his favorite theme. *De ecclesia numquam satis.* "The Church," he says, "is now what the earthly paradise was. Therefore those who slay men by seducing them from the Church are sons of Satan." Just as unity was the characteristic mark of the Roman Empire, so unity must be the distinctive mark of the spiritual commonwealth, the Church of God. To be out of the unity of Christ's Mystical Body is, in Augustine's eyes, to be not merely a heretic, but a pariah, an outcast, without country or home or kindred.

As St. Paul may be said to have been Christocentric, filled with Christ, breathing His spirit in all his utterances, so Augustine may be said to have been filled with the Church, Christ's incarnate Spouse, and to breathe reverence and love for her in his every word. How accurately he discerned the importance of unity for her continued existence and growth, the history of the divisions of Christendom in later centuries abundantly testifies.

Not less daring than his conception of the infant Church emerging from the catacombs, and rising from the ruins of the Roman Empire to fashion the civilization of the world, was his conception of the entire creative process as having occurred in a moment of time, with the germinal principles (*rationes seminales*) destined to unfold their latent potentialities into higher and higher forms of evolving life. As a result of God's creative act, there appeared all the elements of the world, not in their present developed and specialized forms, but in a confused and *nebulous* mass. The word nebulous, embodying the core of the famous theory of Kant and Laplace that the world evolved from an original nebula, is Augustine's "*Nebulosa species apparet.*"

A principle of hermeneutics which Augustine emphasized with

great frequency would, if it had been observed by subsequent biblical scholars, have spared Christianity many so-called conflicts between religion and science. The principle emphasizes the need of extreme prudence and caution in determining the meaning of Scripture. His words, which have been taken over by several Pontiffs and made their own, are: "We must be on our guard against giving interpretations which are hazardous or opposed to science, and so exposing the Word of God to the ridicule of unbelievers." He pictures the harm done to the cause of religion when a Christian, by appealing to the Bible, undertakes to lecture a scientist concerning subject matter within the latter's jurisdiction.

"It very often happens," he says, "that there is some question as to the earth or the sky, or the other elements of this world—respecting which one who is not a Christian has knowledge derived from most certain reasoning or observation, and it is very disgraceful and mischievous and of all things to be carefully avoided, that a Christian speaking of such matters as being according to the Christian Scriptures, should be heard by an unbeliever talking such nonsense that the unbeliever perceiving him to be as wide from the mark as east from west, can hardly restrain himself from laughing." Pointing out that we are not to regard the Bible as a textbook of science, nor seek to solve disputes of scientists by quoting a scriptural text, Augustine says: "The Gospels do not tell us that Our Lord said: 'I will send you the Holy Ghost to teach you the course of the sun and the moon'; we should endeavor to become Christians and not astronomers."

By far the most popular and famous of all Augustine's works is his *Confessions*. With the exception of Vergil, no other Latin book has been translated into so many languages and read over such a long period of time. In influence it far exceeds Vergil and ranks next to *The Imitation of Christ* in the sway it has exercised in the minds and hearts of its readers. Modern best sellers rarely remain at the top of the list for more than a year or two, but Augustine's story has remained in the upper bracket since the year 400. Because it lays bare the abiding passions, hopes, fears and yearnings of the human soul, it transcends his period and belongs to the ages. Unlike contemporary works which enjoy the transient popularity of Book-of-the-Month Club selections, points out Bishop Sheen, the

Confessions of St. Augustine has won lasting fame as a Book-of-the-Centuries!

The *Confessions* are an impassioned soliloquy uttered in the presence of God. Written twelve years after his baptism, the book tells the story of his early life. Two contrasting notes echo throughout the narrative: sorrow, shame and penitence for his sins and gratitude and praise to God for his deliverance. Augustine tells us that he wrote it at the suggestion of friends that they might mourn with him in his offenses and join with him in thanking God for the grace of repentance and reformation. "Confession," he says, "is understood in two senses: of our sins and of God's praise." The note of joyous praise is dominant throughout the narrative, and the reader finds himself eager to sound the same exultant refrain.

Though it is in the nature of autobiographies to be personal and distinctive, there is in *Confessions* an element of universality which enables every reader to feel that it is the story of his own soul. Even if he did not actually fall into the sins of Augustine, he realizes the potentiality was there and feels impelled to exclaim: "There, too, go I but for the grace of God." "When I began to read the *Confessions of St. Augustine*," said St. Theresa, "I saw myself there described." Such, too, is the experience of virtually every reader of this moving story, for it is the autobiography of humanity.

Depicted with consummate skill is the ceaseless play of two elemental forces struggling for the mastery: the pull of the flesh and its lusts for sensual gratification and the tug of the spirit and grace for union with God and the peace and joy of a good conscience. It is a vivid dramatization of that internecine strife to which St. Paul bears abiding witness; "I see another law in my members, fighting against the law of my mind, and captivating me in the law of sin, that is in my members."

Shaken to the foundations of his being by the bruising struggle of these two elemental forces within him, he cries out, "Unhappy man that I am, who shall deliver me from the body of this death?" To which his soul replied, "The grace of God, by Jesus Christ our Lord." These are the two leading characters in the dramatis personae of Augustine's moving drama.

Much of the current rash of confessions, especially in pulp magazines, is concocted by editors to provide the reader with a vicarious experience of sinning: seductions are described to tickle the prurience and excite the passions. When he closes the book or magazine he feels he has been drawn through the mire and slime of the gutter. How different is the artistry of Augustine! He portrays the sin and its psychological aftermath in such a way as to provide the reader with a vicarious experience not of the sin but of the shame and repentance.

Thus the reader is stirred not to passion but to a horror of sin and to resolutions of amendment. Instead of feeling befouled he experiences a sense of purgation, atonement, uplift and union with God. When all the lewd, lascivious, and seductive portrayals of vice that have ever been written are but dust and ashes men will still turn to the *Confessions* of the penitent prodigal of Hippo for light to chart the nobler course and strength and courage to follow it.

For more than fifteen centuries the book has brought hope to the sinner, consolation to the frustrated, courage to the fearful, and strength to all. "No one before or since," observes Bishop Fulton J. Sheen, "has written such a psychoanalysis or revelation of a soul. If he shows here and there the thorns in his side, it is only the better to declare how these thorns by the curious germination of Divine Grace can blossom into the rose of Divine Friendship." One ends the reading of this masterpiece profoundly convinced of the truth of the words of Leon Bloy; "The only tragedy in all the world is the tragedy of not being a saint."

What is the secret of the peculiar hold which Augustine has had on the minds and hearts of men for fifteen centuries? It lies in the unquestioned soundness of the answer he gives to the ceaseless cry of the human soul: "How and where shall I find happiness?" Camouflage it though we may, this is the one persistent and irrepressible cry, uttered by every one born of woman, be he peasant or king, simpleton or philosopher, sinner or saint. Augustine answers it in his profound treatises with a logic and erudition that compel the admiration of the scholar, and in the *Confessions* with a simplicity which astonishes the ordinary reader as much as it grips and stirs him. Like his great patron St. Paul, he became "all things to all men" that he might lead them all to God.

To Augustine there are but two supreme and abiding realities: God and the human soul. All his thinking gravitates between these two poles and has for its purpose the uniting of these ultimates. In that union alone man finds the fulfillment of his destiny and everlasting happiness. There are many winding roads between these two poles, many labyrinthine ways that lead to dark gloomy caves of lust and vice wherein the pilgrim may be endlessly detoured, but there is only one straight road: that blazed by the incarnate God, Jesus Christ, who is the way, the truth, and the life.

Christ came to show us the way to heaven, to redeem us, and to incorporate us into Himself. Just as the whole human race was germinally contained in Adam, Augustine points out, so the whole of the new redeemed humanity is contained in the second Adam, the creative Word of God. This redeemed humanity is but the unfolding in space and time of the humanity of Jesus. Of that body Christ is the Head and we are the members: hence Christ is whole and entire only when Head and members are organically united.

So close and intimate is this union, this fellowship of being and life, that Augustine does not hesitate to speak of Christ and His members as one single Christ, one single person. This true, vital, and essential union of our humanity with the new Adam, Jesus Christ, is established by baptism and strengthened by confirmation and the Holy Eucharist. Thus Christianity, Augustine observes, is essentially sacramental, since the sacraments are exclusively concerned with the enactment of the central Christian "mystery": our incorporation into the Mystical Body of Christ and our living in harmonious union with its Head.

Thus beautifully does Augustine develop the Pauline doctrine of the Mystical Body and trace out its profound implications for the individual and for society. Since Christianity, he reasons, is the union of Head and members in one body, so Christian love is a love of the whole body, a social love which excludes no single part or segment. Thus the true Christian is never alone, never isolated, never solitary: conscious of his union with Christ and His members, his sympathy and love go out without reserve to the whole fellowship. Indeed to Augustine all Christendom is but "one Christ, loving himself," and to be a Christian means to be born again of the Holy Spirit and to be incorporated into the Mystical Body and share in the divine life which is grace. These are Augustine's joyous and exultant tidings which soar to a mighty climax as he cries ecstatically, "Christ is my beginning! Christ is my root! Christ is my head!"

"No Father before Augustine," says Karl Adam, "nor theologian after him, has treated this mystical unity so profoundly, or employed it so fruitfully and comprehensively in expounding the essential nature of Christianity and the Church. In this, Augustine was the inspired pupil of an inspired master, the great apostle of the Gentiles."

The character of Augustine both as a man and as a scholar has been briefly indicated in the course of our sketch. None can question the genius of his mind or the greatness of his soul: his infectious enthusiasm, his unceasing search for truth, his affectionate disposition, his big-hearted generosity to the poor and lowly, his passionate love of God and of his fellow man. Even those who differ with him in some phases of his philosophical and theological reasoning cannot but acknowledge the penetrating power of his keen intellect and the logical acumen with which he handled the most profound questions.

Of the four great Fathers of the Western Church he is unquestionably the greatest: more penetrating than Ambrose, his spiritual father; more creative and profound than Jerome, his correspondent; and intellectually far more brilliant than Gregory the Great, his pupil on the papal throne. No other single mind has ever exercised such a profound and far-reaching influence upon Christian thought and life—an influence that has continued for more than fifteen centuries.

What is indeed remarkable is the virtual unanimity with which the great critics of all schools of theological thought, Protestant as well as Catholic, accord Augustine the foremost place among the Fathers and Doctors of the Church. Peter the Venerable reflects the general sentiment of the Middle Ages when he ranks Augustine as second only to the Apostles. What an eloquent tribute St. Thomas Aquinas pays him in citing him more than a thousand times in the *Summa Theologica* alone! Bossuet calls him "the incomparable Augustine" and "the Doctor of Doctors." Christopher Dawson declares that he "was not only the founder of the Christian philosophy of history but was actually the first man in the world to discover the meaning of time."

Not less enthusiastic are Protestant scholars in their admiration of his genius. Harnack reflects the consensus of opinion among them when he says, "Where, in the history of the West, is there to be found a man who, in point of influence, can be compared with him?" Similar is the judgment of Bindeman; "Augustine is a star of extraordinary brilliancy in the firmament of the Church. Since the

Apostles he has been unsurpassed." Schaff sums up the verdict of all when he terms Augustine "a philosopher and theological genius of the first order dominating, like a pyramid, antiquity and the succeeding ages. . . . Compared with the great philosophers of past centuries and modern times, he is the equal of them all; among theologians he is undeniably the first, and such has been his influence that none of the Fathers, Scholastics, or Reformers has surpassed it."

Not a little of the perennial interest in Augustine's works is due to his unrivaled facility in the use of words, to his polished diction and his graceful, brilliant style. He varied it, as Papini points out, to suit his theme and reflect his mood: now it is sonorous and penetrating like Cicero at his best; now pathetic and soulful like romantic prose; now like Tertullian, impetuous and violent; now calm, restrained, and simple, as in a Platonic dialogue. In his style there are reflected, not only the light of a glowing intellect, but also the volcanic rumblings and the seething storms of his restless and tempestuous heart. It is part of the unique genius of Augustine that he speaks to his readers not only with his intellect but with his heart as well. The greatest stylist of his era, he endowed the ancient majesty of Latin prose with a greater pregnancy of meaning and a cadence that is entirely modern.

This does not mean, however, that all his works are equal in literary style. There are passages which betray the violence of the mind's struggle to reshape the fixed and hardened form of words to capture new nuances and meanings. Here Augustine was confronted with the problem, which faces every original thinker venturing into new and unexplored regions in the trackless sea of thought, of putting new conceptions into old words. It is like putting new wine into old wineskins, only to see much of it leak out.

Words are but the hardened shells of old meanings, and they can't easily or quickly reshape themselves to new tenants. Like all finite material things, they lag behind the flight of thought, with its dazzling new twists and turns, and the infinitude of nuances and ideas to which the spirit gives birth. In this respect Augustine was like St. Paul: both struggled with the inherent inadequacy of the medium to carry the full cargo of their meaning. It is the problem which confronts every truly great artist, whether it be in music, painting, sculpture, or literature: "the tragedy," as Papini calls it, "of the eternal Pygmalion surrendering before the unconquerable inflexibility of matter."

Despite that ineluctable handicap, Augustine achieved eminence as a writer because his thought burned its way into the very marrow of his soul and he lived what he thought and felt deeply what he said. Religion became an integral part of his very being: God so filled his soul that he had only to look within himself to study the mysterious action of grace upon his heart and will. The consciousness of his membership in the Mystical Body quickened his desire to mirror the indwelling Christ in his thoughts and actions. His tears of repentance were not mere secretions from his lachrymal glands but blood oozing from a grieving heart. Indeed his thoughts and sentiments stream from such deep fountains within him that his writings on any subject bear the shadow of his autobiography: this is the true secret of his distinctive style and diction.

Though Augustine has passed from this life, he still lives in the minds and hearts of all men who hunger for truth, justice, righteousness, and love, and who seek to find in union with God repose for their restless hearts. He brings before our eyes the timeless and invisible world of the spirit, and helps us to realize that we, wayfarers on a fleeting planet in the skies, have a destiny beyond the realms of time and space; that there awaits us a habitation, not built by hands, eternal in heaven. It is the genius of Augustine that works in every generation the miracle of which Francis Thompson dreamed:

> *O world invisible, we view thee,*
> *O world intangible, we touch thee.*
> *O world unknowable, we know thee,*
> *Inapprehensible, we clutch thee!*

Augustine ends his *Confessions* with the following words: "But Thou, the Good who needeth no good, art always at rest, for Thou art Thy own rest. And what man can make another man understand this? What angel can make another angel grasp it? What angel can convey it to man? From Thee it must be begged; in Thee be sought; at Thy door must one knock: thus, thus will it be received, thus will it be found, thus will it be opened."

In these final words Augustine seeks to drive home to each reader a truth of far-reaching consequence: wisdom and true happiness cannot be bought, or handed over by others like merchandise, but must be gained by personal effort aided by God. Each individual must seek them for himself. Though others may assist him, he himself must struggle for them in the solitude of his own soul. Where will he find them? Though he search throughout the whole universe, he will find them only in God. Thus the whole moving narrative is but the spelling out of the mighty truth which runs as a refrain through every page: "Our heart has been made for Thee, O God, and it shall never rest until it rests in Thee!" In the realization of this truth man finds wisdom and in living it he finds happiness.

The mortal remains of Augustine repose in the Church of St. Peter in Pavia, Italy, and those of his saintly mother, Monica, in the Church of St. Augustine in Rome. Thus even in death the dust of the mother clings to the church consecrated to the memory of her son. No one who reads the story of their pilgrimage and pentrates their living faith in the power of the Crucified can doubt that the union broken at Ostia, when mother and son looked out with wistful eyes toward Carthage across the sea, has its continuance in that celestial Jerusalem, the City of God, to which their eyes and hearts were constantly turned. In the union of both with the heart of the Infinite their restless hearts find rest at last.

JOHN HENRY NEWMAN
Scholar of Oxford

I. FROM THE DARKNESS INTO THE LIGHT

Every great achievement, it has been observed, is but the length-ened shadow of a great man. A movement which has weathered the storms of more than a century and still exercises its influence upon the direction of human thought is indeed no small achievement. Such is the Oxford Movement, which projects into our modern day the mighty figure of John Henry Newman, scholar of Oxford, littéra-teur, philosopher, theologian and cardinal of the Catholic Church.

Toward the close of the last century Lord Coleridge reflected the sentiment of many an Englishman in referring to Newman as "that great man who still survives at Birmingham in venerable age, but with undimmed mental eye and unabated force of genius, a Roman cardinal in title, but the light and guide of multitudes of grateful hearts outside his own communion and beyond the limits of these small islands." The numerous volumes which have issued from the press in recent years about him mirror the constantly widening in-terest among people of every faith in the retiring scholar of Oxford, who still speaks to a listening world from the pages of his mighty books.

Born in London on February 21, 1801, Newman was the eldest son of John Newman, a banker, and of Jemima Fourdrinier of Huguenot extraction. He was of a quiet, retiring nature, finding his recreation less in school games and more in the reading of the Bible and the novels of Scott, which were then in the course of publication. From his mother he received his religious training, which was a modified Calvinism. At sixteen he entered Trinity Col-lege, Oxford, and in the following year he gained a scholarship of sixty pounds, good for nine years. When only twenty-one he was elected a fellow of Oriel, then the acknowledged center of Oxford intellectual life. In 1824 he was ordained and became tutor of Oriel, and later was appointed vicar of St. Mary's, the university church at Oxford.

He took a Mediterranean trip with Froude, whose health was impaired, visiting Sicily, Naples, and Rome. There he met Dr. Wiseman, then rector of the English College, who was destined to play an important part in his later career. Returning alone from Rome to Sicily, he was stricken with a dangerous fever at Leonforte. Recalling in later years the details of this critical illness, Newman saw himself upon his bed, a prey to delirium, with death hovering near, giving final instructions to his Italian servant, but adding the strange words, the memory of which was to haunt him later on: "I shall not die, I shall not die, for I have not sinned against the light . . . God has still a work for me to do."

When the worst of the fever had passed, and he had determined to continue his journey, he remembered himself sitting on the bed of the inn, still weak and sobbing, and saying to his servant, who understood not a word: "I have a work to do in England." What that work was, he had no idea then. But subsequent events were to prove with a vengeance that he had a work to do.

With difficulty he reached Palermo, aching to get home. He crossed the Mediterranean, then France, and was sailing home when the vessel became becalmed in the Straits of Bonifacio. While walking the deck and gazing up at the darkened sky, he composed the poem, *Lead, Kindly Light,* which has become a favorite hymn in all the Christian churches. It reveals to us the state of his mind questing for the light that he might obey the mysterious voice telling him that he had "a work to do."

> *Lead, kindly light, amid the encircling gloom,*
>   *Lead Thou me on!*
> *The night is dark, and I am far from home.*
>   *Lead Thou me on!*
> *Keep Thou my feet; I do not ask to see*
> *The distant scene—one step enough for me.*
>
> *So long Thy power hath blest me, sure it still*
>   *Will lead me on,*

O'er moor and fen, o'er crag and torrent, till
  The night is gone;
And with the morn those angel faces smile,
Which I have loved long since, and lost awhile.

Newman landed in England on July 9, 1833. A few days later, what is called "The Oxford Movement" began. Arriving at Oxford, Newman found his friends greatly excited over the government's bill to suppress a number of the Anglican bishoprics in Ireland. It was regarded by them as a shocking usurpation by the state, a clear manifestation that the government considered the Church its creature, with which it could do as it saw fit. What then became of the Church as a divine institution, apostolic in character, having a charter independent of the state, a conviction which these Anglican divines liked to entertain? Keble declared war against the measure in a sermon on "National Apostasy," which he preached at St. Mary's on July 14, 1833. The sermon was printed, widely distributed, and created a great stir.

Newman later wrote "that he had ever considered and kept the day as the start of the religious Movement of 1833," subsequently known as the Oxford Movement. While Keble first sounded the tocsin, and Pusey spread further the alarm, it was Newman who was the real leader of the crusade. "For hundreds of young men," writes J. A. Froude, "*Credo in Newmannum* was a genuine symbol of faith." His gifts of intellect, his deep spiritual nature, and his transparent honesty of purpose inspired complete confidence.

The sermons which he preached on Sunday afternoons at St. Mary's were events to which all of Oxford, especially the younger men, looked forward with eagerness. Delivered without a gesture or any of the arts of the orator, the sermons gripped the audience with their spiritual insight, their fertility of illustration, their profound sincerity. Each member of the audience hung upon his words as though he only were being spoken to.

"The service was very simple," writes Principal Shairp, "no pomp, no ritualism; for it was characteristic of the leading men of the movement that they left these things to the weaker brethren . . . To call Newman's sermons eloquent would be no word for them; high poems rather they were as of an inspired singer, or the outpourings of a prophet, rapt yet self-possessed. And the tone of voice in which they were spoken, once you grew accustomed to it, sounded like a fine strain of unearthly music. Through the silence of that high Gothic building, the words fell on the ear like the measured drippings of water in some vast, dim cave. After hearing these sermons you might come away still not believing the tenets peculiar to the High Church system; but you would be harder than most men if you did not feel more than ever ashamed of coarseness, selfishness, worldliness, if you did not feel the things of the faith brought closer to the soul."

Newman was stirring Oxford to a religious life and fervor much after the fashion in which Savanarola had shaken fifteenth-century Florence out of its lethargy. While the Dominican prior, his dark eyes flashing fire, thundered from the Duomo, arousing the Florentines to repentance, Newman spoke in a restrained voice which at times fell to a whisper that yet rose to a thunder within the inner ear. From every side disciples flocked to him as to a leader and prophet. His influence at Oxford was supreme.

In championing the divine character of the Anglican Church, Newman had developed the theory of the *via media*. He held that the English Church lay at an equal distance from Rome and Geneva. Being apostolic in origin and doctrine, it anathematized the peculiar tenets of Calvin and Luther, while it protested with equal vigor against "Roman corruptions," excrescences upon the body of primitive truth. Hence he conceived of the Anglican Church as appealing to antiquity, having as its norm the undivided Church, and handing down the teaching of the Fathers in the articles and in the prayer book. Hence his absorption in the study of the Fathers, which, under his influence, became the order of the day at Oxford.

A few weeks after Keble's sermon, Newman started, on his own initiative, *Tracts for the Times*. Their aim was to secure for the Church of England a definite basis in doctrine and discipline, and thus obtain for her some security from the highhanded dealings of the state which her sister institution in Ireland was then experiencing. In 1841 Newman published *Tract 90*, in which he set forth the thesis that the negations in the Thirty-nine Articles of the Anglican creed were directed not against the authoritative doctrines of the Catholic Church but only against exaggerations which had crept in.

A storm of indignation broke out. Newman was reviled as a traitor and characterized as a veritable Guy Fawkes at Oxford. The Bishop of Oxford censured it, and demanded that the tracts cease. For three years condemnations fulminated intermittently from the bench of bishops. Entertaining high ideas of the authority of the episcopacy, Newman regarded their condemnation as an authoritative judgment against him. Ending the tracts, he relinquished the editorship of *The British Critic;* shortly afterward he resigned from St. Mary's and went to Littlemore to live as a layman. It was becoming increasingly apparent even to his reluctant eyes that soon he would be obliged to choose between Rome, the historic center of Christian unity, with its emphasis upon apostolicity of doctrine and of practice, and the Church which Henry VIII had ushered into the world and which felt no need to hark back to the center of unity for its credentials.

Newman was further unsettled by an article which Dr. Wiseman, who had now returned to England, had published in the *Dublin Review*. Wiseman compared the Donatist heretic with the Anglican. Newman had previously made an exhaustive study of the Arians and other heretical sects in the first five centuries, and he found the comparison disturbing. "I must confess," wrote Newman, "that it has given me a stomachache. . . . At this moment we have sprung a leak; and the worst of it is that those sharp fellows, Ward, Stanley and Co., will not let one go to sleep upon it . . . this is a most uncomfortable article on every account."

The more he pondered upon the parallel suggested by Wiseman between the earlier heresies, such as Donatism and Monophysitism, and the Anglican formularies, the more and more obvious it seemed, and by the same token the more difficult did escape become. "There was an awful similitude," he wrote, "more awful because so silent and unimpassioned, between the dead records of the past and the feverish chronicle of the present . . . My stronghold was antiquity. Now here, in the middle of the fifth century, I found, as it seemed to me, Christendom of the sixteenth and nineteenth centuries reflected. I saw my face in that mirror," he adds with horror, "and I was a Monophysite."

Wiseman had quoted with telling effect the famous phrase of St. Augustine, *Securus judicat orbis terrarum*, which may be interpreted, "The sure world judges or decides." In this case it implies that Catholic consent is the judge of controversy. There burst in upon Newman the concept of a living Church, witnessed to in the past by Nicaea, Ephesus, and Chalcedon, and witnessed to at the present by its churches, schools, and monasteries in all the countries of the world. True, the seed had unfolded into a mighty tree, but it had not lost its identity in the phenomenon of world-wide growth. The shadow of Rome as an institution destined by its Founder for mankind in all the ages was overclouding his Anglican compromise, his *via media*. From this time on Newman was on his deathbed, he confessed afterward, as far as his membership in the Anglican Church was concerned.

Newman was not to take a step, however, which would change the whole course of his life without long and deliberate study and prayer. For three years he remained at Littlemore with a band of disciples, seeking light from above that they might chart their course aright. They lived under monastic conditions in great physical austerity and in an atmosphere of anxiety and suspense. To his disciples he assigned the task of writing the lives of the English saints, while he occupied himself with the completion of an essay on the development of doctrine; by this principle he sought to trace the growth of the mustard seed of apostolic teaching into the mature doctrines of the Catholic Church. By more than a decade he thus anticipated Darwin's formulation of the principle of organic evolution which was to win him lasting fame in biology. Newman replaced the static principle hitherto prevailing in religious thought with a dynamic one —the principle of growth, development, evolution.

While Newman was at Littlemore he received letters from a number of his friends urging him to take no step that he would regret later on. Among such pleas was one from his sister, Mrs. John Mozley, reminding him "of those many anxious minds waiting and watching your every motion, who would misunderstand your proceedings, and consider it a beginning of a formal disengaging of yourself from your own Church." She also enclosed a letter from a lady who voiced the plea of many against being deprived of the guidance which they had come to rely upon from Newman. Its sad tone was well calculated to touch Newman's heart.

"I have been thinking," she wrote, "that among all the opinions and feelings your brother is called upon to sympathize with, perhaps he hears least and knows least of those who are, perhaps, the most numerous class of all—people living at a distance from him, and scattered over the country, with no means of communication with him as with one another, yet who all have been used to look up to him as a guide. These people have a claim upon him; he has witnessed to the world, and they have received his witness; he has taught, and they have striven to be obedient pupils. He has formed their minds, not accidentally; he has *sought* to do so, and he has succeeded. He has undertaken the charge, and cannot now shake them off. His words have been spoken in vain to many, but not to them. He has been the means, under Providence, of making them what they are. Each might have gone his separate way but for him.

"To them his voluntary resignation of ministerial duties will be a severe blow. If he was silenced, the blame would rest with others; but giving them up of his own free will, they will have a sense of abandonment and desertion. There is something sad enough and discouraging enough in being shunned and eyed with distrust by neighbors, friends and clergy; but whilst we have had someone to confide in, to receive instruction from, this has been borne easily. A sound from Littlemore and St. Mary's seems to reach us even here, and has given comfort on many a dreary day; but when the voice ceases, even the words it has already spoken, will lose some of their power; we shall have sad thoughts as we read them. Such *was* our guide, but he has left us to seek our own path; our champion has deserted us; our watchman, whose cry used to cheer us up, is heard no more."

When Newman finished reading this letter tears came to his eyes. He suffered tortures from the consciousness of the sorrow he was thus involuntarily bringing to souls who trusted him. In his reply to his sister, his "Dearest Jemima," couched in as affectionate terms as ever, he begs her to trust the motives which direct his course. To his other sister, Mrs. Thomas Mozley, he writes: "I am so drawn to the Church of Rome, that I think it safer, as a matter of honesty, not to keep my living . . . I could not without hypocrisy profess myself any longer a *teacher* and a *champion* for our Church . . . My dear Harriet, you must learn patience, so must we all, and resignation to the will of God."

On September 25, 1843, he bade a tearful farewell to his Anglican congregation at Littlemore. The little church was adorned with flowers in honor of the seventh anniversary of its consecration. There, too, was the tomb of his mother, and on it the flowers were heaped high. As Newman ascended the pulpit, an attitude of tension prevailed, the members sensing that an announcement fraught large with meaning for the future would be forthcoming. Taking as his theme "The Parting of Friends," he spoke slowly in a low voice, passing in review the scenes of separation depicted in the Bible, dwelling at some length upon that of David and Jonathan. His many pauses, the pathos in his voice, told of the anguish in his soul struggling for expression. He ended with the touching plea for the prayers of his people that he might know God's will and do it.

"O my brethren," he said, "O kind and affectionate hearts, O loving friends, should you know anyone whose lot it has been, by writing or by word of mouth, in some degree to help you thus to act; if he has ever told you what you knew about yourselves, or what you did not know; has read to you your wants or feelings, and comforted you by the very reading; has made you feel that there was a higher life than this daily one, and a brighter world than that you see; or encouraged you, or sobered you, or opened a way to the inquiring, or soothed the perplexed; if what he has said or done has ever made you take interest in him, and feel well inclined toward him; remember such a one in time to come, though you hear him not, and pray for him, that in all things he may know God's will, and at all times he may be ready to fulfill it."

Tears were in the eyes of all. Descending the pulpit, Newman received communion and withdrew. Pusey completed the services, struggling to suppress the tears that interrupted his reading. All left Littlemore with a clear feeling that the whole of a mighty past was definitely closed. "I am just returned, half broken-hearted," wrote Pusey, "from the commemoration at Littlémore; the sermon was like one of Newman's . . . People sobbed visibly . . . If our Bishops did but know what faithful hearts, devoted to our Lord and the service of His Church, they are breaking."

The agitation aroused by Newman's farewell sermon was as great at Oxford as at Littlemore. "How vividly comes back the remembrance of the aching blank," remarked Principal Shairp, "the awful pause, which fell on Oxford, when that voice had ceased, and we knew that we should hear it no more. It was as when, to one kneeling by night, in the silence of some vast cathedral, the great bell tolling solemnly overhead has suddenly gone still." There was a widespread feeling that his resignation was but a prelude to his secession, and everybody realized what a staggering blow this would be for the Church of England. "I stagger to and fro like a drunken man, and am at my wit's end," wrote Gladstone to Manning.

Describing the impact of this news upon the intellectual world at Oxford, Stanley says: "No one asked about it in public, but everyone rushed to and fro to ask in private . . . To anyone who has been accustomed to look upon Arnold and Newman as *the* two great men of the Church of England, the death of the one and the secession of the other could not but look ominous, like the rattle of departing chariots that was heard on the eve of the downfall of the Temple of Jerusalem."

While Newman had lost faith completely in the apostolic character of the Anglican Church, he was not yet fully convinced that the Church of Rome was the true Church. He did not wish to act on mere probabilities but desired complete certainty. "My difficulty was this," he wrote later, "I had been deceived greatly once; how could I be sure that I was not deceived a second time? . . . What test had I, that I should not change again, after I had become a Catholic? I had still apprehension of this, though I thought a time would come when it would depart."

For two years Newman waited, praying and searching for the light, seeking to pass from probability to certainty. Some have been surprised at this long delay and have been critical of it. But they can be answered with Newman, echoing the voice of St. Augustine: "Let those make use of severity who are not acquainted with the difficulties of distinguishing error from truth, and in finding the true way of life amidst the illusions of the world." Newman's habit of viewing both sides of a question, weighing the pros against the cons on the scales of logic, further slowed his reaching a definite conclusion. Since his decision would exercise such a profound influence upon those who looked to him for guidance, he felt it doubly necessary to exhaust all means of resistance before surrendering.

Indeed nothing in Newman's life throws into clearer relief the profound sincerity of the man, his unwillingness to act on mere sentiment, his painstaking solicitude for truth, than the protracted inquiry he conducted at Littlemore before taking the final step. Who can fail to admire the transparent honesty of this earnest soul, struggling to dissipate the darkness of uncertainty and to arrive not at the twilight of probability but at the bright light of certainty and truth before he would chart his course upon the troubled waters of the future?

On the one hand were the associations of a lifetime, the pleadings of his sisters, the esteem of his colleagues at Oxford, the reverent affection of the younger men, and the promise of advancement in the Church of his birth. On the other hand was the alien communion of Rome, in which he had few acquaintances and scarcely any friends. His contact with the Catholic clergy had been practically nil. He knew the deep-seated prejudices of the British people against "Romanism," and the social and intellectual ostracism which they tended from long custom to inflict upon its members. His concern, however, was not for a crown, with the honors it would bring, but for the truth, even though it bring him a cross of shame and ignominy.

His prayer was for light to see the truth and courage to follow wherever it might lead, even though it lead him through strange and lonely ways, where his feet never before had trod. Like St. Augustine, who after his conversion in the garden at Milan, remained at his retreat at Cassiciacum for almost a year, preparing himself by prayer and discipline for his baptism and Holy Communion, Newman remained at Littlemore, increasing his austerities and redoubling his prayers. "Lord, that I may see!" was his daily prayer.

Ward and some others had preceded him into the Church of Rome, but still Newman deliberated, awaiting the result of the working of his conscience and of his prayers for light. That he realized what the contemplated step would cost him is evident from a letter he wrote to his sister on March 15, 1845: "I have a good name with many: I am deliberately sacrificing it. I have a bad name with more: I am fulfilling all their worst wishes, and giving them their most coveted triumph. I am distressing all I love, unsettling all I have instructed or aided. I am going to those whom I do not know, and of whom I expect very little. I am making myself an outcast, and that at my age—oh! what can it be but a stern necessity which causes this?"

Meanwhile, Wiseman, puzzled at the long delay, decided to send Father Bernard Smith, a convert and an old friend of Newman's, to Littlemore to note the lay of the land. Newman received him with marked coldness. But the vigilant eyes of Father Smith did not fail to note one telltale detail: Newman dined in gray trousers. To Father Smith, who knew Newman's punctiliousness in the matter of dress, this was evidence that he no longer regarded himself as a clergyman. But the end was not yet. "There was a pause," says Dean Church. "It was no secret what was coming. But men lingered. It was not till the summer that the first drops of the storm began to fall. Then through the autumn and the next year, friends whose names and forms were familiar in Oxford, one by one disappeared, and were lost to it . . . We sat glumly at our breakfasts every morning, and then someone came in with the news of something disagreeable—someone gone, someone sure to go."

The community at Littlemore waited and waited for their leader to give the signal. At last the end of the long vigil of prayer and deliberation came—simply and quietly, without pomp or melodrama. Newman learned that Father Dominic, a Passionist missionary, would be passing through Oxford on the evening of October 8, 1845, and he sent Father Dalgairns to meet him. "At that time," writes Father Dalgairns, "all of us except St. John, though we did not doubt that Newman would become a Catholic, were anxious and ignorant of his intentions in detail. About three o'clock I went to take my hat and stick and walk across the fields to the Oxford 'Angel,' where the coach stopped. As I was taking my stick Newman said to me in a very low and quiet tone: 'When you see your friend, will you tell him that I wish him to receive me into the Church of Christ?' I said: 'Yes,' and no more. I told Father Dominic as he was dismounting from the top of the coach. He said: 'God be praised,' and neither of us spoke again till we reached Littlemore."

On October 9 Newman made his profession of faith and received conditional baptism. The following morning, along with his disciples, Dalgairns, St. John, Stanton, and Bowles, he received Holy Communion from the hands of Father Dominic.

The news of Newman's entry into the Catholic Church aroused intense excitement. "It is impossible," says Mark Pattison, "to describe the enormous effect produced in the academical and clerical world, I may say throughout England, by one man's changing his religion." Gladstone, the prime minister, declared: "I regard Newman's concession as an event as unexampled as an epoch." Later Disraeli, another prime minister, declared "that this conversion had dealt a blow to England from which she yet reeled." Following in Newman's steps came Oakeley, Faber, and a long line of clergymen and Oxford graduates, numbering more than three hundred. "Nothing similar," says Thureau-Dangin, "had been seen since the Reformation."

The procession started by Newman has never stopped. Continuing into our own day, it has brought more than fourteen hundred Anglican clergymen into the Catholic Church. The step cost Newman dearly—his position, his friends, even his family. Did he regret the step later on, as some writers have sought to imply? Twenty years later, at a time when he had reason to complain of the tactics used against him by some of his co-religionists, he openly testified to "the perfect peace and contentment that he had enjoyed since his conversion." He declared "that he had never had one doubt," and that "it was like coming into port after a rough sea; and my happiness on that score remains to this day without interruption."

Newman's life of almost ninety years was split by his conversion into equal parts, both filled with drama, struggle against odds, and achievement. In October 1846 Newman went to Rome, where he was ordained a priest and honored by the Pope with the degree of Doctor of Divinity. Pope Pius IX approved his plan of establishing in England the Oratory of St. Philip Neri, a community of religious with simple vows, and in 1847 Newman set up the house at London, with Father Faber as superior, and later founded oratories at Birmingham and Edgbaston. Here for almost forty years he remained as a recluse, going out occasionally for lectures, but spending most of his time in writing his matchless books, which have enriched all posterity with the genius of his thought.

His sermon, *The Second Spring*, delivered at the Synod of Oscott, on the occasion of the re-establishment of the hierarchy in England, is a masterpiece of chaste and delicate beauty, which Macaulay learned by heart. His *Lectures on the Present Position of Catholics in England* abounds in passages of lively humor, rich imagination, and delicate beauty which held George Eliot in thralldom. "When Newman made up his mind to join the Church of Rome," observes R. H. Hutton, "his genius bloomed out with a force and freedom such as it never displayed in the Anglican community . . . In irony, in humor, in eloquence, in imaginative force, the writings of the later, and as we may call it, the emancipated portion of his career far surpass the writings of his theological apprenticeship."

In 1854 Newman went, at the request of the Irish bishops, to Dublin as rector of the newly established Catholic university. Practical difficulties beset the undertaking and after four years Newman retired. The most valuable outcome of this enterprise was his volume of lectures entitled, *Idea of a University*, which has remained as the classic in this field from the day it first appeared. The following passage illustrates its graceful ease of diction and its pregnancy of thought:

"A university neither confines its view to particular professions on the one hand, nor creates heroes or inspires genius on the other. Works indeed of genius fall under no art; heroic minds come under no rule; a university is not a birthplace of poets or of immortal authors, of founders of schools, leaders of colonies, or conquerors of nations. It does not promise a generation of Aristotles or Newtons, of Napoleons or Washingtons, of Raphaels or Shakespeares, though such miracles of nature it has before now contained within its precincts.

"Nor is it content on the other hand with forming the critic or the experimentalist, the economist or the engineer, though such too it includes within its scope. But a university training is the great ordinary means to a great but ordinary end; it aims at raising the intellectual tone of society, at cultivating the public mind, at purifying the national taste, at supplying true principles to popular enthusiasm and fixed aims to popular aspiration, at giving enlargement and sobriety to the ideas of the age, at facilitating the exercise of political power, and refining the intercourse of private life.

"It is the education which gives a man a clear conscious view of his own opinions and judgments, a truth in developing them, an eloquence in expressing them, and a force in urging them. It teaches him to see things as they are, to go right to the point, to disentangle a skein of thought, to detect what is sophistical, and to discard what is irrelevant."

Since 1841 Newman had been under a cloud, *sub luce maligna,* as far as concerned the great masses of cultivated Englishmen who never could bring themselves to understand how such a gifted mind could take the step he did. Conscious of the suspicion with which he was viewed, Newman had begun in 1842 to gather biographical and other memoranda waiting for the opportunity to vindicate his career. The occasion was offered him by Charles Kingsley, a novelist of note, who in reviewing Froude's "History of England" in *Macmillan's Magazine* for January 1864, incidentally asserted:

"Truth for its own sake has never been a virtue with the Roman clergy. Father Newman informs us that it need not be, and on the whole ought not to be, that cunning is the weapon which Heaven has given to the saints wherewith to withstand the brute male force of the world which marries and is given in marriage. Whether his notion is doctrinally correct or not, it is, at least, historically so." .

When Newman protested Kingsley replied by referring to Newman's sermon, "Wisdom and Innocence," published in 1844, before Newman's conversion. "It was in consequence of this sermon," he wrote, "that I finally shook off the strong influence which your writings exerted on me, and for much of which I still owe you a deep debt of gratitude. I am most happy to hear from you that I mistook your meaning; and I shall be most happy, on showing me that I have wronged you, to retract any accusation as publicly as I have made it."

In response to a further letter Kingsley remarked that he liked the tone of Newman's letter, and in his proposed apology expressed his "hearty pleasure" at finding Newman "on the side of truth in this or any other matter." Newman objected to this as well as to the no less ambiguous remark that "no man knows the meaning of words better than Dr. Newman." Kingsley refused to do more, maintaining that he had done as much as one English gentleman could expect from another. Exasperated beyond measure, Newman felt that the only manner in which he could secure redress was by publishing the correspondence, thus submitting the controversy to the fairness of the British public. The result was a masterpiece of controversial irony, unsurpassed in the English language for the vigor of its biting satire.

"Mr. Kingsley," Newman wrote, "begins by exclaiming: 'Oh, Oh, the chicanery, the wholesale fraud, the vile hypocrisy, the conscience-killing tyranny of Rome! We have not far to seek for evidence of it! There's Father Newman to wit; one living specimen is worth a hundred dead ones. He, a priest, writing of priests, tells us that lying is never any harm.' I interpose, 'You are taking a most extraordinary liberty with my name. If I said this, tell me when and where.' Mr. Kingsley replies: 'You said it, reverend sir, in a sermon which you preached as a Protestant, as Vicar of St. Mary's, and published in 1844, and I could read you a very salutary lecture on the effects which that sermon had at the time on my own opinion of you.' I make answer: 'Oh . . . *not*, it seems, as a priest speaking of priests; but let us have the passage.'

"Mr. Kingsley relaxes: 'Do you know, I like your *tone*. From your *tone* I rejoice—greatly rejoice—to be able to believe that you did not mean what you said.' I rejoin: '*Mean* it! I maintain I never *said* it, whether as a Protestant or as a Catholic!' Mr. Kingsley replies: 'Waive that point.' I object: 'Is it possible? What! Waive the main question? I either said it or I didn't. You have made a monstrous charge against me—direct, distinct, public; you are bound to prove it as directly, as distinctly, as publicly, or to own you can't!'

"'Well,' says Mr. Kingsley, 'if you are quite sure you did not say it, I'll take your word for it—I really will.' *'My word!'* I am dumb. Somehow, I thought that it was my *word* that happened to be on trial. The *word* of a professor of lying that he does not lie! But Mr. Kingsley reassures me. 'We are both gentlemen,' he says. 'I have done as much as one English gentleman can expect from another.' I begin to see: he thought me a gentleman at the very time that he said I taught lying on system. After all it is not I, but it is Mr. Kingsley who did not mean what he said."

Kingsley would have done well to have escaped as quickly as possible from an untenable position. Newman was the last man in England who could be charged with insincerity. In his quest for truth he had sacrificed more than any man in the Church of England and had received in return an obscure post in an alien communion. Uncompromising in his loyalty to the truth, he should have been the last man for Kingsley to choose for his cruel and unjust attack. "But Kingsley," as Arnold Lunn well observes, "was as incapable of understanding Newman's subtle and complex mind as a prize fighter of grasping the Einstein theory." Foolishly persisting in this attack, he wrote a pamphlet, *What Then Does Dr. Newman Mean?* It was a rehash of all the familiar anti-Roman charges now worn threadbare. Again he gave Newman a splendid opportunity.

Newman seized it to vindicate not only his own career but his espoused faith, which was now assailed. The result was the *Apologia pro Vita Sua,* the simple confidential tone of which revolutionized the popular estimate of its author. Written as a series of fortnightly articles, it achieved an instant success. Newman appealed to the fairness of the British public to decide the merits of the controversy. And not in vain. For with all their ingrained prejudices against Romanism, the essential fairness of the English public and their fine sense of sportsmanship enabled them to appreciate the superior logic of Newman's reasoning and the greater deftness of his controversial strokes. He gained a smashing victory among all classes.

They applauded the honesty and courage of a man who, splashed with slander and abuse by an opponent who then sought to withdraw, pursued him until his honor and truthfulness were vindicated beyond all cavil. The *Apologia* was written under the stress of great emotion and at a furious speed. Newman wrote sometimes for twenty hours at a stretch. In consequence, as literature it is uneven. But in spite of the speed with which it was ground out, it is permeated with a deep earnestness which echoes even between the lines, and is aglow with an irrepressible passion to vindicate the truth. In none of his other works do the character, personality and forthrightness of the author shine forth more luminously.

"No finer triumph of talent in the service of conscience," says William Barry, "has been put on record. From that day the Catholic religion may date its re-entrance into the national literature. Instead of arid polemics and technical arguments, a living soul had revealed in its journey toward the old faith wherein lay the charm that drew it on. Reality became more fascinating than romance, the problem which staggered Protestants and modern minds—how to reconcile individual genius with tradition, private judgment with authority—was resolved in Newman's great example." The place of the *Apologia* among the great masterpieces of autobiographical writing is secure.

Amid the acclamations of Catholics and non-Catholics alike, Newman turned now to the formulation of the philosophy which would justify his action. He began *A Grammar of Assent*, the most closely reasoned of all his works. In it the author avoids abstractions and metaphysics and focuses attention upon the problem of concrete affirmation, its motives, and its relation to the personality of the individual. Hitherto interest had been centered on the objective grounds for assent, while the subjective or psychological steps leading to the affirmation remained largely unexplored.

The author brought to the problem a penetrating insight into the workings of the human mind and heart, a rare capacity for subtle analysis, and a vast amount of experience in examining and analyzing the psychological factors which lead to a decision of the will. Without sacrificing the rights of pure logic, Newman restores the will to its rightful place and emphasizes the influence of the moral resonance of the individual's character in providing that proper disposition, that *pia credulitas*, which is a prerequisite to the act of faith. In short, assent is not a mere mechanical echo of the syllogism, but a distinct psychological act in which the will and the moral resonance of the individual play vital and important parts.

In common with Kant, Newman considered the witness of conscience, "the categorical imperative," among the supreme evidences of a deity both immanent in the universe and yet transcending it. He states that it would be easier for him to doubt his own existence than the existence of "Him who lives as an All-seeing, All-judging Being in my conscience." To him conscience is the inward revelation of God: Catholicism is the external and objective one. He held that the reason by which men guide themselves is *implicit* rather than *explicit*, and stressed the need of varied and converging proofs. The work served as a sequel and a crown to the *Development of Doctrine* and completes the author's philosophy. It was composed with painstaking care, some portions of it being written ten times, and it abounds in passages of psychological penetration, deft analysis, and logical power.

In *Christianity and Scientific Investigation* Newman developed the thesis that theology was a deductive science, while physics and the other natural sciences were inductive. Hence there could be no real collisions between these two bodies of knowledge. They moved in essentially different orbits, and the appearance of conflict would occur only from the scientist invading the domain of theology or the theologian trespassing upon the territory of science. He thus sought to provide a concordat which would prevent a recurrence of the Galileo imbroglio.

Some of the friends of Newman belong to a type known in history as "Liberal Catholics," though the term has never found a hospitable welcome in the Church. In 1864 he wrote of Montalembert and Lacordaire: "In their general line of thought and conduct I enthusiastically concur and consider them to be before their age." He speaks of "the unselfish aims, the thwarted projects, the unrequited toils, the grand and tender resignation of Lacordaire"—a description which might well be applied to himself. It will be recalled that on his deathbed Lacordaire said: "I die a repentant Christian but an unrepentant Liberal."

In many of his lectures Newman stressed the inadequacy of knowledge alone to provide the motive power for action in the face of passion and habit. "Carve the granite with a razor," he wrote, "moor the vessel with a thread of silk, then you may hope with such

keen and delicate instruments as human knowledge and human reason to contend against those giants, the passions and the pride of
men." Will power, strength of character, and those driving forces
which spring from deep religious convictions are necessary to hold
to its charted course the human bark tossed about on the turbulent
seas of angry passions.

In the midst of inner travail and suffering that came from the
blighting of his cherished hopes, Newman was accustomed to turn
to the writing of poetry in which he found relief. *The Dream of
Gerontius* is the most beautiful of his poems, and is indeed a masterpiece of nineteenth-century English poetry. Unlike the composition
of his philosophical works which occasioned always the pains of
travail, the writing of his poetry was done with ease. Thus he wrote
The Dream of Gerontius with a facility which called for scarcely any
erasures. When completed, he attached so little importance to it that
he threw it into the wastepaper basket, where it would have been
lost forever had not a friend chanced to come upon it and prevailed
upon Newman to publish it anonymously. It met with instant success and has continued to grow in popularity. Later it was made the
subject of an oratorio by Sir Edward Elgar, a distinguished musician.

In this poem the author seeks to penetrate the veil that cloaks
the mystery of the soul's adventuring immediately after death when
it finds itself midway between time and eternity. He follows the soul
into purgatory and describes the scenes of the other world, peopled
with angels and demons, with a grandeur of imagery that reminds
one of Dante but is more detached from earthly influences and more
wrapped in the contemplation of the spiritual. Newman was much
touched when he learned toward the close of his life of the refreshment of spirit which General Gordon had found in it when shut up
at Khartoum and preparing to sacrifice his life for his country's cause.
He kept his heroic death vigil, reading this poem and scoring with
pencil lines the passages which most appealed to him.

To Newman poetry was not only an outlet for the emotions, but
it was also a means of disciplining and chastening them. To his sensitive soul much of the ceremony and ritual, the processions, vest-
ments, and shrines of the Catholic Church were suffused with poetry.
The former was poetry in action, the latter was poetry crystallized
in art.

"Poetry," he said, "is a method of relieving the overburdened mind;

it is a channel through which emotion finds expression, and that a safe, regulated expression. Now what is the Catholic Church, viewed in her human aspect, but a discipline of the affections and passions? What are her ordinances and practices but the regulated expression of keen, or deep, or turbid feeling, and thus a cleansing, as Aristotle would word it, of the sick soul?

"She is the poet of her children; full of music to soothe the sad and control the wayward, wonderful in story for the imagination of the romantic; rich in symbol and imagery, so that gentle and delicate feelings, which will not bear words, may in silence intimate their presence or commune with themselves. Her very being is poetry; every psalm, every petition, every collect, every versicle, the cross, the mitre, the thurible, is a fulfilment of some dream of childhood or aspiration of youth. Such poets as are born under her shadow, she takes into her service; she sets them to write hymns, or to compose chants, or to embellish shrines, or to determine ceremonies, or to marshal processions; nay, she can even make schoolmen of them, as she made St. Thomas, till logic becomes poetical."

II. THE END CROWNS THE WORK

It was part of the tragedy of Newman's life that after having made so costly a sacrifice to follow the conviction of his conscience, he was looked at askance by so many of his former Anglican friends, and on the other side by many of the "old" Catholics. He regarded the tendency of certain other converts, such as Manning, Archbishop of Westminster, W. G. Ward, editor of the *Dublin Review*, and F. W. Faber, head of the Oratory at London, to overstress the papal claims as more calculated to antagonize the British public than to attract them. Many of the converts were strong papalists, with pronounced inclinations to overstate the papal authority in both temporal and spiritual matters.

Thus W. G. Ward would have relished immensely having a Papal Bull delivered each morning with *The Times*. He wanted the Pope to decide every question that arose, and seemed to look forward with impatience to the day when the Pope would be issuing Bulls on every subject. From such extremes Newman's delicate soul shrank in horror. While he respected the authority of the Pope and believed in his infallibility in matters of faith even before the dogma was formally proclaimed, he thought it wiser to stress the reasonableness of doctrine than merely to show its authoritativeness.

In his *Roman Converts,* Arnold Lunn terms him a "minimizer," as Talbot did before him. But this is scarcely accurate. A "realizer" would be a better term. For it was because of his keen realization of the temper and prejudices of the British mind of his day that he endeavored to soften the needlessly harsh statement of certain Roman doctrines which Ward, Faber, and others were frequently making. Understanding from his own experience as an Anglican divine how certain ultra-Romanizing tendencies were inclined to grate on British sensitivities, none too friendly even to the restrained statement of Roman claims, he sought to avoid any unnecessary waving of the red flag before the British bull.

An instance in point is the language used by Cardinal Wiseman in his Pastoral announcing the re-establishment of the regular hierarchy in England, with himself as primate. Writing from the Catholic atmosphere of Rome, the newly appointed cardinal seems to have forgotten momentarily the anti-Roman prejudices of the British public, and addressing his letter from "without the Flaminian gate," declares: "Till such time as the Holy See shall think fit otherwise to provide, we shall govern and continue to govern the counties of Middlesex, Hertford and Essex as ordinary therefor with the islands annexed as administrators with ordinary powers."

A storm of indignant protest followed. "John Bull snorted," remarked Arnold Lunn. "He wrote to *The Times* explaining that he'd see Wiseman damned before Wiseman governed as ordinary or as extraordinary a yard of British soil." Even the prime minister, Lord John Russell, joined in the hue and cry. The "No Popery" campaign was in full swing again. Why? Because of a needlessly arrogant and haughty manner of stating a simple fact, unobjectionable in itself. Because of a complete lack of delicacy in dealing with latent anti-Roman prejudices, which with a discerning and tactful statement would have remained dormant, but which were jolted into furious activity by the bombastic and domineering language used.

Because Newman had a profound understanding of the British mind and knew its sensitive spots, he opposed all his life the needlessly harsh statement of doctrine, of Roman claims and viewpoints which Manning, Talbot, Ward, and others seemed bent on using.

In the language of our day, he did not believe in "rubbing the fur the wrong way"—at least not needlessly. In a letter to Phillips de Lisle in 1848, he wrote: "It is no new thing with me to feel little sympathy with parties, or extreme opinions of any kind." While he did not, of course, approve any minimizing of the truth or any compromise with falsehood, he did approve a gracious, kind, and appealing statement of any doctrine or viewpoint.

Manning thought he was transplanting the "Oxford tone into the Church," while Ward used harsher language. But when the hue and cry broke out against the formal proclamation of the dogma of papal infallibility by the Vatican Council in 1870, it was Newman who came to its defense, and whose presentation more than those of any of the ultra-papalists, told with the British public. He had previously opposed the definition as untimely, but when Gladstone, the prime minister, accused the Catholic Church of having "equally repudiated modern thought and ancient history," Newman sprang to her defense.

In a letter nominally addressed to the Duke of Norfolk, he gave a masterly vindication of the rights of conscience and showed the harmonious roles which authority and reason play in the formulation of the verdict of the individual conscience. Probably no other writer in England or elsewhere has so stressed the important role which conscience plays in the spiritual life, and no one has laid greater emphasis upon its finality as the court of last appeal. Passages concerning it abound in practically all his works.

"What is the main guide of the soul," he asks, "given to the whole race of Adam, outside the true fold of Christ as well as within it, given from the first dawn of reason, given to it in spite of that grievous penalty of ignorance which is one of the chief miseries of our fallen state? It is the light of conscience, 'the true Light,' as the Evangelist says, 'which lighteth every man that cometh into the world.' Whether a man be born in pagan darkness, or in some corruption of revealed religion; whether he has heard the name of the Savior of the world or not; whether he be the slave of some superstition, or is in possession of some portions of Scripture, in any case, he has within his breast a certain commanding dictate, not a mere sentiment, not a mere opinion, or impression, or view of things, but a law, an authoritative voice, bidding him do certain things and avoid others.

"It is more than a man's self. The man himself has not power over it, or only with extreme difficulty; he did not make it, he cannot destroy it. He may silence it in particular cases or directions; he may distort its enunciations; but he cannot—or it is quite the exception if he can—he cannot emancipate himself from it. He can disobey it, he may refuse to use it; but it remains.

"This is conscience; and, from the nature of the case, its very existence carries on our minds to a being exterior to ourselves; else, whence its strange, troublesome peremptoriness? I say its very existence throws us out of ourselves, and beyond ourselves, to go and seek for Him in the height and depth, whose voice it is. As the sunshine implies that the sun is in the heavens, though we may see it not; as a knocking at our doors at night implies the presence of one outside in the dark who asks for admittance, so this word within us necessarily raises our minds to the idea of a teacher, an unseen teacher.

"Conscience holds of God, and not of man, as an angel walking on the earth would be no citizen or dependent of the civil power. Conscience is not a long-sighted selfishness, nor a desire to be consistent with oneself! But it is a messenger from Him, who, both in nature and in grace, speaks to us behind a veil, and teaches and rules us by His representatives. Conscience is the aboriginal Vicar of Christ, a prophet in its informations, a monarch in its peremptoriness, a priest in its blessings and anathemas, and, even though the eternal priesthood throughout the Church should cease to be, in it the sacerdotal principle would remain and would have a sway."

It was not only in his writings that Newman paid homage to the thin small voice within, but in his life as well. He not only preached obedience to that inner voice, he practiced it. He bore eloquent testimony to his uncompromising loyalty to its whispering when, in tears, he descended from the pulpit at Littlemore and turned his back upon his beloved Oxford. When later as a Catholic he found himself frequently put in an infavorable light before the officials at Rome, he scorned the slightest approximation to toadyism, engaging in no flattery or sycophancy, but relied solely upon the testimony of an approving conscience.

This trait in his character is illustrated in a reply he wrote to Monsignor Talbot. The younger son of Lord Talbot of Malahide, he had entered the Church in 1847, had become the Pope's chamberlain and the trusted agent of Manning in Rome. As such he had used his strategic influence to thwart Newman in many ways. After the great success of *Apologia*, however, he relented to the extent of inviting the oratorian to Rome. He reminded him that he would "derive great benefit from revisiting Rome and showing himself to the ecclesiastical authorities" and pointed out that as a preacher he would enjoy at Rome "a more educated audience of Protestants than could ever be the case in England." What a tempting opportunity to curry favor he was dangling before Newman's eyes! Did Newman rush to accept? He sent the following reply:

Dear Monsignor Talbot,
—I have received your letter inviting me to preach in your church at Rome to an audience of Protestants more educated than could ever be the case in England. However, Birmingham people have souls, and I have neither the taste nor the talent for the sort of work which you have cut out for me. And I beg to decline your offer.

I am, yours truly,
JOHN H. NEWMAN

In this brief note the character of the oratorian, devoid of obsequiousness and utterly lacking any tendency to truckle, stands plainly revealed. He might have saved himself many a jolt if he had stooped to curry favor, but it simply was not in his make-up. He was to learn from bitter experience that manly independence and a scorn for the arts of the sycophant offer no passport to preferment in a world where climbing and crawling are performed in much the same attitude. But he held to it to the bitter end. Then, strangely enough, when he least expected it, recognition, glorious, overwhelming, world-wide, came to him.

It was this trait in Newman's character which compelled even Dean Inge, who wastes no affection upon the Catholic Church, to pay tribute. "Newman's confidence toward God," he writes, "rested on an unclouded faith in the divine guidance, and on a very just estimate of the worthlessness of contemporary praise and blame. There have been very few men who have been able to combine so strong a faith with a thorough distrust of both logic-chopping and emotional excitement, and who, while denying themselves these aids to conviction, have been able to say, calmly and without petulance, that with them it is a very small thing to be judged of man's judgment."

Newman was simply practicing what he had preached in one of his sermons. "What," he asks, "can increase their peace who believe and trust in the Son of God? Shall we add a drop to the ocean, or grains to the sand of the sea? We pay indeed our superiors full reverence, and with cheerfulness as unto the Lord; and we honor eminent talents as deserving admiration and reward; and the more readily act we thus, because these are little things to pay." Such unworldliness as this, observes R. H. Hutton in words singularly well chosen, "stands out in strange and almost majestic contrast to the eager turmoil of confused passions, hesitating ideals, tentative virtues, and groping philanthropies, amidst which it was lived."

Newman engaged in a number of projects of great promise which, because of circumstances over which he had no control, failed to materialize. We have already seen how his valiant effort to found a great national university in Ireland failed because of lack of organized support of the Irish bishops.

Another project which stirred his enthusiasm and seemed rich in promise was a new translation of the Bible which Cardinal Wiseman had induced him to undertake. The Douay Bible, while a great improvement on the Rheims edition, lacks the dignity and charm of the Authorized Version. No one realized this more painfully than Newman, whose ear was delicately attuned to its harmonies and whose style was so largely influenced by its chaste cadences. If there was any one man in the English-speaking world who was superbly gifted to turn out a masterpiece of simple beauty and dignity it was Newman.

Friends who heard about it were elated. Newman threw himself into the enterprise with unbounded energy. He enlisted contributors and was already at work, when alas, obstacles again appeared. Booksellers and publishers with a large stock of the Douay Bible launched vigorous protest. Wiseman yielded. And again one of Newman's great undertakings died aborning. What a priceless loss for the English-speaking world!

Who can calculate the far-reaching influence of the inspired Word expressed in Newman's sentences of stately majesty and simple beauty, cadences which would live in the memory and keep ever fresh their precious cargoes of eternal truth? In many respects this would appear to be one of the most tragic frustrations of all of Newman's great undertakings. To him may be applied the phrase which

Horace wrote about Daedalus seeking to fly to the heights of heaven on the wings of Icarus: *Si non tenuit, tamen magnis excidit ausis*— Even though he succeeded not, it was in a brave and gallant undertaking that he failed.

Another enterprise which augured much was his acceptance of the editorship of *The Rambler*. This was a journal conducted by an able group of laymen, of whom Lord Acton, the historian, was one. Newman had been prevailed upon by Cardinal Wiseman to assume the editorship with a view of directing its policy. But the ill-fortune which attended his many other efforts to serve the Church of his adoption pursued him here. An article which he contributed, "On Consulting the Laity in Matters of Doctrine," was delated to Rome by Bishop Brown of Newport, who denounced it as heretical.

There was some talk of summoning Newman himself to Rome. That it stirred him deeply is evident from the following: "Call me to Rome—what does that mean? It means to sever an old man from his home, to subject him to intercourse with persons whose languages are strange to him—to food, and to fashions, which are almost starvation on one hand, and oblige him to dance attendance on Propaganda week after week, and month after month—it means death. This is the prospect which I cannot but feel probable, did I say anything, which one bishop in England chose to speak against and report. Others have been killed before me.

"Lucas went of his own accord indeed, but when he got there—oh! how much did he, as loyal son of the Church and Holy See as ever was, what did he suffer because Dr. Cullen was against him? He wandered, as Dr. Cullen *said* in a letter he published in a sort of triumph, he wandered from Church to Church without a friend, and hardly got an audience from the pope. And I too should go from St. Philip to Our Lady, and to St. Peter and St. Paul, and to St. Laurence and to St. Cecilia, and if it happened to me, as to Lucas, should come back to die."

Newman resigned from the editorship. This was in 1859, after a mere two months of incumbency.

Wilfred Ward, his biographer, regards the following five years as the saddest in Newman's life. The oratorian chafed under the restraint placed upon him. He craved greater freedom to express himself without being pounced upon by the authorities. He contrasted sadly the present restraint with the magnificent freedom which characterized the great intellectual periods of the Church's past—a freedom without which the highest scholarship cannot thrive. He thought wistfully of the liberty which Thomas Aquinas, Peter Lombard, Alexander of Hales, Bonaventure, and other intellectual giants of the Church enjoyed—the freedom to defend their theses in the open arena against all challengers, the freedom to clash and with sturdy blows to pound out on the anvil of controversy the nuggets of truth from the ore of speculation and theory.

In 1863 Newman wrote to Miss E. Bowles: "This age of the Church is peculiar. In former times there was not the extreme centralization now in use. If a private theologian said anything free, another answered him. If the controversy grew, then it went to a bishop. The Holy See was but the court of ultimate appeal. *Now* if I as a private priest put anything into print, Propaganda answers me at once. How can I fight with such a chain on my arm? It is like the Persians driven to fight under the lash. There was true private judgment in the primitive and medieval schools—there are no schools now, no private judgment (in the religious sense of the phrase), no freedom, that is, of opinion. That is, no exercise of the intellect. No, the system goes on by the tradition of the intellect of former times."

In explanation of the conditions then prevailing, it should be recalled that the Church in England had been in a state of siege for several centuries. Since the time of Henry VIII her monasteries had been confiscated, her schools and churches seized, her hierarchy suppressed, her clergy scattered, and the overwhelming portion of her children torn from her by violence. At the beginning of the nineteenth century the Catholic population numbered only about 160,-000, and they were anxious only to be let alone. Neither priests nor people had any mood for controversy in the open arena. They were quite content to let sleeping dogs lie.

Moreover the scenes of horror and bloodshed ushered in by the French Revolution were still fresh in the Church's memory, while the rumblings of the approaching storm in Italy, portending the seizure of the papal states, were being heard with an ominous frequency. The nerves of churchmen were jumpy and jittery. They had enough dangers to contend with, without inviting more from controversy on delicate and disturbing questions. Warfare, persecutions, states of siege, do not encourage speculative controversies and are not conducive to academic freedom. There have been few periods, either before or since, when the officials of the Church had such little relish for academic controversies as at Newman's time.

During all his life Newman retained a deep love for Oxford, the Alma Mater which had nurtured him with her best and had honored him with an outpouring of reverence and affection which she had given to few, if any, of her other children. Among the many sacrifices which he made in entering the Church of Rome, few exacted heavier toll in heartthrobs and in tears than the resulting exile from the institution where he had dreamed his dreams, seen his visions, and hurled his defiance at the worldliness without, with all the high idealism of a young divine. When about to take the momentous step, he felt instinctively that it would mean a long farewell to the place that was dearest to him in all England and to the scenes that would live hereafter only in his memory. His foreboding proved all too true. But once again in almost fifty years, and that in graying age, did he set foot in Oxford, though occasionally from a distance he saw its storied spires.

Newman's love for Oxford was reciprocated by all connected with the venerable institution—dons, tutors, fellows, and even undergraduates. Describing the spell that Newman cast upon all at Oxford and the awe and reverence which the students experienced at the sight of him, Principal J. C. Shairp of Oxford writes: "In Oriel Lane light-hearted undergraduates would drop their voices, and whisper, 'There's Newman,' as, with head thrust forward, and gaze fixed at some vision seen only by himself, with swift noiseless step he glided by. Awe fell on them for a moment, as if it had been some apparition that had passed. . . . What are the qualities that inspired these feelings? There was, of course, learning and refinement. There was genius, not, indeed, of a philosopher, but of a subtle and original thinker, an unequalled edge of dialectic, and these all glorified by the imagination of a poet. Then there was the utter unworldliness, the setting aside of all the things which men most prize, the tamelessness of soul which was ready to essay the impossible. Men felt that here was,

> *One of the small transfigured band*
> *Which the world cannot tame."*

Those sentiments toward Newman still persist. During our student days at Oxford we found that the mention of his name never failed to stir an immediate response. Time has dealt tenderly with his memory, which after a century is still fresh and green. We walked into old St. Mary's and read the record carved in stone proudly proclaiming Newman's pastorate. We gazed at the pulpit from which he delivered so many of his masterly sermons, holding spellbound university don and undergraduate alike. We visited his old room in Trinity and, looking out the leaded window, recalled not without emotion his description of his last visit there: "There used to be snapdragon growing on the walls opposite my freshman's room there, and I had for years taken it as the emblem of my own perpetual residence, even unto death, in my university."

Returning, we passed by his statue, which seemed to echo the words of Matthew Arnold anent Newman; "A man never to be named by any son of Oxford without sympathy, a man who alone in Oxford of his generation, who alone of many generations, conveyed to us in his genius that same charm, that same ineffable sentiment, which this exquisite place itself conveys." Newman has come to symbolize the culture and the learning of Oxford and its distinctive charm.

Something of the sentiments tugging at his heartstrings when about to leave his Alma Mater he reveals to us in *Loss and Gain.* Herein he describes how the convert, Charles Reding—the pseudonym for himself—about to leave Oxford, "passed through Bagley wood, and the spires and towers of the university came to his view, hallowed by how many tender associations, lost to him for two whole years, suddenly recovered—recovered to be lost forever! There lay old Oxford before him, with its hills as gentle and its meadows as green as ever. At the first view of that beloved place he stood still with folded arms, unable to proceed.

"Each college, each church, he counted them by their pinnacles and turrets. The silver Isis, the grey willows, the far-stretching plains, the dark groves, the distant range of Shotover, the pleasant village where he had lived with Carlton and Sheffield—wood, water, stone, all so calm, so bright, they might have been his, but his they were not. Whatever he was to gain by becoming a Catholic, this he had lost; whatever he was to gain higher and better, at least this and such as this he never could have again. He could not have another Oxford, he could not have the friends of his boyhood and youth in the choice of his manhood."

With such deep attachment to Oxford, it was only natural that Newman should think of establishing a house of the Oratory there. In 1864 he set himself to achieve this goal. This he did with no pretense at deciding the controversy concerning the attendance of Catholics at Oxford, but merely with the thought that the students actually there should not be left without any of the ministrations of religion. This, he felt, was the surest way to lose them. But the opposition raised by Manning among the English bishops and among his friends at Rome thwarted the plan.

Newman's bishop, Dr. Ullathorne, keenly regretted this failure. A pious and zealous man, he was anxious to utilize Newman's great talents for the cause of religion at Oxford. The hostility, tactless and unjust, directed against his ablest priest by high-placed ecclesiastics distressed him. In June 1866 he reopened the matter, petitioning the Propaganda to permit the establishment of an oratory at Oxford.

Six months later he received a reply permitting the proposed foundation, but directing him to discountenance Dr. Newman's taking up residence there. The bishop, not wishing to hurt Newman by telling him of the restriction, and thinking that he could remove it by personal representations, simply informed Newman that the plan had been accepted. Newman was enthusiastic. It looked as though his dream of many years of returning to his old Alma Mater to champion the religion which he had embraced was at last to be realized.

He believed that truth is its own defense, and though its spokesmen be outnumbered, the odds are with it still. He had long felt that the policy of isolation from the great intellectual center of English life was calculated only to lessen the little influence which Catholics were then exercising, and to render it even more negligible. They had the teachings of Christ, he reasoned, in their apostolic purity. They had the great traditions of the Schoolmen. They had a masterly system of theology wrought out with marvelous consistency. Above all, they had the promise of the Holy Ghost to be with them all days. And while at certain times that pentecostal fire seemed to be but smoldering, it never failed to blaze up ever and anon to manifest its undying character. Why not, then, go into this great stronghold of intellectual life, present the Church's heritage of divine truth, and welcome the fullest discussion from every quarter?

To Newman it seemed almost to be lacking in faith to doubt the capacity of the truths of Christ and the Apostles to sustain themselves when placed fearlessly before the eyes and the minds of men. He opposed the policy of timid isolation. He scorned the shelter of the ivory tower. Like St. Paul going to the Acropolis to present the teaching of the Crucified to the scholars of Athens, Newman yearned to carry the apostolic faith to the chief intellectual fortress of England, Oxford University.

He was doubly elated at the prospect of returning under such circumstances to the campus upon which he had not set foot since the time he left it, as an outcast and an exile without kindred or abiding place, to join the alien communion of Rome more than a quarter of a century ago. With the permission of his ordinary, Newman issued a circular, appealing for funds. The sum of five thousand pounds was quickly raised. A site was purchased. Newman packed his trunk and, sunshine on his face, talked of the approaching fulfillment of his dream.

Then the opposition broke. Broke from a double quarter. On the one hand, his old colleagues of Tractarian days, Keble and Pusey, who had remained with the Anglican Church, grew alarmed at the prospect of an invasion of Oxford by such a formidable representative of Rome. The memory of the influence Newman had exercised among the faculty and with the students, whose creed was *Credo in Newmannum*, was still with them. What devastation might he not work now as the spokesman of Rome?

They sounded the tocsin, and a cry of protest sprang up from Anglican leaders at Oxford. On the other side, Manning, equally alarmed, led the opposition from within the Church. Rallying a number of the bishops behind him, he made representations through his agent, Monsignor Talbot at Rome, that Newman's presence would draw many Catholic students to Oxford and would further engender "a certain Anglo-Catholicism" in which the English national spirit would prevail over the Roman or Catholic one.

Fighting desperately to stave off another of the many defeats which crowned his efforts to serve the Church he loved, Newman sent his faithful disciple, Ambrose St. John, to Rome, with precise instructions as to the answers which were to be made to the objections raised. He was to point out that, even though there was a danger of increasing the attendance, this would be more than counterbalanced by the advantage of an Oratory church, which would provide the ministrations of religion for students already there, who otherwise would be neglected. But all in vain. His fellow convert, Manning, like himself, a former Oxford man, made his views prevail at Rome. The Propaganda directed Bishop Ullathorne to "take heed lest Dr. Newman should do anything which might favor in any way the presence of Catholics at the university."

It was a great blow to Newman. It was all the more bitter because those who on the representations of his critics had decreed his exclusion, had never even taken the trouble to question him concerning his own views and plans. Still more was he cut to the quick when Cardinal Reisach, who came to collect information on the Oxford question, avoided an interview with him. What strange nemesis was dogging this man's footsteps, mocking his high purposes, blighting his hopes, and dooming to ignominious failure his many valiant undertakings to serve the Church in as effective a manner as his intellect could devise? Strachey pictures him a forlorn figure, Manning and Talbot smiling in triumph, while Newman stands at the gate with his bag, packed all in vain, looking wistfully toward the spires of his beloved Oxford, from which he was bidden to remain an exile forever, weeping bitterly. Such would seem to be the usual verdict.

But did he really fail? Go to Oxford today and see. The music of his voice has died, but the melody of his dream lingers on. Yes, it lingers on in abiding stone, in the impressive foundations established by the great religious orders of the Church, in Campion Hall of the Jesuits, in St. Benet's Hall of the Benedictines, in the House of the Salesians, in the Hall of the Franciscans, in the Foundation of the Dominicans with the significant inscription over its portals; "After a long exile the sons of St. Dominic have returned!" Black-robed Jesuits, brown-robed Franciscans, and white-robed Dominicans are in the lecture halls, laboratories, and libraries. Catholic students, both undergraduates and graduates, are there in abundance: among the chaplains who have ministered to their needs are such gifted scholars as Monsignors Arthur Barnes and Ronald Knox, the latter a son of an Anglican bishop. At long last Newman's dream has come true.

We discussed with Cardinal Bourne the work of the Catholic foundations at Oxford. A few years previous, there was some agitation for the establishment of a national Catholic university. The cardinal along with other leaders of the Church opposed the project as unwise. "While I do not wish to speak about what is the best arrangement for other countries, where conditions are different," said His Eminence, "I am certain that for the Church in England the establishments we have at Oxford and Cambridge offer the best facilities for Catholic higher education. They are the two great historic centres of intellectual life in England, and our hope is to utilize them more and more. To cut ourselves off from these two great universities, and to try to establish a university off by ourselves would be the height of folly, if not positively suicidal. The graduates of Oxford and Cambridge have the ear of the English public and are at least listened to with respect."

"What effect does Oxford have upon the faith of the Catholic students?" we inquired. "Instead of weakening them," replied the cardinal, "we can say now on the basis of a long experience that with the provisions made for them, attendance at Oxford strengthens them. The graduates of Oxford are supplying the Church with a splendid type of scholarly lay leadership." The remarkable growth which the Church in England has experienced in the last half century is attributable in no small degree to the vigorous work of her able lay apostolate.

How happy would be the Church in any country to claim the able Catholic apologists and scholars who have issued from Oxford in recent decades! That brilliant controversialist, Arnold Lunn, clashed swords with Father Knox, only to surrender his sword at last and ask his erstwhile duelist to receive him into the Church which not long before had opened its hospitable arms to receive Knox himself. Well indeed might Newman have smiled, as he looked down from the eternal hills upon this latest corroboration of the wisdom of his plan.

The frustration of his many noble undertakings, calculated to try the soul of the strongest man, Newman bore with a patience that was little short of heroic. Shortly after the thwarting of his Oxford project, a correspondent in Rome made an anonymous attack upon Newman's orthodoxy in the *Weekly Register*. This was the spark which kindled into a flame the long-smoldering indignation of the Catholic laity at the many unjust attacks made upon one of the noblest and holiest souls in the Church in England. A mass meeting of the laity was called. A testimonial, signed by two hundred of the most distinguished English Catholics, was presented to him.

In it they served notice that "every blow that touched him inflicted a wound on the Catholic Church in England." Newman was deeply touched. "The attacks of the opponents," he replied, "are never hard to bear when the person who is the subject of them is conscious in himself that they are undeserved; but in the present instance I have small cause indeed for pain or regret at their occurrence, since they have at once elicited in my behalf the warm feelings of so many dear friends who know me well, and of so many others whose good opinion is the more impartial for the very reason that I am not personally known to them. Of such men, whether friends or strangers to me, I would a hundred times rather receive the generous sympathy than have escaped the misrepresentations which are the occasion for showing it."

There comes at last an end to everything. And an end to the series of disappointments which had crowned Newman's undertakings had come. Likewise an end to the suspicions under which he had labored for almost thirty years. This ostracism of a saintly genius had been due chiefly to his former friends, Manning, Ward, and Talbot. In 1877 Newman was elected an honorary Fellow of Trinity College, and in February of the following year, after an absence of thirty-two years, he returned to the Oxford whose spires only he had seen from a distance in the intervening years. Appearing in his university robes as the guest of the president of Trinity College, he was warmly applauded by the students and faculty.

In the same month, Pope Pius IX died, and Leo XIII, who had also lived in exile from the Curia since 1846, and who had learned from experience the meaning of Vergil's phrase, *haud ignora mali* (not ignorant of evil), ascended the chair of Peter. The Duke of Norfolk and other Catholic peers approached Cardinal Manning about securing the honor of the cardinalate for Father Newman. Leo XIII had apparently already made up his mind to so honor Newman and readily acceded to their request. A letter of the Cardinal Secretary of State announced to Newman "that the Holy Father, highly appreciating the genius and erudition which distinguished him, his piety, the zeal which he displayed in the exercise of the holy ministry, his devotion and filial attachment to the Holy Apostolic See, and the signal services he had for long years rendered to religion, had decided on giving him a public and solemn proof of his esteem and good will," and that he would proclaim his elevation to the Sacred College in the next Consistory.

On May 12, 1879, he was created a cardinal, amid the universal rejoicing of the British people, Catholic and non-Catholic alike. The event was without a parallel in modern times, as no simple priest without duties in the Roman Curia had been raised to the cardinalate. Congratulations poured in upon him from such distant countries as Australia, New Zealand, as well as from all parts of America. Newman received the exalted honor with simple dignity and with a complete absence of personal vanity. "The cloud is lifted from me forever," he said to his brothers of the Oratory.

"The Roman Church has been less unpopular in England," observes Dean Inge, "since Newman received from it the highest honor which it can bestow. Throughout his career he was a steadfast witness against tepid and insincere professions of religion, and against any compromise with the shifting currents of popular opinion. All cultivated readers, who have formed their tastes on the masterpieces of good literature, are attracted, sometimes against their will, by the dignity and reserve of his style, qualities which belong to the man, and not only to the writer.

"Like Goethe, he disdains the facile arts which make the commonplace reader laugh and weep. *'Ach die zärtlichen Herzen! ein Pfuscher vermag sie zu rühren!'* Like Wordsworth, he might say, 'To stir the blood I have no cunning art.' There are no cheap effects in any of Newman's writings . . . He was loved and honored by men whose love is an honor, and he is admired by all who can appreciate a consistently unworldly life . . . He has left an indelible mark upon two great religious bodies. He has stirred movements which still agitate the Church of England and the Church of Rome, and the end is not yet in sight."

The remaining eleven years of his life the aging cardinal spent in the quiet of the oratory at Edgbaston, answering the many correspondents who solicited his guidance in matters of conscience, re-editing his works, and in meditation and prayer. In 1886, Bishop Ullathorne dedicated to Cardinal Newman, his former priest and subject, his last spiritual work in commemoration of "forty years of a friendship and confidence which has much enriched my life." Touched by the testimony of affection from the venerable prelate, who had stood bravely by him in his many trials, the cardinal wrote the following note of thanks, which Dr. Ullathorne terms "a memorial and a treasure for all time":

"How good has God been to me in giving me such kind friends! It has been so all through my life. They have spared my mistakes, overlooked my defects, and found excuses for my faults. God reward you, my dear Lord, for your tenderness toward me, very conscious as I am of my great failings. You have ever been indulgent towards me; and now you show me an act of considerate charity, as great as you can, by placing my name at the beginning of the last work of your long life of service and sacrifice. It is a token of sympathy which, now in my extreme age, encourages me in the prospect of the awful journey which lies close before me."

In the following year Dr. Ullathorne paid a visit to the aged cardinal at Edgbaston and on returning narrated the following touching incident, which showed that the humility and simplicity of Newman had not been impaired by the honor of the cardinalate: "I have been visiting Cardinal Newman today. He is much wasted, but very cheerful . . . We had a long and cheery talk, but as I was rising to leave, an action of his caused a scene I shall never forget, for its sublime lesson to myself. He said in low and humble accents, 'My dear Lord, will you do me a great favor?' 'What is it?' I asked.

"He glided down to his knees, bent down his venerable head, and said, 'Give me your blessing.' [A general rule of the Church's ritual ordains that the lower dignitary should kneel before the higher one.] What could I do with him before me in such a posture? I could not refuse without giving him great embarrassment. So I laid my hand on his head and said: 'My dear Lord Cardinal, notwithstanding all laws to the contrary, I pray God to bless you, and that His Holy Spirit may be full in your heart.' As I walked to the door, refusing to put on his biretta as he went with me, he said: 'I have been indoors all my life, whilst you have battled for the Church in the world.' I felt annihilated in his presence; there is a saint in that man."

No trace of the former suspicions and hostilities now remained. To an allusion to the party which had so long opposed him in England and in Rome, Newman replied: "Let bygones be bygones," adding with a smile, "besides, they have all come round to my side now." His declining years were full of serenity and peace. By a happy reversal of fortune, the man who had gone through so many internal crises, had encountered such prolonged opposition from within the Church as well as from without, now found himself at peace with the world and with himself. All England had become proud of him, and the universal acclamation of his elevation to the cardinalate became prolonged into a kind of apotheosis such as few men have experienced in their lifetime. In March 1844 he wrote: "For myself, now, at the end of a long life, I say from a full heart that God has never failed me, never disappointed me, has ever turned evil into good for me."

The calm of a long evening was drawing to a close. Shortly before his death he asked some of the brothers of the oratory to sing him Faber's hymn, "The Eternal Years." "Many people," he said, "speak well of my 'Lead, Kindly Light,' but this is far more beautiful. Mine is of a soul in darkness—this is of the eternal light." After a brief illness he passed away peacefully on August 11, 1890, surrounded by his brethren of the oratory. His body lies beside that of his faithful disciple, Ambrose St. John, in Rednall on the quiet Lychey Hills where he had so often gone to pray in silence and meditate, "alone with the Alone."

On his tomb is inscribed the epitaph written by himself, an epitaph that would tell, he thought, the story of his pilgrimage: *Ex umbris et imaginibus in veritatem*—from the shadows and the symbols into the truth. With his passing the race lost a soul distinguished alike for sanctity and for scholarship. Though dead, he still speaks to us from the pages of his mighty books, speaks of his vision of the truth which led him at times through strange and lonely waters, but brought him safely at eventide to the harbor of peace and rest. Poor tired soul, he has passed at last from the tumult of controversy into the silence of the beyond where the eternal Truth speaketh without the noise or confusion of words. May he find there the rest he craved —under the everlasting arms and in the light that shall not fail!

G. K. CHESTERTON
God's Crusader

I. RISE TO FAME

Gilbert Keith Chesterton was one of England's outstanding writers of prose and poetry in the first half of the twentieth century, and is generally recognized as its greatest master of paradox. Familiarly known to the world as "G.K.C.," he displayed in the literary field something of the versatile genius of a Leonardo da Vinci, winning recognition as a literary critic, essayist, novelist, poet, journalist, playwright, lecturer, and illustrator. Not only was he a brilliant literary craftsman but also a fresh, original, and even a profound thinker. Looming up above all these diverse talents was a character singular in its childlike innocence, refreshing simplicity, rollicking good humor and charm. Indeed no writer of his generation was more widely loved by the masses as well as by the notables, with whom he engaged in endless debate, than this knight of Battersea, this crusader for the rights of the "uncommon" common man.

Born on Campden Hill, London, May 29, 1874, he was the elder son of Edward Chesterton, head of the well-known Kensington firm of auctioneers and real-estate agents. His mother, Marie Louise Grosjean, was of French and Scottish blood, and her maternal ancestors, the Keiths of Aberdeen, gave Chesterton his middle name. He attended St. Paul's School from 1887 to 1892, and at sixteen he started the junior debating club and a magazine known as *The Debater*. It contains exceptionally good work for a boy of that age, who was moreover almost two years behind his contemporaries in his regular schoolwork.

Even at this early age he was already the kind of being that he was to remain all his life: absent-minded, good-natured, yet stubbornly loyal to his ideals and convictions and willing to defend them against all comers. A tall, awkward, untidy scarecrow, he sat at his desk, drawing pictures all over his blotter and his books. His thoughts strayed far from his lessons and came to grips with deep problems beyond his years. Such is the picture of the growing boy, disclosed by his friends and confirmed by his notebooks.

So promising were his drawings that his parents decided to send him, not to Oxford, but to the Slade School of Art; during part of that time, he continued to study English literature at London University. "If my father had been a duke instead of a nice man," Chesterton later remarked, "I should have gone to Oxford or Cambridge and learned the insane optimism of the idle rich." It was not long before it became apparent that writing, not drawing, was his primary talent.

Nevertheless his fondness for drawing, in which he had unquestioned ability, remained with him all his life. He drew the illustrations for Hilaire Belloc's novels and he would often complete the sketches for one of these in a couple of hours. In *The Colored Lands*, published in 1938 after his death, are presented samples of his work at different periods. Even when thinking at his desk or when talking, he would frequently be drawing or painting.

In his *Autobiography* G.K. presents a vivid and fascinating picture of his early childhood. He is grateful to his country, his parents, and his home for all that they gave him. "I regret," he says, "that I have no gloomy and savage father to offer to the public gaze as the true cause of all my tragic heritage; no pale-faced and partially poisoned mother whose suicidal instincts have cursed me with the temptations of the artistic temperament . . . I look back to that landscape of my first days with a pleasure that should doubtless be reserved for the Utopias of the Futurist."

In the experience of his childhood we glimpse the beginnings of his philosophy. He sees childhood not as an isolated fragment or as an excursion into fairyland, but as his real life. That reality was beautiful, radiant in the clear light of an eternal morning, and it had a sort of wonder in it, as if the world were as new as himself. "What was wonderful about childhood," he says, "is that anything in it was a wonder. It was not merely a world full of miracles; it was a miraculous world."

Recalling the period of his attendance at St. Paul's, Chesterton recalls, "I was one day wandering about the streets in that part of North Kensington, telling myself stories of feudal sallies and sieges, in the manner of Walter Scott, and vaguely trying to apply them to the wilderness of bricks and mortar around me." Confirming this picture is the recollection of Mr. Fordham, a schoolmate of G.K. "I can see him now," he recalls, "very tall and lanky, striding untidily along Kensington High Street, smiling and sometimes scowling as he talked to himself, apparently oblivious to everything he passed."

In his last year at St. Paul's Gilbert entered a competition for a prize poem and won it. The subject chosen was St. Francis Xavier. Gilbert was then but in the sixth form, and the prize had never previously been won by any but an eighth-form student. Immediately afterward Gilbert was amazed to find the following notice on the bulletin board: "G. K. Chesterton to rank with the Eighth. F. W. Walker, High Master." When Mrs. Chesterton visited the master to seek his advice about her son's future, he remarked, "Six foot of genius. Cherish him, Mrs. Chesterton, cherish him."

Toward the end of his school life Gilbert's voice had not yet broken, so his mother took him to a doctor for an examination. The physician reported that his brain was the largest and most sensitive he had ever seen. Physically and mentally he was on an unusually large scale and probably for that reason of a slow rate of development. Such is a not infrequent occurrence in the childhood of men of exceptional endowment.

Leaving the art school in 1895, Gilbert found the next two years very trying. First he went through a period of extreme skepticism, then he became engrossed with Walt Whitman's principle of jubilant acceptance of the universe. Later he came to see Whitman's outlook as a mood and not a philosophy.

Despite the headmaster's characterization of Gilbert as a genius, neither of his parents dreamed of his making a livelihood by writing alone. Since he was clearly unfitted for the business of a real-estate agent, he worked for a time in two publishing houses and then turned to journalism. This became his profession and in later years, when he won fame as a novelist, essayist, and poet, he would claim no other title than that of journalist.

In 1899 Gilbert was working on the *Speaker* with a group of young liberals whose general outlook was congenial to his own. His great friendship with Belloc had begun, and the latter deeply influenced his social thinking. Even more important, he had become engaged to Frances Blogg, the eldest daughter of a London diamond merchant. A devout Anglo-Catholic five years his senior, she revived his moribund spiritual life and provided the practical touch that he so desperately needed.

His first published volumes were both verse. Financed by his father, *The Wild Knight,* mostly in the Swinburne manner, was widely acclaimed: *Greybeards at Play,* a collection of humorous poems, illustrated by the author, proved equally successful. Published in 1900, they evoked a crop of enthusiastic reviews and aroused much curiosity as to who G.K.C. was. As a result of these successes he became a regular contributor to the London *Daily News* in 1901, and maintained this connection the rest of his life.

On June 28 of the same year, Gilbert and Frances were married at Kensington Parish Church. During the first year of their married life, they resided in a house in Edwards Square, Kensington, and then they moved to the Overstrand Mansions, Battersea, where the rest of their London life was spent. For that reason G.K. was often called the "knight of Battersea." The marriage was a happy one, made all the happier by the generous action of Frances in channeling the current of her life unreservedly into the greater river of her husband's. With the devoted bride looking after his many needs, Gilbert was now able to concentrate upon his literary work, which ventured into an ever increasing variety of fields.

With his strong dislike for imperialism, jingoism, and Chauvinism, Chesterton went against the tide of national feeling in opposing the Boer War. The Liberal party joined with the Conservatives in backing it. Such leading Fabian Socialists as Bernard Shaw, Mr. and Mrs. Sidney Webb, Hubert Bland, Cecil Chesterton and the "semidetached Fabian H. G. Wells united in beating the drums of war. Despite that formidable alignment, Gilbert stood like a rock of adamant in opposition.

Asked by a correspondent in the *Daily News* about his stand, G.K. replied, "The unreasonable patriot is one who sees the faults of his fatherland with an eye which is clearer and more merciless than any eye of hatred, the eye of an irrational and irrevocable love." Waging a battle against such overwhelming foes strengthened and deepened that independence of judgment which was to characterize his whole life. "Chesterton was the one British writer, utterly unknown before," observed Cyril Clemens, an American writer, "who built up a great reputation, and it was gained, not through nationalistic support, but through determined and persistent opposition to British policy."

G.K. thought of the Boers as fellow humans who might well have been farmers of Sussex or of Kent, and he bitterly opposed the imperialism which was to take the lives of so many of them. In 1904 he wrote *The Napoleon of Notting Hill* in fantastic illustration of his thesis against jingoism and he outlined it more soberly in his long introductory chapter to *England a Nation*, a symposium of young liberals.

In the period from 1900 to 1910 Chesterton formulated his basic philosophy in twenty books and innumerable articles. In 1903 he crossed swords with Robert Blatchford, the editor of the *Clarion*, an inveterate foe of the Christian religion and a believer in determinism. After a well-reasoned refutation of Blatchford's views on God and religion, G.K. comes to grips with his opponent's denial of free will and consequently of moral responsibility.

Blatchford had contended that bad surroundings inevitably and necessarily produce bad men. Having seen the virtue and even the heroism of many of the poor in the most abject poverty, Chesterton was furious at "this association of vice with poverty, the vilest and the oldest and the dirtiest of all the stories that insolence has ever flung against the poor." He proceeded to show that men can and do lead heroic lives in spite of unfavorable environments, because man possesses the sovereign gift of freedom of the will.

"More numerous," said Chesterton, "than can be counted in all the wars and persecutions of the world, men have looked out of their little grated windows and said, 'At least my thoughts are free.' 'No, No,' says the face of Mr. Blatchford, suddenly appearing at the window, 'your thoughts are the inevitable result of heredity and environment. Your thoughts are as material as your dungeons. Your thoughts are as mechanical as the guillotine.' So pants this strange comforter, from cell to cell.

"I suppose Mr. Blatchford would say that in his Utopia nobody would be in prison. What do I care whether I am in prison or no, if I have to drag chains everywhere? A man in his Utopia may have, for all I know, free food, free meadows, his own estate, his own palace. What does it matter? He may not have his own soul."

In another essay Chesterton comes to grips with Blatchford's denial of the supernatural and of original sin. In discussing the Fall, G.K. uses one of his most brilliant illustrations. We speak, he points out, of a manly man but not of a whaly whale. "If you wanted," he says, "to dissuade a man from drinking his tenth whiskey, you would slap him on the back and say, 'Be a man.' No one who wished to dissuade a crocodile from eating his tenth explorer would slap it on the back and say, 'Be a crocodile.' For we have no notion of a perfect crocodile; no allegory of a whale expelled from his Whaley Eden."

Not less devastating is his reply to Blatchford's contention that the Gospel miracles are to be rejected because experience is against their occurrence. "There was a great Irish Rationalist of this school," replied Chesterton, "who when he was told that a witness had seen him commit a murder said that he could bring a hundred witnesses who had not seen him commit it."

Blatchford had also argued that no English judge would accept the evidence for the Resurrection. G.K. answers that possibly Christians have not all got "such an extravagant reverence for English judges as is felt by Mr. Blatchford himself. The experiences of the Founder of Christianity have perhaps left us in a vague doubt of the infallibility of Courts of Law."

In his three short essays dealing with Blatchford's attacks upon theism in general and Christianity in particular, we see the early formulation of G.K.'s own philosophy and religious faith, which was to be set forth in explicit and detailed form in his great work *Orthodoxy*. In all his writings, however, it is doubtful that there is anything more pregnant with thought or brilliant in expression than these three essays. He reaches the heights of eloquence in replying to Blatchford's contention that Christianity produced chiefly tumult and cruelty.

G.K. replies by pointing out that when some new truth or ideal is suddenly placed before mankind, and they find it enormously attractive, the chance of coining or losing it drives them mad. It has substantially the same effect in the moral world that the finding of gold has in the economic realm. It upsets values, stirs a new ferment, and creates a kind of cruel "gold rush." He illustrates it by citing the excesses to which the masses went in the French revolution in their furious and savage pursuit of liberty and fraternity, making the streets of Paris run with blood.

"The mere flinging," he says, "of the polished pebble of Republican Idealism into the artificial lake of eighteenth century Europe produced a splash that seemed to splash the heavens, and a storm that drowned ten thousand men. What would happen if a star from heaven really fell into the slimy and bloody pool of a hopeless and decaying humanity? Men swept a city with the guillotine, a continent with a sabre, because Liberty, Equality, and Fraternity were too precious to be lost. How if Christianity was yet more maddening because it was yet more precious?

"But why should we labour the point when One who knew human nature as it can really be learnt, from fishermen and women and natural people, saw from his quiet village the track of this truth across history, and, in saying that He came to bring not peace but a sword, set up eternally His colossal realism against the eternal sentimentality of the Secularist?"

Blatchford had further sought to discredit the Hebrew and Christian religions by arguing that they began as local things; that their god was a tribal god; that they gave him material form, and attached him to particular places. Chesterton replies by pointing out that this really serves as an argument for the validity of biblical experience. What could be more natural than for the simple rude people of early times to regard a revelation as local and to connect it with the particular hill or river where it happened? This has a far more credible look than if these simple people had talked cosmic philosophy from the beginning. If they had, they would have been suspected of "priestcraft" and forgeries and third-century agnosticism.

With a blend of logic, wit, discernment, and common sense, G.K. exposes the shallowness of Blatchford's argument. "If there be such a being as God," he says, "and He can speak to a child, and if God spoke to a child in the garden, the child would, of course, say that God lived in the garden. I should not think it any less likely to be true for that. If the child said: 'God is everywhere; an impalpable essence pervading and supporting all constituents of the Cosmos alike'—if, I say, the infant addressed me in the above terms, I should think he was much more likely to have been with the governess than with God.

"So if Moses had said God was in Infinite Energy, I should be certain he had seen nothing extraordinary. As he said He was a Burning Bush, I think it very likely that he did see something extraordinary. For whatever be the Divine Secret, and whether or no it has (as all people have believed) sometimes broken bounds and surged into our world, at least it lies on the side furthest away from pedants and their definitions, and nearest to the silver souls of quiet people, to the beauty of bushes, and the love of one's native place."

Chesterton concludes by pointing out the curious paradox that the very arguments Blatchford has urged against Christianity are in reality the very reasons why an intelligent person should believe in it. "His book," he remarks, "is really rich and powerful. He has undoubtedly set up these four great guns of which I have spoken. I have nothing to say against the size and ammunition of the guns. I only say that by some strange accident of arrangement he has set up those four pieces of artillery pointing at himself. If I were not so humane, I should say: 'Gentlemen of the Secularist Guard, fire first.'"

Here was no dry-as-dust apologetics but one that sparkled with wit, throbbed with humor, and scintillated with the brilliance of penetrating insight and discernment while at the same time it pulverized the opponent's arguments. Here was something new on the English scene. It was no wonder that the reading public sat up and took notice of the arrival of a new and delightful type of Christian apologist. The cogency of his reasoning, matched by a clarity and charm of expression, was a refreshing contrast to the vagueness and chaotic formlessness of many of his contemporaries. Obstreperously impatient of cant and humbug of every kind, G.K. considered dullness a symptom of inadequate understanding, vagueness a sure sign of confused thinking, and pomposity a smoke screen for pretense and incompetence: against such a loathsome trinity the knight of Battersea had sworn eternal enmity, and in all his writings he gave them a wide margin.

Chesterton's wit spiced both his thought and expression. He attributes to St. Thomas Aquinas "that instantaneous presence of mind which alone really deserves the name of wit": an attribute which he himself possessed and which shines forth in virtually all his writings.

"What single book would you choose," he was once asked, "if you were cast on a desert island?" Quick as a flash he replied, "Thomas' *Guide to Practical Shipbuilding*."

One of his famous pleasantries was his observation on the so-called emancipation of women, over which there was then much crowing. "Twenty million young women," he remarked, "rose to their feet with the cry, 'We will not be *dictated* to,' and proceeded to become stenographers."

The first book in which Chesterton formulated his maturing thought on the serious problems of life was *Heretics*, published in 1905. With penetrating insight he analyzes the writings of his contemporaries and shows that none of them presents a satisfactory philosophy of life. Laying bare the cheerless morality of Ibsen, he shows that it is purely negative and lacks positive standards of human happiness and true virtue. He shows how the militarism and cosmopolitanism of Kipling miss the more human loyalties to home and nation, and how the feverish Utopias of Wells are planned without any regard for the real nature of man. Equally unsatisfying are the aesthetic subjectivity of George Moore and the unrealistic panaceas of Shaw.

With biting invective he attacks the prevalent contempt for absolute or fixed standards of morality, for definite convictions and for dogma. "Trees," he remarks, "have no dogmas. Turnips are singularly broad-minded . . . To know the best theories of existence and to choose the best from them (that is, to the best of our own strong conviction) appears to us the proper way to be neither bigot nor fanatic, but something more firm than a bigot and more terrible than a fanatic, a man with a definite opinion. But that definite opinion must in this view begin with the basic matters of human thought, and these must not be dismissed as irrelevant—as religion, for instance, is too often in our days dismissed as irrelevant . . . We who are Christians never knew the great common sense which inheres in that mystery until the anti-Christian writers pointed it out to us."

The whole work is a brilliant defense of the philosophy of theism, of the necessity of dogma, and of fixed standards of judgment in every sphere: ethics, politics, art and literature. He points out that it is impossible to speak of anything being good or improved unless there is agreement on the fundamental criteria. Not less than a vessel, man needs the rudder of fixed principles to guide him, otherwise he travels like a rudderless ship in meaningless circles. Bucking the tide and defying the fashion of the day, G.K. came out as an avowed dogmatist who maintained that the chief function of human reason is to discover the meaning of life and the destiny of the human soul.

Chesterton sought the answers to these questions, in the words of Plato, "with his whole soul." The instincts of childhood, authority, tradition, homely common sense, wide reading, a sympathetic understanding of the poor, an appreciation of the individual value of man, and a penetrating, vigorous and balanced intelligence combined with an inborn congeniality with what is wholesome and enduring in society to shape his philosophy. Optimist, traditionalist, mystic, medievalist, and democrat he was, but never at the expense of reason.

The gradual shaping of his philosophy of life was like the slow, steady growth of a mighty sequoia: an advance in unified complexity, in firmness, strength, and fullness, but always true to the original direction. Of him might be applied with exceptional aptness Tertullian's famous phrase, *"anima naturaliter Christiana"*—the soul is naturally Christian. Slowly but unmistakably he was progressing to the vantage point where he would see that the Christian philosophy is the only one which gives meaning and purpose to human life. Once that profound conviction entered into the possession of him, there was no twisting, no detours, no turning back. Such was the flow of the sap and the line of the grain in the sequoia of his robust and stalwart character.

In *Fads and Fancies* we get an insight into the influences which helped to shape the direction of his thought. "My first impulse to write," he says, "and almost my first impulse to think was a revolt of disgust with the Decadents and the aesthetic pessimism of the nineties. It is now almost impossible to bring home to anybody, even to myself, how final that *fin de siècle* seemed to be; not the end of the century but the end of the world. To a boy his first hatred is almost as immortal as his first love. He does not realize that the objects can alter; and I did not know that the twilight of the Gods was only a mood. I thought that all the wit and wisdom of the world was banded together to slander and depress the world, and in becoming an optimist I had the feeling of becoming an outlaw."

In that instinctive revolt against pessimism in philosophy and decadence in art and morality is contained the germ of his whole philosophy. In his *Autobiography* he discloses certain gropings after truth in spiritualism and an intellectual struggle in which he plumbed the dark depths of doubt, but the native vigor of his mind justified and strengthened his confidence in human knowledge and rescued him from the clammy claws of skepticism.

Further light is thrown upon the direction of his thinking and the shaping of his permanent outlook in *The Defendant,* a collection of his early essays. These are a defense of the common simple things which most of his contemporaries either did not advert to or did not consider worth defending. In a passage in the introduction G.K. describes in typical apocalyptic imagery a remote valley in some interminable upland: here is a place strewn with rocks and boulders that must surely have been the scene of the stoning of some prehistoric prophet. What was the primal blasphemy, the unutterable thing at which men stopped their ears? The simple assertion that grass is green and that birds sing in the spring!

"The thread on which these essays are strung like beads," observes Hugh Kelly, "is the strange law in history by which man tends to underrate his happiness and the things in life that are of greatest value." No small portion of Chesterton's work consisted in revealing to men the common things that they had come to overlook, to show them a new heaven and earth that was indeed a very ancient one.

During the years in which his philosophy was gradually taking shape, G.K. turned his hand frequently to the field of belles-lettres. His studies of *Robert Browning* and of *Charles Dickens* won him fame as a literary critic and that of *G. F. Watts* established him as an art critic. The British public marveled at the versatility of his talents: it seemed no difficult feat for him to play the role of poet, novelist, artist and art critic, essayist, philosopher, journalist, sociologist, and theologian, and to play them all with distinction. Here surely was a genius of a rare order—a sort of literary Michelangelo.

All that had gone before was, however, but a clearing of the ground for *Orthodoxy,* one of his greatest works. It is remarkable that even he was able to write it at thirty-five. It is a sort of autobiography, not so much an argument for orthodoxy as the story of how he discovered orthodoxy as the only satisfactory answer to the perplexing riddle of the universe.

He had been tempted to become a prophet, like those featured in *Heretics,* by stressing one aspect of truth and ignoring others. This would have attracted a great crowd of disciples. He was able to resist the temptation, however, by the perception of the many-sided unity of truth. It would be easy to take one side of truth and magnify it into all of truth:

> . . . *a sage feels too small for life,*
> *And a fool too large for it.*

Reverence for truth in all its many-sidedness and a childlike humility in the presence of nature and the universe as created by God made him forego the meretricious glory of the prophet who trumpets one aspect of reality and is mute about its many other facets. The exposition of truth demands sobriety and restraint; otherwise it is distorted into a half-truth or deformed into a falsehood. How could he pose, he asked, as the original and independent architect of his own intellectual universe any more than he could pose as the creator of sun, moon, and earth. "God and humanity made it," he remarks of the philosophy he discovered, "and it made me."

"I was a pagan," he says, "at the age of twelve and a complete agnostic at the age of sixteen." Slight or negligible had been the religious influences of his home, his early surroundings, and school: they had furnished him with no answers for the questionings which arose from his immensely active mind and his wide reading. Unfamiliar with any work of Christian apologetics, he ranged over the whole field of rationalistic and agnostic literature. It was the great balance of his nature as much as the vigor of his intelligence that enabled him to see the inadequacy of these systems of philosophy.

"It was Huxley, Herbert Spencer, and Bradlaugh," he remarks, "who brought me back to orthodox theology. They sowed in my mind the first wild doubts of doubt." These philosophers claimed to explain the universe and human life; they offered simple explanations, but they achieved their simplicity by overlooking or denying all that was discordant or complex or interesting or significant or human in life.

Rationalism put one in the strait jacket of a single idea and achieved an explanation of the universe that had the narrow logicality of a maniac's delusion. Materialism took all the mystery and fascination out of life and left one with a dreary waste that was not worth bothering about. Determinism left no place for hope, courage, romance, or sacrifice. After listening to the prophets and philosophers of his day—Tolstoy, Ibsen, Nietzsche, Swinburne, Whitman, Shaw, and Schopenhauer—Chesterton found they could give no explanation of the universe that would satisfy his head and heart, and make it a place worth living in.

During all this time he was fashioning a philosophy of his own, trying to fit into some sort of a coherent pattern the fundamental ideas which reason, experience, instinct, and common sense were imposing on him. This ultimate attitude to the universe was something very distinctive and immensely influential in all his life and thought: a strange elemental joy in the presence of nature, a feeling that life and all common things were precious beyond all price, that they were gifts which might easily have gone astray, but whose safe delivery was a stroke of rare good luck. As a little child he had felt exactly like Robinson Crusoe making an inventory of the things he had saved from the wreck. How precious they all were! What a calamity if any of them had been lost!

"The trees and the planets," he writes, "seemed like things saved from the wreck; and when I saw the Matterhorn I was glad that it had not been overlooked in the confusion; I felt economical about the stars as if they were sapphires (they are called so in Milton's Eden); I hoarded the hills. For the universe is a single jewel, and while it is a natural cant to talk of a jewel as peerless, yet of this jewel it is literally true. This cosmos is indeed without peer and without price: for there cannot be another one."

With this feeling of joy was mingled the feeling that gratitude was due for the gifts received. "The test of all happiness," he observes, "is gratitude; and I felt grateful, though I hardly knew to whom." He also had the conviction that things must be respected, that they must in some way be paid for, that with the gift went certain conditions which must be observed.

Summarizing the ultimate attitudes and the deepest convictions at which he had arrived, G.K. says: "I felt in my bones; first, that this world does not explain itself. It may be a miracle with a supernatural explanation; it may be a conjuring trick, with a natural explanation. But the explanation of the conjuring trick, if it is to satisfy me, will have to be better than the natural explanations I have heard. The thing is magic, true or false. Second, I came to feel as if magic must have a meaning, and meaning must have some one to mean it. There was something personal in the world, as in a work of art; whatever it meant it meant violently.

"Third, I thought this purpose beautiful in its old design, in spite of its defects, such as dragons. Fourth, that the proper form of thanks to it is some form of humility and restraint: we should thank God for beer and Burgundy by not drinking too much of them. We owed, also, an obedience to whatever made us. And last, and strangest, there had come into my mind a vague and vast impression that in some way all good was a remnant to be stored and held sacred out of some primordial ruin. Man had saved his good as Crusoe saved his goods; he had saved them from a wreck. All this I felt and the age gave me no encouragement to feel it. And all the time I had not even thought of Christian theology."

This theology came with the answers to the deepest questionings of his mind and heart. Like many of his contemporaries, Chesterton had fancied Christianity a philosophy that had been tried and found wanting. It was only when he realized that the answers he was finding for himself always fitted into the Christian view of things that he began to turn toward it. To his surprise he discovered that he was not blazing a trail, but that he was traveling over a broad highway made smooth by the feet of countless pilgrims. He was not approaching a new Jerusalem which he had somehow assembled, but the old Jerusalem, the Christian Church. When this truth dawned upon him he felt as foolish as "the man who landed (armed to the teeth and talking by signs) to plant the British flag on that barbaric temple which turned out to be the pavilion at Brighton."

What he had thought was a new vision of things, a new pattern of the universe, he now discovered was a vision and a pattern which Christianity had been offering to men for nineteen centuries. The universe with its complex and bewildering system of categories and its baffling orders of reality had been for him a great lock which none of the skeleton keys of contemporary philosophers would fit. Now he had found the key that fitted perfectly all the complexities of the cosmic lock.

Having been thus brought up against the Christian religion in this startling manner, Chesterton determines to study it. The results of this examination are presented in the second half of *Orthodoxy*. He found in it a balance and moderation, a huge and heroic sanity of thought and conduct, and the best root of human energy and sound ethics. It alone seemed broad and strong enough to moderate and harmonize the divergent and discordant virtues. "The modern world," he finds, "is full of Christian virtues gone mad." Since the

Reformation "the virtues have gone mad because they have been isolated from each other and are wandering alone."

Making an especial appeal to him were the Christian doctrines of creation and original sin: they solved many of the difficulties which had long perplexed him. A thousand small but converging facts had convinced him that man was not at his best, that he was in a fallen state. Hence the doctrine of original sin was the echo of his instinct. It lifted the curtain and enabled him to see that God's gift was good, but that man had violated the conditions of the gift.

"God had written not so much a poem," he writes, "but rather a play; a play he had planned as perfect, but which had necessarily been left to human actors and stage-managers who had since made a great mess of it . . . My sense that happiness hung on the crazy thread of a condition did mean something when all was said: it meant the whole doctrine of the Fall. Even those dim and shapeless monsters of notions which I have not been able to describe, much less defend, stepped quietly into their places like colossal caryatides of the creed . . . And my haunting instinct that somehow good was not merely a tool to be used, but a relic to be guarded, like the goods from Crusoe's ship—even that had been the wild whisper of something originally wise, for, according to Christianity, we were indeed the survivors of a wreck, the crew of a golden ship that had gone down before the beginning of the world."

Possessing an uncanny genius for absorbing the contents of a book with incredible speed, as by a psychic osmosis, Chesterton's mind became a mighty storehouse which was further enriched by his own reflections. This enabled him to cast an intensely new light upon the perennial philosophy of Christianity upon which so much had been written. His discovery that Christianity represented a new balance that constituted a liberation was specially needed for his age. He showed how Christianity "made moderation out of the still crash of two impetuous emotions."

"The more I considered Christianity," he says, "the more I felt that while it had established a rule and order, the chief aim of that order was to give room for good things to run wild." It managed to make the lion lie down with the lamb and yet keep its royal ferocity. Heresy lops off a part of truth and thus impairs liberty: orthodoxy prevents any one idea from devouring another, and thus preserves the whole truth and safeguards freedom. Such is the justification of councils, definitions, and even repressive measures: they serve as bastions for the defense of reason as well as of the faith. They prevent the suicide of thought which results when this delicate balance is lost.

"The Church," he says, "could not afford to swerve a hair's breadth on some things if she was to continue her great and daring experiment of the irregular equilibrium. Once let one idea become less powerful and some other idea would become too powerful. It was no flock of sheep the Christian shepherd was leading, but a herd of bulls and tigers, of terrible ideals and devouring doctrines, each one of them strong enough to turn to a false religion and lay waste the world.

"Remember that the Church went in specifically for dangerous ideas; she was a lion tamer. The idea of birth through a Holy Spirit, of the death of a divine being, of the forgiveness of sins, or the fulfilment of prophecies, are ideas which, any one can see, need but a touch to turn them into something blasphemous or ferocious . . . A sentence phrased wrong about the nature of symbolism would have broken all the best statues in Europe. A slip in the definitions might stop all the dances; might wither all the Christmas trees or break all the Easter eggs. Doctrines had to be defined within strict limits, even in order that man might enjoy general human liberties. The Church had to be careful, if only that the world might be careless."

Instead of orthodoxy being something tame and boring, as many imagine, it is a thrilling romance. "People," he remarks, "have fallen into a foolish habit of speaking of orthodoxy as something heavy, humdrum, and safe. There never was anything so perilous or so exciting as orthodoxy. It was sanity: and to be sane is more dramatic than to be mad. It was the equilibrium of a man behind madly rushing horses, seeming to stoop this way and to sway that, yet in every attitude having the grace of statuary and the accuracy of arithmetic."

Chesterton then points out how the Church with superhuman dexterity and wisdom has steered her flying chariot away from the snares set up on the highway of progress by all the heresies of history. "To have fallen into any of those open traps of error and exaggeration," he concludes, "which fashion after fashion and sect after sect set along the historic path of Christendom—that would indeed have been simple. It is always simple to fall; there are an infinity of angles at which one falls, only one at which one stands. To have fallen into any one of the fads from Gnosticism to Christian Science would indeed have been obvious and tame. But to have avoided them all has been one whirling adventure; and in my vision the heavenly chariot flies thundering through the ages, the dull heresies sprawling and prostrate, the wild truth reeling but erect."

Here was a new, exciting, and fascinating view of the Christian Church, her rugged sanity and uncompromising insistence upon orthodoxy to safeguard the many-sided unity of truth and protect the human mind against the menace of unreason. Here was a new light bringing out beauties long hidden in old truths. Such was the enthralling picture which emerged after G.K. had focused the genius of his mind, imagination, mysticism, ecstasy, poetry, and joy upon the transcendent reality which the God-man, Jesus Christ, had planted as the one central, eternal, and divine institution in a landscape of time and space, His homestead in a world of men.

Chesterton's previous works had already established his reputation as a brilliant literary craftsman: *Orthodoxy* stamped him as a profound and penetrating thinker and prompted Wilfred Ward to rank him with Butler, Coleridge, and Newman. It was clear now that Christianity had a champion who would never lack a wide and appreciative audience when he took up his pen in its defense.

In the following year G.K. wrote *George Bernard Shaw*, a discerning study of the thought and writings of the gifted Irish-born playwright. Between these two men there was a warm personal friendship in spite of their radical differences of thought on many subjects. It is no small tribute to G.K.'s immense and unfailing charity that he managed to vent his criticisms without ever engaging in bitterness or wounding the feelings of his friend. Indeed in the midst of his severest strictures he was able to mirror his affection for the man and his admiration for his dramatic skill and unquestioned artistry. Thus after the appearance of the book, Shaw wrote him, "I liked it very much, especially as it was so completely free from my own influence."

These two men carried on many debates as well as a lifelong correspondence. In reading their letters, one is impressed with the warmth and depth of their friendship and of the sincerity of their appreciation of each other's literary talents. Shaw repeatedly urged G.K. to turn his versatile pen to the writing of plays, and one is inclined to regret that G.K. did not hearken to his advice and write

more than *Magic, The Judgment of Dr. Johnson,* and *Surprise*: the
only three plays in his enormous literary output.

In 1909 the Chestertons moved from their modest flat in Battersea
and went to live at Beaconsfield, a country village, where they remained for the rest of their lives. Here they had a lovely garden
in which G.K. took much pleasure and which appears in the background of many of his stories. Grieved at having no child of their
own, the Chestertons surrounded themselves with children: nieces
and nephews, godchildren and young neighbors. G.K. had a special
love for little children and this shines forth in not a few of his poems.
The following from his notebook is typical:

> *Sunlight in a child's hair.*
> *It is like the kiss of Christ upon all children.*
> *I blessed the child: and hoped the blessing*
> > *would go with him*
> > *And never leave him;*
> *And turn first into a toy, and then into a game*
> > *And then into a friend,*
> *And as he grew up, into friends*
> > *And then into a woman.*

As a youth, Chesterton was tall and rather slim, but in his twenties
he began to put on weight. "It was not ordinary fatness," says his
schoolmate E. C. Bentley; "I believe some gland trouble must have
been at the root of it." At any rate he grew heavier every year,
reaching the incredible weight of 350 pounds! He became a legendary figure, wearing a large flapping hat and an ample cloak. He
carried a swordstick and managed to get lost on every possible and
impossible occasion.

His absent-mindedness was as enormous as his size and has been
the theme of innumerable stories. Typical of a thousand is this one.
After setting out from home to give a lecture in some midland town,
he wired his wife: "Am in Market Harborough. Where ought I to be?"

In 1910 Chesterton set forth his social creed in *What's Wrong with
the World.* It became a best seller: a rare achievement for a social
and philosophical treatise in English-speaking countries. In it G.K.
sets forth some basic principles on the nature of man, marriage,
family, the child and its education. He shows that historically and
of his nature man needs the family, and for its protection the family

needs property, which unregulated capitalism can destroy not less than socialism.

"It is the negation of property," he writes, "that the Duke of Sutherland should have all the farms in one estate: just as it would be the negation of marriage if he had all our wives in one harem." He goes on to show that property is a condition for the ordinary man's development. "Property," he points out, "is the art of the democracy." The latter is most solidly established when property and wealth are widely distributed, and each family owns its own home.

During the war of 1914–18 he suffered a critical illness. "I wonder," the doctor heard him murmur as he was lifted into a water bed, "if this bally ship will ever get to shore." For many months he hovered between life and death. Under the devoted nursing of his wife, he gradually recovered his health and vigor. "I am afraid," he wrote at once to Shaw, "you must reconcile yourself to the dismal prospect of my being more or less like what I was before; and any resumption of my ordinary habits must necessarily include the habit of disagreeing with you."

In 1917 G.K. published his sketchy but fascinating *Short History of England*. This was followed in 1919 by *Irish Impressions* and in 1920 by *The New Jerusalem*. "These books," points out Maisie Ward, "all mark stages in that mental voyage of discovery in which Chesterton, historically and in the contemporary world, was approaching nearer and nearer to the Roman Catholic Church." His progress was impeded by the exhausting pressure of a multitude of duties and commitments of every kind.

Some years previously his brother Cecil and Belloc had started a newspaper called first the *Eye Witness* and later the *New Witness* to fight corruption in public life and to uphold the liberties of the poor against a growing bureaucracy. When Cecil joined the Army in 1916, Gilbert took over the editorship: Cecil's death in France in December 1918 placed the whole burden permanently upon Gilbert's shoulders and produced a chronic condition of fatigue.

To recover from this, Gilbert, along with his wife, set out in 1919 on a trip to Palestine and returned home by way of Rome early in 1920. The following year they left for a lecture tour in the United States. These travels deepened G.K.'s awareness of the world-wide character of the Catholic Church and brought him closer to her threshold. In Baltimore he was invited to visit Cardinal Gibbons, and felt himself touching "the end of a living chain" that went back to Peter the Fisherman. Upon his return home the thoughts and sentiments, which had for years been drawing him toward Rome, were to find their flowering in the greatest event of his life: his entrance into the Catholic Church. That faith became the axis around which his whole world revolved.

II. EMBRACES THE FAITH

To tell the story of Chesterton's conversion it is necessary to trace the progress of his thought and the influences which led to his acquiring an accurate and even penetrating understanding of the Catholic faith. This can be done through a study of his numerous books, his debates on religious topics, his personal correspondence and his life. Oddly enough, it won't be found in his *Autobiography,* where the references to it are disappointingly few.

Referring to the fact that many converts have to work their way through a swarm of lies and libels about the Catholic Church, G.K. relates that in his case it was at worst a matter of slights rather than slanders. "I owe it," he says, "to the liberal and Universalist atmosphere of my family, of Stopford Brooke and the Unitarian preachers they followed, that I was always just sufficiently enlightened to be out of the reach of Maria Monk." The latter was the author (at least in name) of a notorious work, depicting convents as prisons in which nuns were kept against their will, and reeking with the vilest slanders.

After passing through a youthful stage of agnosticism, Chesterton thought his way into theism and Christianity and joined the Anglican Church, of which his wife was a devoted member. After lengthy study and reading his brother Cecil entered the Catholic Church shortly before World War I. G.K.'s sojourn in the Holy Land deepened his insight into the antiquity of the Church, its supranational character and the unbroken continuity of apostolic succession. He was deeply stirred during a visit to the Church of Ecce Homo in Jerusalem.

Returning from Jerusalem, Gilbert wrote from Alexandria to his friend Maurice Baring: "I will only say here that my train of thought, which really was one of thought and not fugitive emotion, came to an explosion in the Church of Ecce Homo in Jerusalem: a church which the guidebooks call new and the newspapers call Latin." G.K. had reached the stage where he had a firm belief in the divinity of Christ, in the sacraments, in the priesthood and—what was of vital importance—in the authority of the Church.

Chesterton's admiration for the Church had been steadily growing through the years, and his keen eye was quick to perceive in her those paradoxical qualities which he acclaimed with an enthusiasm and a brilliance unsurpassed by any of her members. He recognized the Mother Church of Christendom as the greatest conservative force in the world, yet the most adventurous. She possesses the mellow wisdom of two thousand years and the eager enthusiasm of youth; she discarded the heresies of fifteen centuries ago which have become the novelties of today. She does not embrace every new scientific theory that is marshaled into the public square with the blare of trumpets and the beating of drums because she does not wish to be a widow the day after tomorrow.

She smiles at the deadly seriousness of the nationalists sitting in the saddle of all the countries today and seeking to remake the world: she smiles because she has seen the idol of nationalism, along with many others, rise and fall. When Edith Cavell, one of the noblest martyrs of our modern religion of nationalism, was about to face the firing squad of earnest German soldiers, intent upon the service of the fatherland, she cried out: "I see now that patriotism is not enough." The cry stirred the people of England as though it were a great and startling discovery. To the Church, however, it was as ancient as the commandment to love one's neighbor. It is no wonder that, after perceiving these attributes of the Church, Chesterton was drawing ever closer to her.

G.K. had a few close Catholic friends who helped him in his progress toward the Church. Hilaire Belloc was one of these. For this great scholar and independent thinker, Gilbert had almost unbounded respect, admiration, and affection. So close were they in thought and in friendship, that Shaw coined the name "Chesterbelloc" for the two of them. Profoundly appreciative of all that the Catholic faith meant to him, Belloc naturally wanted to share the source of his happiness with his friend. What could be a better expression of genuine friendship? So from the Reform Club, Manchester, on December 11, 1907, he wrote the following letter:

My dear Gilbert,

I am a man afraid of impulse in boats, horses and all action though driven to it. I have never written a letter such as I am writing now, though I have desired to write some six or seven since I became a grown man. In the matter we discussed at Oxford I have a word to say which is easier to say on paper than by word of mouth, or rather, more valuable. All intellectual process is doubtful, all inconclusive, save pure deduction, which is a game if one's first certitudes are hypothetical and immensely valuable if one's first certitude is fixed, yet remains wholly dependent on that.

Now if we differed in all main points I would not write thus, but there are one or two on which we agree. One is *"Vere passus, immolatus in cruce pro homine."* Another is in a looking up to our Dear Lady, the blessed Mother of God.

I recommend to you this, that you suggest to her a comprehension for yourself, of what indeed *is* the permanent home of the soul. If it is here you will see it, if it is there you will see it. She never fails us. She has never failed me in any demand.

I have never written thus—as I say—and I beg you to see nothing in it but what I say. There is no connection the reason can seize— but so it is. If you say "I want *this*" as in your case to know one way or the other—She will give it you: as She will give health or necessary money or success in a pure love. She is our Blessed Mother.

I have not used my judgment in this letter. I am inclined to destroy it, but I shall send it. Don't answer it.

> *Yours ever,*
> H. BELLOC

At top of letter: "My point is: If it is right, She knows. If it is not right, She knows."

No one can read this letter without admiring the forthright honesty and manly courage of Belloc in broaching a subject from which so many Catholic laity shy. He put it in such a way that no offense could be taken, and made it transparently clear that he simply wanted to share a precious treasure with a friend he esteemed so highly. In other words, he was bearing witness to the beauty,

holiness, and life-giving character of his faith, as Christ wants all
His followers to do.

From his conversations with Chesterton, Belloc knew that Gilbert
was singularly free from that strange Protestant prejudice that sets
the Mother of God against God the Son. From his early boyhood
Gilbert had respected and admired Our Lady. This admiration shines
forth in the following lines written in early youth:

The Nativity of Botticelli

Do you blame me that I sit hours before this picture?
But if I walked all over the world in this time
I should hardly see anything worth seeing that is not
*   in this picture.*

It was on the profound reality of Mary's help that Belloc rightly
felt that they both could meet. The words evidently struck deep in
G.K.'s mind, for it was to her he first made the promise to take the
step that would bring him into the fold of her divine Son. This he
discloses in the following passage from *The Well and the Shadows:*
"Now I can scarcely remember a time when the image of Our
Lady did not stand up in my mind quite definitely, at the mention
or the thought of all these things. I was quite distant from these
things, and then doubtful about these things; and then disputing with
the world for them, and with myself against them; for that is the
condition before conversion. But whether the figure was distant, or
was dark and mysterious, or was a scandal to my contemporaries,
or was a challenge to myself—I never doubted that this figure was
the figure of the Faith; that she embodied, as a complete human
being still only human, all that this Thing had to say to humanity.
The instant I remembered the Catholic Church, I remembered her;
when I tried to forget the Catholic Church, I tried to forget her!
When I finally saw what was nobler than my fate, the freest and the
hardest of all my acts of freedom, it was in front of a gilded and
very gaudy little image of her in the port of Brindisi, that I promised
the thing that I would do, if I returned to my own land."

In his work on Chaucer, G.K. quotes with amusement a learned
critic who said it was "possible" that Chaucer "had passed through a
period of intense devotion, more especially toward the Virgin Mary."
"It is," Chesterton comments. "It does occur from time to time. I do

not quite understand why Chaucer must have 'passed through' this fit of devotion; as if he had Mariolatry like the measles. Even an amateur who has encountered this malady may be allowed to testify that it does not usually visit its victim for a brief 'period'; it is generally chronic and (in some sad cases I have known) quite incurable."

In *The Queen of Seven Swords* Chesterton expresses his "chronic" love of Our Lady:

> *And men looked up at the woman made for the morning*
> *When the stars were young,*
> *For whom more rude than a beggar's rhyme in the gutter*
> *These songs were sung.*

Another of G.K.'s close friends was Maurice Baring. Frances Chesterton frequently remarked that of all her husband's friends there was none he loved more than Baring. Gifted as a novelist, dramatist, poet, critic, and historian, Baring was a member of the great banking family, related to most of the aristocracy and intimate with most of the rest; his generosity had enabled the Chestertons to take the trip to the Holy Land.

In 1909 he was received into the Catholic Church at the Brompton oratory. He referred to his conversion as "perhaps the only action of my life which I am quite certain I have never regretted." Like Belloc, he too knew how much the faith would mean to Chesterton, and he encouraged him to look into it seriously.

After Chesterton returned from his trip to Jerusalem and Rome in April 1920, he wrote to Baring that he would call on him shortly. "As you may possibly guess," he continued, "I want to consider my position about the biggest thing of all, whether I am to be inside it or outside it. I used to think one could be an Anglo-Catholic and really inside it; but if that was (to use an excellent phrase of your own) only a Porch, I do not think I want a Porch, and certainly not a Porch standing some way from the building. A Porch looks so silly, standing all by itself in a field. Since then, unfortunately, there have sprung up round it real ties and complications and difficulties; difficulties that seemed almost duties. But I will not bother you with all that now; and I particularly do not want you to bother yourself, especially to answer this unless you want to. I know I have your sympathy; and please God, I shall get things straight."

A month or so later he wrote a brief note to Baring saying that he had to leave for America sooner than he had expected. In closing, he says, "I have pretty well made up my mind about the thing we talked about. Fortunately the thing we talked about can be found all over the world."

Chesterton had many ties with the Anglican Church. He had lectured to a large audience of Anglo-Catholics at Albert Hall and had been highly acclaimed; the deep joy of his early conversion to Christianity was linked with Anglicanism and so too were many friendships and the continued attachment of Frances to it. But the reference to it as a porch, leading into the Church and not the Church itself, revealed the progress of his thinking. A man of immense charity, he did not wish to hurt his Anglican friends and particularly the devoted wife to whom he was so deeply attached. Yet truth had claims upon his loyalty which he could not in conscience ignore, and its claims were becoming increasingly articulate and urgent.

In a letter to Baring he tells of his addressing the Anglo-Catholics at Albert Hall and says: "I felt it like a farewell . . . A young Anglo-Catholic curate has just told me that the crowd there cheered all references to the Pope, and laughed at every mention of the Archbishop of Canterbury. It's a queer state of things. I am concerned most, however, about somebody I value more than the Archbishop of Canterbury: Frances, to whom I owe much of my own faith, and to whom therefore (as far as I can see my way) I also owe every decent chance for the controversial defense of her faith. If her side can convince me, they have a right to do so; if not, I shall go hot and strong to convince her. I put it clumsily, but there is a point in my mind."

Father Ronald Knox was another warm friend of Chesterton, who offered a helping hand as the great littérateur was struggling to reach the port. The son of the Anglican Bishop of Manchester, Knox completed a brilliant course at Oxford and was ordained in 1912 as a priest of the Church of England. Exhaustive studies carried on over five years convinced him of the divine foundation of the Catholic Church and of her exclusive authority to teach in the name of Christ. In 1917 he was received into the Catholic Church and two years later was elevated to the priesthood.

In a series of undated letters G.K. wrote Knox of the factors delaying his anticipated entrance. "I could not explain," he wrote, "what I mean about my wife without saying much more. I see in principle it is not on the same level as the true Church; for nothing can be on the same level as God. But it is on quite a different level from social sentiments about friends and family. I have been a rottenly irresponsible person till I began to wear the iron ring of Catholic responsibilities. But I really have felt a responsibility about her, more serious than affection, let alone passion. First, because she gave me my first respect for sacramental Christianity; second, because she is one of the good who mysteriously suffer . . .

"I have, however, a more practical reason for returning to this point. So far as my own feelings go, I think I might rightly make application to be instructed as soon as possible; but I should not like to take so serious a step without reopening the matter with her, which I could do by the end of a week."

The critical illness of Chesterton's father and his subsequent death further delayed G.K. He was then engrossed in doing everything possible for his bereaved mother and that involved him in business matters which were always immensely distracting to him. Eventually G.K. got around to discussing the matter with his wife and wrote Father Knox: "In our conversation my wife was all that I hope you will some day know her to be; she is incapable of wanting me to do anything but what I think right; and admits the same possibility for herself: but it is much more of a wrench for her, for she has been able to practice her religion in complete good faith; which my own doubts have prevented me from doing."

Chesterton was next obliged to leave for a week of lecturing in Holland. Shortly after his return he wrote Father Knox that he had another talk with his wife and as a result he invited Father O'Connor, an old friend of the family, to come to help him take the final step. "Frances," he wrote, "is just at the point where Rome acts both as the positive and the negative magnet; a touch would turn her either way; almost (against her will) to hatred, but with the right touch to a faith far beyond my reach. I know Father O'Connor's would be the touch that does not startle, because she knows him and is fond of him; and the only thing she asked of me was to send for him."

In replying on July 17, 1922, Father Knox said: "I'm awfully glad to hear that you've sent for Father O'Connor and that you think he's likely to be available. I must say that, in the story, Father Brown's powers of neglecting his parish always seemed to me even more admirable than Dr. Watson's powers of neglecting his practice; so I hope this trait was drawn from life."

From the time they first met in 1904, Father (later Monsignor) John O'Connor had been a close friend of the Chestertons, had tramped over the heath with Gilbert on long walks, and was genuinely admired and loved by both. It was only natural for Frances to suggest him as the ideal priest to prepare her husband for his entrance into the Church. He was an able and scholarly priest, who seems to have been as much at home in the drawing room of notables as in the simple homes of the workers in factories and stores. Chesterton immortalized him as the "Father Brown" of his detective stories.

Father O'Connor was delighted to come to Beaconsfield and prepare his old friend for the most important step in his whole life. After several sessions with Gilbert, he had a little talk with Frances.

"There is only one thing," he said, "troubling Gilbert about the great step—the effect it is going to have on you."

"Oh!" she replied, "I shall be infinitely relieved. You cannot imagine how it fidgets Gilbert to have anything on his mind. The last three months have been exceptionally trying. I should be only too glad to come with him, if God in His mercy would show the way clear, but up to now He has not made it clear enough to me to justify such a step."

Accordingly Father was able to reassure Gilbert on that point that afternoon. "We discussed at large," he said, "such special points as he wished, and then I told him to read through the Penny Catechism to make sure there were no snags to a prosperous passage. It was a sight for men and angels all the Friday to see him wandering in and out of the house with his fingers in the leaves of the little book, resting it on his forearm whilst he pondered with his head on one side."

Father Ignatius Rice, O.S.B., another old and dear friend, came over from the abbey at Douai for the reception ceremony. He tells of finding Gilbert in an armchair reading the catechism, "pulling faces and making noises as he used to do when reading." At that time there was no Catholic church at Beaconsfield, so the ceremony took place in a part of the Railway Hotel, which was used as a temporary chapel. G.K. made his profession of faith and Father O'Connor baptized him and heard his confession. Chesterton was exultant with joy and gladness, "quoting poetry and jesting in the highest spirits," and on returning home wrote the beautiful sonnet on his conversion. It was the happiest day in his life! He had reached the port toward which he had been struggling for many years.

The joy and gladness which filled his heart shines forth in the poem he wrote that afternoon, in which he describes his conversion as a new light that transfigures his life and indeed gives him a new life.

The Convert

> After one moment when I bowed my head
> And the whole world turned over and came upright,
> And I came out where the old road shone white,
> I walked the ways and heard what all men said.

> . . . . .

> They rattle reason out through many a sieve
> That stores the sand and lets the gold go free:
> And all these things are less than dust to me
> Because my name is Lazarus and I live.

Deeply devoted to his mother, he writes to tell her of the step he has taken and to assure her it will not impair their relations or their love.

My dearest Mother,

I have come to the same conclusion that Cecil did about needs of the modern world in religion and right dealing, and I am now a Catholic in the same sense as he, having long claimed the name in its Anglo-Catholic sense. I am not going to make a foolish fuss of reassuring you about things I am sure you never doubted; these things do not hurt any relations between people as fond of each other as we are; any more than they ever made any difference to the love between Cecil and ourselves. But there are two things I should like to tell you, in case you do not realize them through some other impression.

I have thought about you, and all that I owe to you and my father, not only in the way of affection, but of the ideals of honor and freedom and charity and all other good things you always taught me: and I am not conscious of the smallest break or difference in those ideals; but only of a new and necessary way of fighting for them. I think, as Cecil did, that the fight for the family and the free citizen and everything decent must now be waged by the one fighting form of Christianity. The other is that I have thought this out for myself and not in a hurry of feeling . . . I believe it is the truth.

Here G.K. expresses a conviction which echoes and re-echoes throughout most of his subsequent writing: the Catholic Church is the "one fighting form of Christianity" most capable of leading the battle of free men for all the decencies of human life. In the *New Witness* he answered a newspaper suggestion that the Church ought to "move with the times."

"The Cities of the Plain might have remarked that the heavens above them did not altogether fit in with their own high civilization and social habits. They would be right. Oddly enough, however, when symmetry was eventually restored, it was not the heavens that had been obliged to adapt themselves . . . The Church cannot move with the times; simply because the times are not moving . . .

"The Church has the same task as it had at the beginning of the Dark Ages; to save all the light and liberty that can be saved, to resist the downward drag of the world . . . We do not want, as the newspapers say, a Church that will move with the world. We want a Church that will move the world. We want one that will move it away from many of the things towards which it is now moving; for instance, the Servile State."

When Belloc received word that his old friend had at last taken the step which he had ventured to suggest to him fifteen years ago, he was overjoyed. He immediately wrote G.K. a note of hearty congratulations and paid an eloquent tribute to the faith which meant more to him than life itself. He pointed out that he can do this latter appropriately now, whereas before G.K. had taken the step it might have seemed like selected pleading.

"The Catholic Church," he wrote, "is the exponent of *Reality*. It is true. Its doctrines in matters large and small are statements of what is. This it is which the ultimate act of the intelligence accepts. This it is which the will deliberately confirms. And that is why Faith though an act of the Will is Moral. If the Ordnance Map tells us that it is 11 miles to [a place] then, my mood of lassitude as I walk through the rain at night makes it *feel* like 30, but I use the Will and say 'No. My intelligence has been convinced and I compel myself to use it against my mood. It is 11 and though I feel in the depths of my being to have gone 20 miles and more, I *know* it is not yet 11 I have gone.'

"I am by all my nature of mind sceptical . . . And as to the doubt of the soul I discover it to be false: a mood: not a conclusion. My conclusion—and that of all men who have ever once *seen* it—is the Faith: Corporate, organized, a personality, teaching. A thing, not a theory. It . . .

"I am alone and unfed, the more do I affirm the Sanctity, the Unity, the Infallibility of the Catholic Church. By my very isolation do I the more affirm it, as a man in a desert knows that water is right for man: or as a wounded dog, not able to walk, yet knows the way home. The Catholic Church is the natural home of the human spirit. The odd perspective picture of life which looks like a meaningless puzzle at first, seen from that *one* standpoint takes a complete order and meaning, like the skull in the picture of the Ambassadors."

Like Belloc, Maurice Baring was deeply stirred at the news of Chesterton's conversion. Not only had he written gracious but restrained words of encouragement to G.K., but he had prayed most fervently for him and had enlisted others to do the same.

"Nothing for years," he wrote, "has given me so much joy. I have hardly ever entered a church without putting up a candle to Our Lady or to St. Joseph or St. Anthony for you. And both this year and last year in Lent I made a Novena for you. I know of many other people, better people far than I, who did the same. Many Masses were said for you and prayers all over England and Scotland in centres of Holiness. I will show you some day a letter from some Nuns on the subject. A great friend of mine, one of the greatest saints I have known, Sister Mary Annunciation of the Convent Orphanage, Upper Norwood, used always to pray for you. She, alas, died last year.

"Did I ever quote you a sentence of Bernard Holland on the subject of Kenelm Henry Digby when the latter was received?

"'Father Scott . . . who, at last, guided him through the narrow door where one must bend one's head, into the internal space and freedom of the eternal and universal Catholic Church.' *Space* and *freedom:* that was what I experienced on being received; that is what I have been most conscious of ever since. It is the exact opposite of what the ordinary Protestant conceives to be the case . . .

"I was received into the Church on the Eve of Candlemas 1909, and it is perhaps the *only act* in my life, which I am quite certain I have never regretted. Every day I live, the Church seems to me more and more wonderful; the Sacraments more and more solemn and sustaining; the voice of the Church, her liturgy, her rules, her discipline, her ritual, her decisions in matters of Faith and Morals more and more excellent and profoundly wise and true and right, and her children stamped with something that those outside Her are without. There I have found Truth and reality and everything outside Her is to me compared with Her as dust and shadow. Once more God bless you and Frances. Please give her my love. In my prayers for you I have always added her name."

In the warmth of this letter the reader can feel the deep affection Baring had for G.K., which was so fully reciprocated. Even the scoffing agnostic Bernard Shaw took time to write to G.K. about his conversion. With typical Shavian wit and humor he pictures his huge friend going to confession, struggling to get his portly figure into the little box and shaking it so violently as to make the "poor devil" on the other side wish that G.K. had become a fire worshiper instead. It was but a bit of the good-humored raillery and banter in which the two friendly adversaries constantly indulged.

In *The Catholic Church and Conversion* G.K. discusses the broad general problem of conversion and indicates the obstacles and the helps toward that goal. Occasionally he illustrates his points by references to his own experience as a pilgrim who found his way. It is these occasional references which throw the most light upon the mental processes through which G.K. went as he slowly worked his way to the Church's threshold.

Chesterton makes it transparently clear that conversion to the Catholic Church, while aided by divine grace, is a thoroughly rational process: the intellect reaches a conclusion as a result of the weight of evidence and the laws of logical reasoning. "To become a Catholic," he says, "is not to leave off thinking, but to learn how to think. It is so in exactly the same sense in which to recover from palsy is not to leave off moving but to learn how to move . . . What is now called free thought is valued, not because it is free thought but because it is freedom from thought; because it is free thought-lessness."

In seeking to retrace his steps out of the shrine of truth back into the wilderness, G.K. experiences the difficulty common to many, if not most, converts. That difficulty was expressed by a convert who said to Chesterton, "I cannot explain why I am a Catholic; because now that I am a Catholic I cannot imagine myself as anything else." Chesterton then points out that the common charge of Protestants that the Catholic Church is afraid of the Bible never impressed him. Why? Because he grew up in a world in which the Protestants who had previously indicted the Church for not making sufficient use of the Bible were just then excitedly discovering that they did not believe the Bible themselves.

"The next step in progress," as G.K. vividly puts it, "consisted in a man kicking his father for having locked up a book of such beauty and value, a book which the son then proceeded to tear into a thousand pieces." Here Chesterton is referring to the attacks made on the Bible by the so-called Higher Criticism, which turned out to be much more of an onslaught on Protestant Bible-worship than on Roman authority.

"The Church," he says, "is a house with a hundred gates; and no two men enter at exactly the same angle. Mine was at least as much Agnostic as Anglican, though I accepted for a time the borderland of Anglicanism; but only on the assumption that it could really be Anglo-Catholicism. There is a distinction of ultimate intention there which in the vague English atmosphere is often missed. It is not a difference of degree but of definite aim."

He mentions the divisions within the Anglican Church: the High Churchmen and the Low Churchmen, all of whom are primarily concerned with saving the Church of England. Some think they can save it by making it Catholic, or calling it Catholic, or believing that it is Catholic. But G.K. did not start out with the idea of saving the English Church but of finding the Catholic Church. "If the two were one," he says, "so much the better; but I had never conceived of Catholicism as a sort of showy attribute or attraction to be tacked on to my own national body, but as the inmost soul of the true body, wherever it might be. It might be said that Anglo-Catholicism was simply my own uncompleted conversion to Catholicism."

Another charge which fills many Protestants with fear and dread had no effect upon him: the alleged wickedness of Rome and its ministers, from the highest to the lowest. It is that vague fear which so often prevents a truth seeker from coming at once and with confidence to a rectory, often causing him to linger agonizingly long in the wilderness. "Why," asks G.K., "should a man who wanted to be wicked encumber himself with special and elaborate promises to be good? . . . Would any man make himself poor in order that he might become avaricious; or take a vow of chastity frightfully difficult to keep in order to get into a little more trouble when he did not keep it? All that early and sensational picture of the sins of Rome always seemed to me silly even when I was a boy or an unbeliever; and I cannot describe how I passed out of it because I was never in it."

After outlining other charges which are falsely made by her adversaries to keep people from knowing the enthralling truth about the Church, Chesterton comes to the principle of nationalism: this he says the British, like many other nations, have erected into a religion. Patriotism is a duty of the citizen, but his duty does not end there: it must go beyond national boundaries and embrace all humanity. "The Catholic Church," he says, "loves nations as she loves men; because they are her children. But they certainly are her children, in the sense that they are secondary to her in time and process of production . . .

"Secondary loyalties are secondary in time and logic to the law of universal morality which justifies them. And if the patriot is such a fool as to force the issue against that universal tradition from which his own patriotism descends, if he presses his claim to priority over the primitive law of the whole earth—then he will have brought it on himself if he is answered with the pulverizing plainness of the Book of Job. As God said to the man, 'Where were you when the foundations of the world were laid?' We might well say to the nation, 'Where were you when the foundations of the Church were laid?'"

Chesterton had always staunchly defended patriotism and had at times even rendered himself suspect by sympathizing with the patriotism of other people. He defended patriotism, however, as a part of a larger morality, as one of the duties of man and not as his whole duty. He ends his penetrating analysis of the morality of patriotism and nationalism by saying: "But it is absurd to treat the

Church as a novel conspiracy attacking the State, when the State was only recently a novel experiment arising within the Church. It is absurd to forget that the Church itself received the first loyalties of men who had not yet even conceived the notion of founding such a national and separate state; that the Faith really was not only the faith of our fathers, but the faith of our fathers before they had even named our fatherland."

Having exploded the stock charges, libels, and false alarms about the Church, G.K. comes in the third chapter to what he calls the real obstacles: the virtues and the truth of Catholicism. The truth seeker who has gotten an insight into the Catholic faith is no longer afraid of its alleged vices but very much afraid of its virtues. Thus he has forgotten all the old foolishness about the cunning lies of the confessional in his lively and understandable alarm over its truthfulness. Chesterton thinks it is perhaps just as well that people go through this stage before discovering how very little there is to be afraid of. Absolution, like death and marriage, is a reality that each man ought to find out for himself.

"It will be enough to say," remarks G.K., "that this is perhaps the supreme example of the fact that the Faith is a paradox that measures more within than without. If that be true of the smallest church, it is truer still of the yet smaller confessional-box, that is like a church within a church. It is almost a good thing that nobody outside should know what gigantic generosity, and even geniality, can be locked up in a box, as the legendary casket held the heart of the giant. It is a satisfaction, and almost a joke, that it is only in a dark corner and a cramped space that any man can discover that mountain of magnanimity."

Chesterton points out that when the truth seeker has passed the stage of being bothered by the ordinary anti-Catholic propaganda, he has arrived at the crucial point where one foolish word from inside does more harm than a hundred thousand foolish words from outside. The latter he has grown accustomed to, like a blind hail or rain beating upon the Ark; but the voices from within, even the most casual and accidental, he is already disposed to consider as holy or more than human. This is a point which Catholics should always remember and act accordingly.

On the basis of his own experience, G.K. outlines three stages or states of mind through which the convert ordinarily passes. The first is when he imagines himself to be entirely detached or even indifferent. Chesterton thought he was in this stage when he investigated fifteen specific charges against the Church and found them all false. At the time he was doing this apparently for the mere logical pleasure of disentangling an intellectual injustice. "I had," he remarks, "no more idea of becoming a Catholic than of becoming a cannibal. I imagined that I was merely pointing out that justice should be done even to cannibals."

The second stage is that in which the inquirer begins to be conscious not only of the falsehood but of the truth, and becomes enormously excited to find that there is far more of the latter than he had ever expected. This is not so much a stage as a progress, which continues for a considerable time. "This process," says G.K., "which may be called discovering the Catholic Church, is perhaps the most pleasant and straightforward part of the business; easier than joining the Catholic Church and much easier than trying to live the Catholic life. It is like discovering a new continent full of strange flowers and fantastic animals, which is at once wild and hospitable."

During this period the truth seeker catches numberless glimpses of great ideas that had been hidden from him by the prejudices of his provincial culture: these stirring discoveries characterize the adventurous and varied second stage of conversion. It is, in general, the stage in which the individual is subconsciously trying to be converted.

The third stage, the truest and most terrible, is that in which the individual is trying to escape. He has come too near the truth, forgetting that truth is a magnet. It is impossible to be just to the Catholic Church and remain in a state of neutrality. The moment one ceases to pull against it, he feels a tug toward it; the moment he ceases to shout it down, he begins to listen to it with pleasure; the instant he tries to be fair to it, he begins to be fond of it. When that fondness has passed a certain point it begins to assume the tragic and menacing grandeur of a great love affair.

The individual has the feeling of having committed or compromised himself; of having been caught in a trap, even if he is glad to be so caught. But for quite some time he is more terrified than glad. It is possible that a misunderstanding of this profound and complex psychological experience is responsible for the legend that Rome is a mere trap. That legend misses, however, the whole point. It is not the Pope who set the trap or the priests who baited it: the trap is simply the truth. The individual took the two previous steps eagerly on his own account, out of interest in the truth, but he was pulled into the last alarming step because he had come within the magnetic field of the truth. In short the truth has seized him, pulled him from his doubt and uncertainty, and imprisoned him; for when one opens the door of his mind to truth, he finds that he has no longer taken possession of it but it has taken possession of him.

Illustrating this alarming third step by his own experience, Chesterton says: "I for one was never less troubled by doubts than in the last phase, when I was troubled by fears. Before that final delay I had been detached and ready to regard all sorts of doctrines with an open mind. Since that delay has ended in decision, I have had all sorts of changes in mere mood; and I think I sympathize with doubts and difficulties more than I did before. But I had no doubts or difficulties just before. I had only fears; fears of something that had the finality and simplicity of suicide. But the more I thrust the thing into the back of my mind, the more certain I grew of what Thing it was. And by a paradox that does not frighten me now in the least, it may be that I shall never again have such absolute assurance that the thing is true as I had when I made my last effort to deny it."

In this frank and honest disclosure of the changes in mood and the strange fears which beset him after he had become intellectually convinced, one sees at work the aggregate of forces which held him back so long from taking the step which had become inevitable. Here one sees the swarm of crawling phobias and vague unfounded misgivings which subconsciously caused him to procrastinate so long behind the smoke screen of so many external happenings: the sickness of his wife, the death of his father, the lecture trips to Holland and America, his preoccupation with the *New Witness* and even its unpalatable business affairs, and his long-drawn-out concern about his wife's reaction to his taking the final step.

These are mentioned as the causes of his protracted delay in a long series of letters to Maurice Baring and especially to Father Knox, dating from 1919 to 1932 and reproduced in Maisie Ward's splendid biography of Chesterton. Doubtless these things did distract G.K. and tend to delay the supremely important step; but back of them there were the subjective factors which he pulled into the open only after the event.

In the light of all this, one reads with deeper appreciation and understanding the full meaning of his revealing utterance: "There is in the last second of time or hairbreadth of space, before the iron leaps to the magnet, an abyss full of all the unfathomable forces of the universe. The space between doing and not doing such a thing is so tiny and so vast." About ten years had elapsed since Chesterton had first spoken to Father O'Connor about his intention of embracing the faith and three years since he wrote Baring about the "explosion" in the Church of Ecce Homo. By this G.K. doubtless meant the intense and irresistible urge to take the step which he and Baring had been discussing for some time.

"At the last moment of all," says Chesterton, "the convert often feels as if he were looking through a leper's window. He is looking through a little crack or crooked hole that seems to grow smaller as he stares at it; but it is an opening that looks towards the Altar. Only, when he has entered the Church, he finds that the Church is much larger inside than it is outside. He has left behind him the lopsidedness of lepers' windows and even in a sense the narrowness of Gothic doors; and he is under vast domes as open as the Renaissance and as universal as the Republic of the world. He can say in a sense unknown to all modern men certain ancient and serene words: *Romanus civis sum;* I am not a slave."

Thus far G.K. has been subjecting the experience in this crucial last stage to a penetrating psychological analysis. But he is quick to perceive that, after the psychologist has spoken his last word, there remains a mystery which only the action of divine grace can solve. Faith is a gift of God. Man can perceive the truth and achieve full intellectual conviction, but that is not an act of faith. To elicit the latter requires a movement of the will, aided by divine grace, whereby the intellect accepts a teaching not merely on the authority of human reason but on the authority of God the revealer.

It is a considerable step, points out Chesterton, from the inference that a dogma of the faith represents a human truth to the inference that it is a divine truth. "When we come to that conviction of divine authority, we come to the more mysterious matter of divine aid. In other words, we come to the unfathomable idea of grace and the gift of faith."

One of the marks of the Church which made a compelling appeal to G.K. is her universality. Disavowing any unfriendliness toward the sects, he points out that it is simply a historical fact that the Catholic Church is *the* Church and not a sect. The Catholic Church stands alone. She does not merely belong to a class of Christian churches, nor to a class of human religions. She is the one, holy, Catholic, Apostolic Church founded by Christ for the salvation of all mankind and commissioned to teach all nations in His name, and she received this divine commission more than fourteen centuries before a single Protestant sect saw the light of day.

The Church is this *sui generis,* and it is not intolerance but loyalty to her divine Founder and a decent respect for her own divine character which prompts her to hold aloof from all the myriad changing, splitting, bickering creeds of men. To place them on a par with herself would be not an act of broad-mindedness but of treason to her divine Founder. So clearly and vividly did Chesterton perceive this basic truth that he is inclined to make its perception the decisive step in leading to conversion.

"Now conversion," he says, "consists very largely, on its intellectual side, in the discovery that all that picture of equal creeds inside an indifferent cosmos is quite false. It is not a question of comparing the merits and defects of the Quaker meeting-house set beside the Catholic cathedral. It is the Quaker meeting-house that is inside the Catholic cathedral; it is the Catholic cathedral that covers everything like the vault of the Crystal Palace; and it is when we look up at the vast distant dome covering all the exhibits that we trace the Gothic roof and the pointed windows . . . The principle of life in all these variations of Protestantism, in so far as it is not a principle of death, consists of what remained in them of Catholic Christendom; and to Catholic Christendom they have always returned to be recharged with vitality."

Paradoxically enough, as G.K. points out, becoming a Catholic broadens the mind, especially about the reasons for so acting. "Standing in the center," he says, "where all roads meet, a man can look down each of the roads in turn and realize that they come from all points of the heavens. As long as he is still marching along his own road, that is the only road that can be seen, or sometimes even imagined . . . Catholic philosophy is a universal philosophy found to fit anywhere with human nature and the nature of things . . .

Education does not cease with conversion, but rather begins. The man does not cease to study because he has become convinced that certain things are worth studying; and these things include not only the orthodox values but even the orthodox vetoes."

Chesterton chuckled over the felicity of Father Ronald Knox's remark that the Catholic Church manages to carry on by hook or crook. But the hook is that of the fisherman and the crook is that of the shepherd: by the hook the convert is caught and by the crook he is kept. He points to the galaxy of the best minds in Great Britain who since Newman's time have entered the Church in such huge numbers as to resemble a landslide.

This brings G.K. to the subject of the occasional drifter, the unfortunate prodigal who surrenders his inheritance for a mess of pottage. Such individuals, he points out, do not abandon their faith for Protestantism but for paganism. "Most of them," he continues, "abandon it for something that is really too simple to be called an *ism* of any kind. They abandon it for things and not theories . . . They leave it to have a high old time." In short, they leave it not because of the claims of reason but of passion. How penetrating is this analysis of the basic cause of leakage: the riotous triumph of the libidinal instincts over the reason and conscience of man.

What drifting there is, observes Chesterton, is chiefly among the young, and the work of reclaiming them is largely that of instructing them better and then developing in them a deeper spiritual life, which will anchor them in the faith. "It is not a controversy," he says, "between two philosophies, as was the Catholic and the Calvinist, or the Catholic and the Materialist. It is a controversy between philosophers and philanderers . . . But the very laws of life are against the endurance of a revolt that rests on nothing but natural passion; it is bound to change in its proportion with the coming of experience; and, at the worst, it will become a battle between bad Catholics and good Catholics, with the great dome over all."

Recurring to the theme of conversion proper, G.K. advises the inquirer to face any Catholic doctrine which seems to him to be false and, if he faces it long enough, he will probably find it to be the greatest truth of all. "I have found this myself," he says, "in that extreme logic of free will which is found in the fallen angels and the possibility of perdition. Such things are altogether beyond my imagination, but the lines of logic go out towards them in my reason.

Indeed, I can undertake to justify the whole Catholic theology, if I be granted to start with the supreme sacredness and value of two things: Reason and Liberty. It is an illuminating comment on current anti-Catholic talk that they are the two things which most people imagine to be forbidden to Catholics."

Chesterton closes his discussion of conversion proper with a personal reference that is both moving and eloquent. "Supposing," he says, "I were so miserable as to lose the Faith, could I go back to that cheap charity and crude optimism which says that every sin is a blunder, that evil cannot conquer or does not even exist? I could no more go back to those cushioned chapels than a man who has regained his sanity would willingly go back to a padded cell. I might cease to believe in a God of any kind; but I could not cease to think that a God who had made men and angels free was finer than one who coerced them into comfort.

"I might cease to believe in a future life of any kind; but I could not cease to think it was a finer doctrine that we choose and make our future life than that it is fitted out for us like an hotel and we are taken there in a celestial omnibus as compulsory as a Black Maria. I know that Catholicism is too large for me, and I have not yet explored its beautiful or terrible truths. But I know that Universalism is too small for me; and I could not creep back into that dull safety, who have looked on the dizzy vision of liberty."

That vigorous and well-reasoned statement of his inability ever to go back to the errors of his Protestant past is splendidly supplemented by the closing paragraph of a letter he wrote to Maurice Baring shortly after his conversion. "Of course," he says, "there are a hundred things more to say; indeed the greatest argument for Catholicism is exactly what makes it so hard to argue for it. It is the scale and multiplicity of the forms of truth and help that it has to offer. And perhaps, after all, the only thing that you and I can really say with profit is exactly what you yourself suggested; that we are men who have talked to a good many men about a good many things, and seen something of the world and the philosophies of the world and that we have not the shadow of a doubt about what was the wisest act of our lives."

To a mind so many-faceted as Chesterton's, which perceived the myriad charms of the Church and understood the mellow wisdom which enabled her to view with serenity the colossal trifles and the outworn novelties which were shaking the creeds of the sects asunder, it is no easy matter to point to the one set of credentials which appealed to him most. The one fact above all others, however, which overwhelmed him with its cogency and which is the common denominator of all her credentials, is the simple fact that *Catholicism is true.* "The difficulty of explaining 'why I am a Catholic,'" says Chesterton, "is that there are ten thousand reasons all amounting to one reason: that Catholicism is true."

In seeking to portray the various stages of Chesterton's conversion with their respective clusters of thoughts and feelings, we have drawn largely upon his little book, *The Catholic Church and Conversion.* In our opinion it is worthy to rank high among his great works and deserves much more recognition than it has received. For more than forty years we have been especially interested in the experience of conversion, have instructed and received hundreds of converts and studied with great care the accounts of legions of conversions. Yet we are startled and amazed at the many penetrating insights displayed by G.K. into this profound spiritual experience, where nature and grace work hand in hand in the mysterious process of leading a soul from darkness into the light.

Psychologists, theologians, and mystics have sought to trace out the complex pattern of the various psychic and spiritual forces operating in this strange, fascinating and awesome experience. We would be at a loss, however, to name any of them who have penetrated more deeply or thrown more light upon the process than Chesterton. It is an evidence of the uncanny versatility of his genius that he could penetrate so deeply into so many different fields. This will again come to light when we discuss his treatment of the philosophy of St. Thomas.

The announcement of G.K.'s conversion stirred widespread interest throughout the English-speaking world. It was akin to that which was aroused by the entrance of Newman into the Church. A prominent Anglican clergyman, Canon Headderly, voiced at that time the criticism of many against "the general muddleheadedness" of the Church which caused the departure of so gifted a writer.

"We have never had such an apologist as G. K. Chesterton," he declared, "and yet he has hardly ever figured at a church meeting. We prefer the dull logic of some dry-as-dust professor from Oxford to the sparkling paradox of the greatest wit of the century. Religion is still groaning under the weight of Puritanism and kill-joys in this country. Mr. Chesterton would lift us up, but we won't let him. We are still scared by mid-Victorian arguments about science and miracles. G.K.C. would deliver us, and keep us orthodox at the same time.

"But we would rather not be set free. Any one who courteously and fairly explodes Puritan fallacies is doing more good than he knows to the cause of true religion in England. Puritanism has virtually destroyed Sunday in thinking to preserve it. It has made religion suspected. It has taken away joy and beauty and love while it was doing the work of angels who make merry in heaven. Most of this sad work has been through sheer lack of humor, and this is partly why it can only be undone by humorists like Chesterton."

"He approached the Catholic Church," said Belloc, "gradually but by a direct road. He first saw the city from afar off, then approached it with interest and at last entered. Few of the great conversions in our history have been so deliberate or so mature. It will be for posterity to judge the magnitude of the event. We are too near it to see it in scale."

III.   SCALES NEW HEIGHTS

Shortly after receiving Chesterton, Father O'Connor ventured to predict that G.K. would do better work than ever. His prediction was fully realized when *St. Francis of Assisi* appeared the following year and *The Everlasting Man* two years later. The former quickly achieved a wide circulation on both sides of the Atlantic and still remains one of his most popular works. In it G.K. shows his capacity to plumb the depths of mysticism and to catch the peculiar radiance and unique charm of the God-intoxicated *Poverello* of Assisi.

"He was above all things," says Chesterton, "a great giver; and he cared chiefly for the best kind of giving which is called thanksgiving. If another great man wrote a grammar of assent, he may well be said to have written a grammar of acceptance; a grammar of gratitude. He understood down to its very depths the theory of thanks; and its depths are a bottomless abyss." In St. Francis, G.K. saw the living embodiment of his thought that thanksgiving is a duty and a joy and that we should love not "humanity" but each human.

Though less popular, *The Everlasting Man* is more profound: it is the *Orthodoxy* of his Catholic life. In *Orthodoxy* G.K. had traced his own discovery of Christianity: in *The Everlasting Man* he shows what the Christian revelation has meant for mankind as a whole. "I desire," he says, "to help the reader to see Christendom from the outside in the sense of seeing it as a whole against the background of other historic things; just as I desire him to see humanity as a whole against the background of natural things. And I say that in both cases when seen thus, they stand out from their background like supernatural things."

Professor William Lyon Phelps of Yale wrote to thank the author for "a magnificent work of genius and never more needed than now. I took out my pencil to mark the most important passages, but I quickly put my pencil in my pocket for I found I had to mark every sentence." In maturity and depth of thought it surpasses *Orthodoxy*.

In 1926 Frances Chesterton joined her husband at the communion rail and her joy in the practice of her new-found faith was as complete as his. She came in as a result of her own independent study and not merely because of Gilbert's example. When she had made up her own mind, she wrote Father O'Connor, "It isn't true to say that I've only followed Gilbert. I've had a hard fight not to let my love for him lead me to the truth. I knew you would not accept me for such motives."

Entrance into the Church, the Mystical Body of Christ, exercised upon her the same rejuvenating, exhilarating, and joyous influence that it had upon Gilbert. Maisie Ward Sheed, who knew her well, remarks, "I have never known a happier Catholic than she was, once the shivering on the bank was over and the plunge had been taken. One would say she had been in the Church all her life."

In 1930 Chesterton came to America for the second time, and while here gave an extensive course of lectures on Victorian literature and Victorian history at the University of Notre Dame, which honored him with the LL.D. degree. On this campus Chesterton left many pleasant and delightful memories. With him came his wife and his secretary, Dorothy Collins; they took a home just off the campus and got more intimately acquainted with the American people than on their visit to this country nine years before.

G.K. lectured entirely without notes: he quoted long passages of prose and poetry with ease and consummate art. He spoke in a somewhat high-pitched voice, and used none of the tricks of the conventional orator: he held the audience by his brilliant thought, wit, humor, and remarkable fluency. He had such a superb command of language that he seemed to find the precise word and phrase without effort. When he would tell a joke, he would laugh as uproariously as any in the audience, and he constantly radiated good humor.

The president's chauffeur John Mangan would call each evening for him. John reports that G.K. would take only about five minutes to walk up and down on the porch while he gathered his thoughts. But if any little children came along, he would always stop to talk to them. That seemed to be the only immediate preparation needed, so prodigious was his store of knowledge and so remarkable his memory along literary and scholarly lines.

John reports that his chief difficulty was in getting G.K. into the automobile: he solved it by getting him to back into it. But then there was the problem of getting him out. "I brought him to the main building one evening," relates John, "but when he tried to get out, he got stuck in the door. When the president, Father Charles O'Donnell, tried to help him with a suggestion, G.K. said it reminded him of the suggestion made to him by an old Irishwoman. 'Why,' she asked, 'don't you get out sideways?' 'Unfortunately, madam,' he replied, 'I have no sideways.'"

While at Notre Dame G.K.'s love of little children was apparent. Whenever he would encounter them he would stop and talk to them. He would put a number of questions to them and frequently burst out into hearty laughter at their answers. He seemed to be completely at home with them and to share their innocence.

While here, Chesterton attended the football game with Navy and immensely enjoyed the contest as well as the cheering of the students. It inspired him to write a famous poem, *The Arena*, dedicated to the university. Its main building is crowned with a golden dome upon which is enshrined the statue of Our Lady, after whom the university is named. In the poem he pictures first the golden image on "the gilded house of Nero" that stood for all the horrors of the pagan amphitheater. Then comes in contrast another image:

I have seen, where a strange country
Opened its secret plains about me,
One great golden dome stand lonely with its golden image, one

Seen afar, in strange fulfilment,
Through the sunlit Indian summer
That Apocalyptic portent that has clothed her with the Sun.

The students shout "Notre Dame" as they watch the fortunes of the fray and Chesterton sees Our Lady presiding fittingly even over a football contest.

> *And I saw them shock the whirlwind*
> *Of the world of dust and dazzle:*
> *And thrice they stamped, a thunderclap; and*
>   *thrice the sand-wheel swirled;*
> *And thrice they cried like thunder*
> *On Our Lady of the Victories,*
> *The Mother of the Master of the Masterers of*
>   *the World.*

On November 5, 1930, the university for the first time in its history called a special convocation of the faculty and student body to confer a degree, honoring Chesterton with an LL.D. The citation characterized Chesterton as "a man of letters recognized as the ablest and most influential in the English-speaking world of today, a defender of the Christian tradition, whose keen mind, right heart, and versatile literary genius have been valiantly devoted to eternal truth, goodness and beauty, in literature and in life."

From Notre Dame, G.K. went to lecture in various cities in the United States and Canada. In New York he debated with the noted trial lawyer and orator, Clarence Darrow, before an audience of four thousand in Mecca Temple, taking the affirmative side of the question, "Will the World Return to Religion?" At the close of the debate a vote was taken: Chesterton received 2359 to 1022 for Darrow: a glowing tribute to the superiority of brilliant thought over merely polished oratory.

In Chicago, G.K. engaged in a debate with Dr. Horace J. Bridges of the Ethical Cultural Society on the topic, "Is Psychology a Curse?" In introducing Chesterton, Bishop George C. Steward quoted Oliver Hereford's delightful verse:

> *When plain folks such as you and I*
> *See the sun sinking in the sky,*
> *We think it is the setting sun:*

But Mr. Gilbert Chesterton
Is not so easily misled;
He calmly stands upon his head,
And upside down obtains a new
And Chestertonian point of view.
Observing thus how from his nose
The sun creeps closer to his toes
He cries in wonder and delight.
How fine the sunrise is tonight!

In New York, Chesterton was taken to the famous Times Square where hundreds of multicolored neon lights flashed arresting and picturesque advertisements. Glancing at the brilliant display, G.K. chuckled, "What a paradise this must be for a man who can't read."

Chesterton lectured on such paradoxical subjects as, "The Perils of Health," "Shall We Abolish the Inevitable?" and "The Ignorance of the Educated." At Toronto the chairman—a professor of English— thought that there must have been an error in the title as printed, and announced that Mr. Chesterton would lecture on, "The Ignorance of the *Un*educated."

In London, Chesterton debated with Cosmo Hamilton on the subject, "There Is No Law in England." G.K. made so overwhelming a case that his opponent decided the only way of replying was to twist the subject into "there are no laws in England," and "go off at 1,000 tangents like a worried terrier." In the *Daily Sketch* Hamilton gives a vivid picture of G.K. in this debate.

"To hear Chesterton's howl of joy," he writes, "when he twigged how I had slipped out, to see him double himself up in an agony of laughter at my personal insults, to watch the effect of his sportsmanship on a shocked audience who were won to mirth by his intense and pea-hen-like marks of joy was a sight and a sound for the gods.

"Probably Chesterton has forgotten this incident but I haven't and never will, and I carried away from that room a respect and admiration for this tomboy among dictionaries, this philosophical Peter Pan, this humorous Dr. Johnson, this kindly and gallant cherub, this profound student and wise master which has grown steadily ever since . . . It was monstrous, gigantic, amazing, deadly, delicious. Nothing like it has ever been done before or will ever be seen, heard and felt like it again."

In 1933 Chesterton turned his attention to that great figure towering above all Christian philosophers, St. Thomas Aquinas. When Shaw heard that G.K. was going to write a book on the Angelic Doctor, he wrote in glee to Mrs. Chesterton: "Great news this about the Divine Doctor. I have been preaching for years that intellect is a passion that will finally become the most ecstatic of all the passions; and I have cherished Thomas as a most praiseworthy creature for being my forerunner on this point." Others, however, felt quivers of apprehension, wondering how G.K. could treat such a subject adequately without years of research on the Doctor's voluminous writings and on the still more voluminous commentaries written by highly trained specialists who had devoted their lives to the study of Thomistic philosophy.

In an incredibly short time G.K. dictated his book. When it appeared, it astonished and amazed the experts. One of the greatest of them, Etienne Gilson, who has given two of the most famous of philosophical lecture series—the Gifford Lectures at Aberdeen and the William James Lectures at Harvard—declared, "Chesterton makes one despair. I have been studying St. Thomas all my life and I could never have written such a book." After G.K.'s death he returned to the same theme and prepared the following careful appraisal:

"I consider it as being without possible comparison the best book ever written on St. Thomas. Nothing short of genius can account for such an achievement. Everybody will no doubt admit that it is a 'clever' book, but the few readers who have spent twenty or thirty years in studying St. Thomas Aquinas, and who, perhaps, have themselves published two or three volumes on the subject, cannot fail to perceive that the so-called 'wit' of Chesterton has put their scholarship to shame. He has guessed all that which they had tried to demonstrate, and he has said all that which they were more or less clumsily attempting to express in academic formulas. Chesterton was one of the deepest thinkers who ever existed."

Some rate this the greatest of all Chesterton's books—a work of sheer genius. Multitudes who shy away from the obstruse philosophical works of the Angelic Doctor as well as from the commentaries turned out by learned specialists will find in G.K.'s unpretentious work much of the pith and substance of the thought of one of the greatest philosophers who ever lived.

Chesterton continued to turn out newspaper articles, essays, poetry, and books on an enormous variety of topics, at an amazing speed. His books are said to have passed the hundred mark, and they represent but a fraction of all his published material. Practically all his material was dictated not to a stenographer but directly to a typist. This is all the more remarkable when one remembers that his "writing" is studded with paradoxes which would normally require the greatest travail to produce. In addition to his writing, he engaged in considerable broadcasting over the B.B.C. and became one of its most popular speakers.

After his conversion G.K. remarked, "Conversion calls on a man to stretch his mind, as a man awakening from sleep may stretch his legs." This is precisely the effect which conversion had upon him: his thinking became deeper and more mature, and his style more chaste and restrained. While possessing all the old sprightliness and good humor, he is less exuberant, paradoxical and rhetorical. "He wears," observes Hugh Kelly, "his new Catholic truth lightly—that is to say, he is not hampered or burdened with it; he can move and fight with all his native agility; it is a *decus et tutamen in armis.*" The possession of the full deposit of divine truth has given a mellowness, a quiet and humble assurance and an enhanced kindliness. There is a notable gain in intellectual strength which shows itself particularly in *The Everlasting Man* and in *St. Thomas Aquinas.* Indeed, it would be difficult to conceive of him achieving his amazing penetration of Thomistic thought and philosophy if he were not in possession likewise of the faith of the Angelic Doctor: the rich source of so many insights, perceptions, and inspirations.

The master of whimsy, pun, and paradox walked close to God and in the midst of rollicking good humor achieved a remarkable charity and a genuine holiness of life. The persons with whom he engaged in stormy controversies and public debates were unanimous in affirming the kindliness and charity with which he lubricated all his divergences, disagreements, and even onslaughts. That is a feat which even a saint might envy.

His sense of wit differed markedly from that of Shaw in its lack of satire, barbs, and stabs; the fangs of his sharp logic dripped no venom; he took up the sword to slay the dragons of error and false-hood but not to wound men. Herein lies the secret of the greatest paradox which this master of paradoxes ever achieved: the paradox of becoming the most popular writer of his day, though he was constantly attacking its pet fads, fashions, and fancies; a best seller challenging its cherished ideals of progress and modernity; an acknowledged champion who espoused the religion of an unfashionable minority and upheld it in every word he spoke or wrote. The explanation of this apparent contradiction was his unfailing charity, his warm good humor and disarming kindliness.

"His criticism," says Maurice Evans, "sprang not from disgust but from love. He has that most essential quality, a real knowledge of his fellow-men, and with it an almost mystical appreciation of the common things of life . . . He might well be called the prophet and poet of the man in the street. It is this humanity which gives a solidity and sanity to all his work, which saves his mediaevalism from preciosity and his dissatisfaction from contempt. What for other writers would be an escape is for Chesterton a call to battle against corruption and heresy. From first to last, through polemic, poem and novel, he never ceases to uphold the humanity of the Cross; and we can think of no fitter title for him, nor would he desire one, than the last of the Crusaders."

Hilaire Belloc likewise calls attention to the singular lack of bitterness in G.K.'s writings. "It seems to me," he remarks, "that Gilbert Chesterton at his baptism was visited by three fairies. Two good and one evil. The two good fairies were the Fairy of fecundity in speech and the Fairy of wide appreciation. The bad fairy was struck dead as she entered the church—and serve her right. He was blessed in knowing nothing of the acerbities which bite into the life of writing men." Similar is the judgment of Frank Swinnerton: "One reason for the love of Chesterton was that while he fought he sang lays of chivalry, and in spite of all his seriousness warred against wickedness rather than a fleshly opponent."

The greatest master of paradox who ever lived, G.K. did not use paradox as a mere display of cleverness or frivolity but for the serious purpose of bringing out an aspect of truth generally overlooked. He defined paradox as "Truth standing on her head to attract attention," and the emphasis was on *truth*.

For several years Chesterton had been suffering from chronic exhaustion brought on by overwork. In 1935 his health suffered a sharp decline, and some of his intimate friends prevailed upon him to complete his *Autobiography*, which he had begun several years before. He finished it early in 1936 and the volume appeared in print shortly after his death that same year. In it he says: "So far as a man may be proud of a religion rooted in humility, I am very proud of my religion; I am especially proud of those parts of it that are most commonly called superstition. I am proud of being fettered by antiquated dogmas and enslaved by dead creeds (as my journalistic friends repeat with so much pertinacity), for I know very well that it is the heretical creeds that are dead, and that it is only the reasonable dogma that lives long enough to be called antiquated."

The Catholic faith was the one window through which he could see the supreme truths of human existence shining like stars in the sky: it furnished him with the key to the locked mysteries of the nature of man and the destiny of the human soul. It is on this note of gratitude to God for the gift of faith that he ends his *Autobiography*.

"But for me," he says, "my end is my beginning, as Maurice Baring quoted of Mary Stuart, and this overwhelming conviction that there is one key which can unlock all doors brings back to me my first glimpse of the glorious gift . . . And there starts up again before me, standing sharp and clear in shape as of old, the figure of a man who crosses a bridge and who carries a key; as I saw him when I first looked into fairyland through the window of my father's peep-show. But I know that he who is called Pontifex, the Builder of the Bridge, is called also Claviger, the Bearer of the Key; and that such keys were given him to bind and loose when he was a poor fisher in a far province, beside a small and almost secret sea."

In June Chesterton's condition became critical. Awaking from a sort of reverie, he murmured, "The issue is now quite clear. It is between light and darkness and everyone must choose his side." Monsignor Smith administered Extreme Unction and his old Dominican friend, Father Vincent McNabb, sang the "Salve Regina." This hymn to Our Lady is sung in the Dominican Order over every dying friar. How fitting it was for the biographer of the order's greatest son, St. Thomas, and the ardent suppliant of Our Lady! On the table beside the bed lay Gilbert's pen: Father McNabb picked it up and kissed it reverently. It was the sword which G.K. had wielded with such valor and chivalry in behalf of God, the Church, the Faith, and all the fundamental decencies of human life. As the words of the hymn, "And show Jesus, the blessed fruit of thy womb, to us after this exile," were echoing about him, the old warrior quietly breathed his last. It was June 14, 1936, the Sunday within the Octave of Corpus Christi, the same feast as on his reception into the Church fourteen years earlier.

When the news spread abroad the people of England were saddened, for he had won a place in their hearts. On hearing the news of his death over the radio a writer at the London *Times* exclaimed, "Good God! That isn't *our* Chesterton, is it?" "A hollow groan of grief," wrote Hugh Kingsmill to Cyril Clemens in America, "echoed that morning all over England." When Chesterton's barber heard of his passing he was heartbroken and went out from the shop, leaving his customer unshaved. Shaw wired Frances: "This makes me feel more than ever out of it. Why does he perish in the prime, whilst I lay superfluous? If there is anything I can do to help or comfort you, let me know at once, even tho it run to three figures."

In his cable the Holy Father called Chesterton a "gifted Defender of the Catholic Faith," and offered his sympathy not only to the widow but to all the people of England. They had lost their most brilliant writer, the Church had lost a stalwart champion, and the world had lost a literary genius of first magnitude. Messages of sympathy and tributes poured in from all parts of the English-speaking world. From them Frances chose for the memorial card the following beautiful tribute from Walter de la Mare, which might well serve also as his epitaph:

> *Knight of the Holy Ghost, he goes his way*
> *Wisdom his motley, Truth his loving jest;*
> *The mills of Satan keep his lance in play,*
> *Pity and innocence his heart at rest.*

ORESTES A. BROWNSON
Defender of the Faith

I. A YANKEE RADICAL

Few among the sociological, political, philosophical, and theological writers of America in the nineteenth century achieved greater eminence than Orestes Augustus Brownson. Endowed with an intellect of unusual penetration and logical acumen, he had the faculty of expressing profound thoughts and involved reasoning with a clarity and lucidity rarely surpassed. While his versatile intellect explored many fields, in some of which he blazed new trails, he was primarily a logician, and in that domain it may well be questioned if our country has ever produced his superior.

Born in Stockbridge, Vermont, September 16, 1803, of Sylvester Brownson and Relief Metcalf Brownson, Orestes was one of six children. He had a twin sister, Daphne Augusta. Two years later his father died, leaving the family in straitened circumstances. After four years of struggle to keep the family together, the mother found it necessary to place Orestes with an elderly couple in Royalton, some fifteen miles distant.

The man was over sixty and his wife near fifty: with this taciturn pair, whose chief concern was to teach him to be honest, industrious and God-fearing, the boy led a somber and lonely life. "Properly speaking," he wrote many years later, "I had no childhood . . . Brought up with old people, and debarred from all sports, plays and amusements of children, I had the manners, the tone, and tastes of an old man before I was a boy."

With no young companions, the lonely boy turned eagerly to the meager library which the elderly couple had filled with religious tomes. Among these were *The Psalms of Watts, The History of the*

Redemption by Jonathan Edwards, Davies' *Sermons*, *The Franklin Primer*, *Philip Quarles* (a novel patterned after *Robinson Crusoe*) and the Bible. "My reading," says Orestes, "was confined to these works, and principally to the Scriptures, all of which I had read through before I was eight, and a great part of which I knew by heart before I was fourteen years old." Here evidently was not merely precocity but prodigy.

The vivid imagery of heaven and hell, nourished by his reading and the gray solitude of his upbringing, colored his youthful imagination and worked itself deep into his emotions. His one diversion was reading, and it washed out the sense of loneliness. "The simple history of the Passion of Our Lord," he wrote in retrospect, "as I read it in the Evangelists, affected me deeply. I hung with delight on the mystery of Redemption, and my young heart often burned with love of our Blessed Lord . . . I was rarely less alone than when alone." It is no wonder that from the first his ambition was to become a minister.

When Orestes was fourteen, his mother brought the family from Vermont to Ballston Spa in northern New York. Here for a few months he attended the local academy, where he studied Latin and Greek, until his earnings ran out and he had to return to work. This was all the schooling he had. He secured a job at a printer's office, where he worked first as an apprentice and later as a journeyman.

At the age of nineteen he joined the Presbyterian Church and dreamed of becoming a missionary. Ballston Presbyterianism was permeated with the gloomy Calvinism of John Knox, and Orestes soon gagged at predestination and total depravity. It seemed monstrous to him that God would predestine people to sin necessarily in order that He might damn them justly. He consulted his minister about this ugly doctrine, and the latter said he hoped it would be changed at the next assembly. This confirmed Orestes in his reaction, and rather than sacrifice his belief in the justice of God, he rejected Presbyterianism, which was doing violence to his reason.

In 1823, at the age of twenty, he taught school in the neighboring town of Stillwater, and the following year left New York for a teaching post in Detroit. Here he was stricken with malaria and was convalescent a considerable part of 1825. After rejecting Presbyterianism he swung to the opposite extreme, embracing Universalism, which asserted little more than the salvation of all men and hence was chief refuge for apostate Calvinists.

In the autumn he applied to the Universalist General Convention for a letter of fellowship as a preacher: the following June he was ordained at Jaffrey, New Hampshire, and then preached at various places in New York. He renewed his acquaintance with Sally Healy, who had once been his pupil in the country school. In the following June they were married. Brownson soon became the editor of *The Gospel Advocate,* the chief publication of the Universalist society.

It soon became apparent, however, that Universalism was no more satisfying to Brownson than Presbyterianism. Placing God in a vague murky obscurity that made Him inaccessible to inquiry, it dulled the demands of reason. Its notion that punishment was merely reformatory blurred all distinction between good and evil: if punishment benefits him who suffers it, the innocent may as well receive it as the guilty. If virtue no longer has its reward or sin its penalty, then all morality is undermined. Subjected to the penetrating scrutiny of Brownson's logical mind, the creed dissolved into a few vague generalities which offered no help to groping and stumbling souls.

Thus disillusioned, Orestes turned increasingly to the advocacy of measures of social reform. Sensitive to social injustice, he was greatly impressed by the reading of William Goodwin's *Political Justice.* In the autumn of 1829 he heard Fanny Wright lecture in Utica and was captivated by her eloquence and her Utopian schemes. Soon he became a contributing editor to the *Free Inquirer,* published in New York by Fanny Wright and Robert Dale Owen. At the same time he became editor of the Genesee *Republican and Herald of Reform,* an organ of the Workingmen's party, dedicated to social democracy.

During these two years he was preaching socialism rather than Christianity, and later spoke of the years 1829–31 as the most anti-Christian period of his life. Abandoning belief in divine revelation, the divinity of Christ, and a future life, he entered the bleak dark realm of agnosticism, shivering in an agony of doubt. After a few months, however, he hearkened to the deepest promptings of his being, and his agnosticism vanished. "I have . . . a witness within," he wrote, "and having this witness, I can find its testimony corroborated by the whole of external nature."

In *Charles Elwood; or the Infidel Converted,* Brownson describes his adventure in agnosticism: it shows that his anguish came from the struggle to believe in things he found essentially unbelievable and not from the terrifying emptiness of actual doubt. Written in the form of a novel, it discloses how the hero destroyed his uncertainty, not by a burning mystical experience, but by a restatement of Christianity. "In logical accuracy," remarked Edgar Allan Poe, "in comprehensiveness of thought, and in the evident frankness and desire for truth in which it is composed, we know of few theological treatises which can be compared with it."

Leaving the Universalists, Brownson began preaching as an independent minister in Ithaca, New York, in February, 1831. In his first sermon he declared: "I do not wish to be called a Universalist. Should I assume the name of any party, it should be Unitarian . . . Unitarian discourses are most practical; their lessons inculcate charity, a refined moral feeling, and universal benevolence."

Later that year he chanced upon a sermon, "Likeness to God," by William Ellery Channing, the noted Boston Unitarian, which kindled Brownson's hitherto vague acceptance of Unitarianism into genuine enthusiasm. "You, sir, have been my spiritual father," he told Channing ten years later. The following year he applied for the Unitarian pulpit in Walpole, New Hampshire, and was accepted. Here he plunged into an intensive study of philosophy and theology, mastered French, learned some German, and gained excited entry into a whole new intellectual world. He delivered frequent sermons and Lyceum lectures and made frequent visits to Boston, where he met the leading Unitarians.

Soon Brownson was writing articles on the French philosophers and on the alliance between Christianity and social progress for such Unitarian journals as the *Christian Register,* the *Unitarian* and the *Christian Examiner.* George Ripley, acting editor of the *Register,* was much impressed by Brownson's "pithy, lucid and direct" style and saw in him an intellect that would be most valuable in reviving the Unitarian cause. With his newly acquired mastery of French, Brownson read the five octavo volumes of Benjamin Constant's *Religion Considered in Its Origin, Its Forms, Its Developments,* and found in them a confirmation of his own confidence in intuition. Thenceforth for many years French philosophy and social theory were among his chief enthusiasms.

In 1834 he was called to the pastorate of the Unitarian Church in Canton, Massachusetts, and Ripley preached the sermon at his installation. There Brownson organized a lyceum and started a library. One summer he was asked by the school committee to examine a Harvard sophomore who wanted to teach at the town school. "The two sat up talking till midnight," Ellery Channing reported later, "and Mr. Brownson informed the school committee that Mr. Thoreau was examined, and would do, and would board with him." These six weeks provided young Thoreau his first continuous association with a mature and provocative intelligence. "They were an era in my life," he wrote Brownson, "the morning of a new *Lebenstag*. They are to me as a dream that is dreamt, but which returns from time to time in all its original freshness."

In the *Christian Examiner* Brownson presented his plan for the "Church of the Future," in which Christianity became essentially a doctrine of social reform. He was working for "the progress of man and society, and the realization of a heaven on earth," as he remarked later. After two busy years in Canton, Brownson moved to Chelsea, across the Mystic River from Boston, where he would be even closer to the laboring men to whom he felt he had a special mission. In Boston he organized "The Society for Christian Union and Progress," to which he preached in the Old Masonic Temple on Tremont Street. In 1836 he published his first book, *New Views of Christianity, Society, and the Church,* as part of his campaign to promote the "Church of the Future," thus indicating that he was already looking beyond Unitarianism.

A striking figure in the pulpit, six feet two inches, slender and handsome, his black hair brushed straight back from his forehead, he impressed all with his dignity and eloquence. In discussions with his friends, however, he tended to shout and pound on the table, and confident of his mastery of logic never hesitated to halt even the Transcendentalist leaders, Emerson, Channing, and Ripley, at all doubtful points. He thus gained a reputation for contentiousness that has survived when most other things about him have been forgotten. "Brownson never will stop and listen," Emerson commented, "neither in conversation, but what is more, not in solitude."

They found him lacking in sympathy, cold, dogmatic, and domineering; Ripley alone pierced through the hard shell of Brownson's proud and haughty bearing to the lonely man within, warmed to him, and became his friend. Probably the others would have been a bit more indulgent if they had but known that the eight lonely years of his boyhood isolation and silence were now being overcompensated. Starved in the bleak and somber solitude of his Puritan foster home, those years were now having their inning, exulting gluttonously over the sound of the voice so long frustrated and suppressed. The exuberance of a lost and orphaned childhood was stealing from unplumbed psychic depths to the surface, causing tempestuous and troublesome waves.

At home Brownson was the stern husband and demanding master who looked to his wife and children for obedience before affection. As his daughter Sarah mentioned years later, he never seemed designed or intended for domestic life: even family affection seemed unable to break through the shell of his abiding loneliness. Studying for long hours, often till the wee hours of the morning, always in his swallow-tail coat, he was so immersed in his ever increasing pile of books that his family saw little of him. His lamp burned constantly, so voracious and even insatiable was his appetite for knowledge—his food and his drink.

While Brownson brought something of the rudeness of the frontier to Boston, he also brought its strength, and this was badly needed. The timid clergy were afraid to touch the burning issues of the day, and the people, bored with monotonous services which snubbed their clamorous needs, were reacting by remaining away. "A notable change," wrote Harriet Martineau, "has taken place. A strong man, full of enlarged sympathies, has not only discerned the wants of the time, but set himself to do what one man may to supply them." She was referring to Brownson's discourse, "The Wants of the Times," delivered in May, 1836, in which he declared the old churches to be failures.

"All over the Christian world," Brownson declared, "a contest is going on . . . between the people and their masters, between the many and the few, the privileged and the underprivileged." In this struggle the Church must espouse the cause of the people, for Jesus is "the prophet of the workingmen." The "Church of the Future," he declared, would combine the spirituality of Catholicism with the humanitarianism of Protestantism in a new synthesis. Protestantism, he wrote in the *Christian Examiner* was no Church, but a chaos of sects attesting the sickness of the time but containing nothing positive enough to serve as a remedy.

In the autumn of 1836 Brownson met with a half dozen of the intellectuals—Ralph Waldo Emerson, George Ripley, F. H. Hedge, Convers Francis, James Freeman Clarke, Bronson Alcott—at Ripley's home, where they formed a loose society known as the Transcendentalist Club. It met also at Brownson's home in Chelsea, and he was generally known as one of its leading members: indeed *Blackwood's Magazine* called him the coryphaeus of the group. "No one loves to break a lance with him," remarked Isaac Hecker, "because he cuts such ungentlemanly gashes."

While retaining its American flavor, the Transcendentalist movement assimilated myriad influences from Europe, and Brownson's chief contribution was as an expositor of European philosophy and social thought, and as a leader in stressing the role of religion in the solution of social problems. In contrast to Emerson, who emphasized the role of the individual and was suspicious of social reformers, Brownson underlined the importance of social institutions as a means of improving the social and economic order. In January 1838 he founded the *Boston Quarterly Review,* to which he contributed articles on literary, philosophical, and political subjects: the latter especially attracted attention throughout the country and brought him into close relations with the leaders of the Democratic party.

Although a steadfast Democrat, Brownson rejected pure democracy, called popular sovereignty or the rule of the will of the majority, contending that government by the will, whether that of a single individual or of many, was mere arbitrary government, easily verging into absolutism and tyranny. He considered constitutions, if not too readily alterable, a wholesome bridle on popular caprice; he objected strenuously to legislation for the especial benefit of an individual or a class; exemption of stockholders in corporations from liability for debts of their corporation, and tariffs to enrich the moneyed class at the expense of mechanics, farmers, and professional people.

In the July 1840 issue of the *Review* he published his article on "The Laboring Classes," in which he developed his line of reasoning to its extreme logical conclusions. He saw in the depression and panic of 1837 the beginning of an acute phase of the class war: industrialism was spawning evils worse than slavery. "Wages," Brownson declared, "is a cunning device of the devil, for the benefit of tender consciences, who would retain all the advantages of the slave system, without the expense, trouble, and odium of being slave holders."

Ridiculing the alleged freedom of the worker to choose his own employment, he pointed out that there was not even true *laissez faire,* that power had already passed to corporations. Monopoly and privilege must be abolished, inheritance of property must cease, and the laborers must be emancipated. On the positive side Brownson demanded the restoration to the worker of his dignity as a person, a return to genuine free competition, and the opportunity for every man to own his own shop or his own farm: thus will he be able to achieve economic security, without which his vaunted political equality with the rich and powerful is hollow mockery.

"Brownson's essay," says Arthur E. Schlesinger, Jr., of Harvard, "is an extraordinary performance. It is clear, direct, compelling and brilliant, written with an intensity of emotion that occasionally burns into genuine eloquence . . . On its critical side the essay is perhaps the best study of the workings of society written by an American before the Civil War. The exigencies of the day somewhat distorted the emphasis . . . The main lines of diagnosis, however, are accepted today; and the method, which no other American of the time used so well, has grown in recent years to be indispensable to social investigation."

Like Carlyle and Ruskin in England, Brownson perceived the injustices of the industrial system by which the rich were becoming richer and the poor poorer. He saw, too, that the abuses could not be eradicated merely by prayer and the enunciation of vague moral principles and glittering generalities, but only by the application of specific remedies of a social, economic, and political character. In sharp contrast was the attitude of most of his fellow Transcendentalists, whose social views were moralistic almost to sentimentality. Thus Channing addressed a group of miserably underpaid English coal miners: "Your true strength lies in growing intelligence, uprightness, self-respect, trust in God, and trust in one another. These cannot fail to secure to you your just share of social privileges." Brownson had discovered that, however admirable "uprightness and self-respect" are, they do not fill empty stomachs.

How far ahead of his time were Brownson's trail-blazing social teachings can be seen when it is remembered that neither in Great Britain nor in New England, where the factory system was developing most rapidly, had the Catholic Church yet developed any specific social program. Not until 1850 was the Catholic hierarchy restored to England, while in New England the Church was exhausting her efforts in the enormous and difficult task of providing the ever-increasing multitude of immigrants with the means of practicing their faith. By 1874, however, Cardinal Manning was stirring England with his address, "Rights and Dignity of Labor," claiming for labor "not only the rights of property but the right of unionization, the right to strike, and the right to have recourse to the civil authorities." It was not until 1891, however, that Leo XIII issued his famous encyclical, *Rerum Novarum,* on the condition of the laboring classes, giving a positive and explicit formulation of Catholic social doctrine. In retrospect Brownson stands out as a great social prophet, aglow with a prophet's vision, though in July 1840 he was but a voice in the wilderness.

The appearance of Brownson's article "The Laboring Classes" caused a great hue and cry: the Democrats were alarmed by the radical measures proposed; the Whigs reprinted the article in enormous quantities and paraded it through the country as evidence of the socialistic leanings of the Democratic high command. Van Buren, candidate for a second term as President, attributed his defeat to it. In Boston it created consternation. The horrified Channing termed Brownson's remedies "shocking" and piously declared, "No good can come but from the spread of intellectual and moral power among all classes."

The stalwart old conservative, John Quincy Adams, sniffed in his study at Quincy and angrily added "Brownson and the Marat-Democrats" to the Transcendentalists, abolitionists, and phrenologists who were disturbing his old age. In a ferocious attack on the article, the *Methodist Quarterly Review* went so far as to charge Brownson with advocating free love as well as political anarchy. Even his old friends shied away from this wild man, whose "shocking" principles were later to become the cornerstone of America's social gospel. What a penalty for the simple crime of perspicacity!

Undaunted by the unprecedented outcry, Brownson returned to the battle in the October issue with a second article on "The Laboring Classes." "We believe," he bravely declared, "property should be held subordinate to man, and not man to property; and therefore that it is always lawful to make such modifications of its constitution as the good of humanity requires." But his careful logical reasoning was lost in the bluster, froth, libel, and circus antics which characterized the presidential election that fall. Torchlight processions of hilarious crowds, carrying banners, marched through the streets, shouting "Tippecanoe and Tyler too" and singing "Little Van is a used-up man."

In the gray November dawn Brownson heard the results: Harrison 234 electoral votes, Van Buren 60. Brownson's candidate had gone down in a landslide to ignominious defeat. Disillusioned and disgusted by the manner in which the electorate had been humbugged by slogans and carried away by a song, Brownson came to see that good government required stronger guarantees than popular suffrage and the popular virtue and intelligence. No longer could he place his trust in the comfortable shibboleth, the voice of the people is the voice of God, which echoes resonantly in so many Fourth of July orations. Something was needed, he sensed, to inform, quicken, strengthen, and uplift the moral and spiritual life of the populace if their voice was to echo the voice of God.

Brownson now began to re-examine his religious position and to turn from the people to God. As his excitement over reform died down, his concern for salvation increased, and he yearned for holiness. "The hard, restless implacably honest and domineering temper of Orestes Brownson has just been greatly softened," reported J. H. Allen, "by a sudden flow of religious feeling in channels which he had thought dried up." He was losing faith in the religion of humanity, which he had heralded with such exuberant eloquence as the creed of the "Church of the Future."

In his writings there began to appear references to the doctrines of the redemption and sanctification of the race, which had long been absent. Imagine the surprise occasioned the readers of the *Quarterly* of January 1842 when they were confronted with the words: "Alas! we have seen enough of mere individual reason. It is impotent when it has not, for its guide and support, the reason of God, speaking not only to the heart, but through revelation and the traditions of the race!" Strange words these from the high priest of reason! Even history, Brownson declared, is inexplicable "save on the hypothesis of a constant intervention in a *special* manner of our ever-watchful Father." This was shocking to the sophisticates who had stripped religion of such a medieval survival as "divine providence."

Up to 1841 Brownson had watered down Christianity to its most innocuous form so that it would make as few demands as possible on the unbeliever. Such a minimizing policy now took on the aspects of desecration: the more he pared down the Christian gospel, he realized, the less reason he had to offer the agnostic to embrace it. He felt ashamed of the timid understatement in his more tepid days. More clearly than ever, he realized that religion is more than the mere projection of one's hopes and aspirations upon the frail canvas of illusion: in the act of faith man makes vital contact with the truest and deepest reality—God. Rooted in the shallow stony ground of mere humanism, his Unitarian and Transcendentalist theories lacked that contact with the divine, and now offered him no support: they were like so many reeds shaken by the wind.

From his study of Pierre Leroux, a follower of Cousin, Brownson gained the sense of hierarchy, which disposed him to look more favorably on the Catholic Church. From him he also got the doctrine of communion: man lives by communion with realities outside himself, with nature, his fellow man, and God. This took Brownson the significant step beyond the subjectivism of his earlier religious views. It suggested to him the Catholic doctrine of grace.

In developing his doctrine of communion, Leroux declared that God elevated certain men into supernatural communion with Himself. Communion with these "providential men"—Jesus, Abraham, Moses, Zoroaster, Confucius, Plato and the like—enabled ordinary individuals to achieve a higher life. This led him to focus his attention upon Christ as a "providential man" or, as he preferred to call Him, a "mediatorial man."

Profoundly stirred as he reflected upon Jesus in this new light, Brownson decided to communicate his new convictions to Dr. Channing, whose sermon had helped to restore him to Christianity ten years ago. Since man cannot by nature commune directly with God, he wrote, there must be a mediator, both God and man, who is essential to man's salvation. It is fatal to reduce this mediator to mere human nature, as was the fashion of the day.

We Unitarians, he continued, misused Jesus: "Jesus became to us a law, an abstract principle according to which man was made." In reality He is much more than this, much more "than a very exemplary sort of man, a very zealous and able reformer, whom we should do well to respect and to remember along with Plato, Alfred,

Luther and Swedenborg." In imparting divine life to His disciples —His "providential men"—He communicated it virtually to all men through the unity, solidarity, and indissolubility of the race.

Brownson concluded by presenting Channing with a dilemma. "If human nature were always what you say it is," Brownson went on, "I cannot conceive what need there was of a redeemer; if it be now what the [Calvinist] church generally affirms, that is, inherently and totally depraved, I am equally unable to conceive what the Redeemer has done . . . Christianity seems to me to assume throughout as its point of departure, man's sinfulness, depravity, alienation from God and heaven." It was Jesus the God-man, the medium of communion and mediation between God and man, whose mission is to redeem man from original sin, who opened up new possibilities of salvation.

"I think, sir," he adds, "I am able to show that the doctrine that human nature became depraved through the sin of Adam, and that it is redeemed only through the obedience of Christ; that the doctrine which teaches us that the Mediator is truly and indissolubly God-man, and saves the world by giving literally his life to the world, are the great 'central truths' of Christianity, and philosophically demonstrable."

This new realization removed the halters from Brownson's deep religious passion. "I can preach now," he continued, "not merely make discursions on ethics and metaphysics . . . I now need to know nothing but Jesus and Him crucified . . . What before was mere thought has now become love; what was abstraction has become life; what was merely speculation has become downright, living earnestness."

It was now crystal clear to Brownson that all the Transcendentalist talk about the religion of humanity, in which he had so long been detoured, was but empty rhetoric; that man cannot lift himself by his own bootstraps but needs a mediator who communicates to him divine life. This means the infusion of supernatural life into natural life: in other words, the grace of God.

Brownson published the letter in pamphlet form under the title *The Mediatorial Life of Jesus:* it is a deeply moving confession of his intense need for religious faith and of his yearning for closer personal relationship with Christ the Mediator and Redeemer. Now an old man, Channing was bewildered by the metaphysics Brownson had introduced into the letter and by his borrowings from foreign philosophers with whose writings Channing was unfamiliar. Construing Brownson's religious affirmations as simply a more vivid expression of his own Unitarianism, he welcomed what he took to be the return of the prodigal son and exhorted him to live calmly and earnestly by his present principles. "God made you," he concluded encouragingly, "for something more than to scatter random shot, although those shot may sometimes be grand ideas and may hit old errors between wind and water." Alas! he was to pass from the scene before Brownson suffered another of those changes of conviction which so distressed the venerable old man.

In his thinking Brownson was drifting farther and farther away from his Transcendentalist friends. They had established Brook Farm, a community venture, in an attempt to work out a way of life. Brownson visited there occasionally and sent his own son Orestes there: though he liked most of the individuals residing there, he could give it in all honesty but limited and halfhearted approval. He had become too religious to enthuse over their vague sputterings about the infinite and their religion of humanity. When he translated their lofty affirmations into simple language they inevitably issued in pantheism, egotism, denial of sin, or some other species of infidelity.

He had lost all sympathy with the Transcendentalist concept of the natural origin of revelation, as expressed in Emerson's well-known lines:

> *Out from the heart of Nature roll'd*
> *The burdens of the Bible old;*
> *The Litanies of Nations came,*
> *Like the Volcano's tongue of flame,*
> *Up from the burning core below,—*
> *The Canticles of Love and Woe.*

Too ruthlessly honest to give them greater praise than he thought they really deserved, Brownson contented himself by saying in an article in the *Democratic Review* that Brook Farm was good because it was simple and unpretending and intended no harm to the State, Church, family, or private property. Between the lines of faint praise, the Transcendentalists could see that their old friend was no longer enraptured over their religion of humanity and the breach between them was widening. "I will own to something of disappointment," Ripley wrote him, "that you should give us so little sympathy or recognition, when a friendly word would have been cheering amidst such a tempest of abuse as fell upon us from the conservative sky."

The stubbornly honest Brownson distinguished carefully, however, between liking persons and giving wholehearted approval to their ideas, and he could not find it in his nature to write words to which his intellect refused consent. His profoundly logical mind, his deep consciousness of sin, and his overpowering sense of the reality of God and the need of His grace rendered their starry-eyed optimism and artless buoyancy increasingly unpalatable and difficult to stomach. So great were the divergencies becoming that a complete break was only a matter of time.

At the end of 1842 Brownson merged his *Boston Quarterly Review* with the *U. S. Democratic Review* of New York, a monthly publication, of which he became a contributing editor. Thus ended for the time being the *Quarterly*, the issues of which are still a living testimony to the candor, vitality, and honesty of its editor, who wrote most of the articles himself. "Take it all in all," lamented W. H. Channing, "it was the best journal this country ever produced." For the new magazine Brownson wrote a series of articles explaining the principles of "Synthetic Philosophy" and a series on the "Origin and Constitution of Government": the latter he rewrote more than twenty years later and published under the title, *The American Republic*, a profound analysis of the principles underlying our government. The doctrines developed in these articles stirred quite a furor and brought complaints from the editor. Discontinuing his connection with it, Brownson again undertook the publication of his own magazine under the new name, *Brownson's Quarterly Review*.

As Brownson's belief in a personal God increased in vigor and vividness, so too did his conviction that, in Newman's words, "since there is a God, the human race is implicated in some terrible aboriginal calamity. It is out of joint with the purposes of its Creator." As original sin carried with it the necessity of grace, involving the infusion of supernatural life into the life of the soul, Brownson perceived the need of a more specific theology to explain these basic realities of the spiritual and moral life. He found himself in agreement with Pascal that the true religion "must give us an explanation of our opposition to God and to our own good. It must teach us the remedies for these infirmities, and the means of obtaining these remedies." The explanation must be definite and detailed, not mere vague assertions about man's proneness to sin and God's providential care and loving kindness. "Brownson's faith grew so powerful," says Schlesinger, "that he finally rushed to the Christian epic of sin and redemption, deeply grounded in the experience of the ages and magnificently realized in Catholic theology."

He perceived that grace must have a channel, and this obviously must be the Christian Church, but he had not yet concluded that this meant specifically the historic Mother Church of Christendom —the Catholic Church. Having little acquaintance with Catholics or Catholic literature, Brownson shared the typical New England prejudices against the "Scarlet Woman" of Rome. The Catholics of that area were for the most part Irish men and women of the working class, who had emigrated from a country in which they and their forefathers had suffered centuries of persecution for the faith and had been denied the opportunity of any but the most elementary schooling.

Nevertheless, his study of the writings of Saint-Simon familiarized him with the idea of hierarchy and thus helped to lessen his distrust of the papacy. Recalling the troubled days of the Tyler administration, he yearned for the deep and serene faith of the Middle Ages and their profound sense of social interdependence. In a series of lectures on the Middle Ages in the winter of 1842–43, he condemned anti-Catholic feeling and called for a new Catholic Church to interpret a universal faith for the modern world, as Rome had done for the Middle Ages. He was favorably impressed by the scholarly lecture of Bishop Hughes of New York on the "Importance of a Christian Basis for the Science of Political Economy."

Fascinated by the ideal of reuniting Christendom on a truly catholic basis, he wrote a series of articles on "The Mission of Jesus" for the weekly journal, the *Christian World*. His purpose was to draw attention to the Church as the medium through which the Son of God redeems mankind. He found himself led by inexorable logic to the disconcerting conclusion: the Catholic Church is the living body of Christ. So shocking was the conclusion that the editor refused to publish the final article.

Yet Brownson still drew back from taking the fatal step. He

seemed to be experiencing the conflicting emotions characteristic of the third stage of conversion, which Chesterton described so vividly: getting so close to the truth as to feel its magnetic pull along with the terrifying and panicky feeling that despite one's effort to resist and even to escape, he is past the point of safe return. The deep ingrained prejudices of forty years were not, however, to be uprooted in a day. While the passage from one Protestant sect to another seemed little more than going from one apartment to another in the same house, entrance into the Catholic Church was a different matter: a break with the whole world in which he had lived and a venture into a new and strange realm from which there is meant to be no return. The commitment is irrevocable.

"To the Protestant mind," he wrote, "this old Catholic Church is veiled in mystery, and leaves ample room to the imagination to people it with all manner of monsters, chimeras, and hydras dire . . . To enter it seemed to me like taking a leap in the dark; and it is not strange that I recoiled, and set my wits to work to find out, if possible, some compromise, some middle ground, on which I could be faithful to my Catholic tendencies without uniting myself with the present Roman Catholic Church . . . Undoubtedly they who are attached to the Roman Catholic fragment have the advantage; but we should labor . . . to effect in the surest and speediest manner possible the reunion of all the fragments, and thus restore the body of Christ to its original unity and integrity."

Brownson's Romeward tendencies became increasingly clear to his friends. "He seems tending toward the Catholic Church," remarked Theodore Parker to a friend. "God bess him, wherever he is! He has a hard head." That hard head Brownson now turned to the difficult and desperate task of finding a way in which he could be faithful to Catholic principles without actually joining the Catholic Church. He planned to proclaim Catholic doctrines within the gates of Protestantism with a view of bringing about the peaceable return of the rebellious sects to the Mother Church.

After disclaiming his intention of becoming a Catholic, Brownson nevertheless told the readers of his *Review:* "I am free to confess that I accept the general theory of that Church as the true theory of the Church of Christ." She may become the nucleus of a reorganization that will ultimately absorb all other communions into herself "because the vital principle, the organic force of the Church, is the indwelling life or Spirit of Christ." Brownson will labor and pray for the reorganization of the Christian world so that it will really be one in spirit, faith and discipline.

"I am neither Protestant nor Romanist," he says, ". . . I look upon Protestantism as a blunder, and as having proved a decided failure . . . In laboring for the rehabilitation of the Church, and for the union of all men . . . we must accept and obey the Law of Continuity."

He declares his acceptance of the Church as the body of our Lord and as the divinely appointed medium of individual and social regeneration and progress. "In this," he acknowledges, "I shall have for enemies the worldly wise, the selfish, the unbelieving, and the indifferent . . . But I shall not be alone; I shall be only one of the still mightier army of the faithful, and shall be encouraged by the saints and the martyrs of all ages, whose prayers I dare invoke, and dare believe will be effectual with the Great Head of the Church, to whose service I have been consecrated, and to which I would consecrate myself anew, and without reserve."

When Isaac Hecker read these words he perceived that Brownson was largely sparring for time until his emotions would permit him to translate his belief into action. Then the awkward compromises, which his present inner perplexity and turmoil had erected, would disappear. Tracing out the logical implications of Brownson's initial premise with an implacability worthy of his master, Hecker wrote in a letter to his mother on May 9, 1843:

"If you grant that the Roman Catholic Church is the true Church, there is, to my thought, no stopping-place short of its bosom. Or even if it is nearest to the truth, you are under obligations to join it. How any one can believe in either one of those propositions, as O.A.B. does, without becoming a Catholic in fact, I cannot conceive. This special pleading of exceptions, the necessity of the case, and improbable suppositions, springs more, I think, from the position of the individual than from the importance or truth of the arguments made use of. Therefore I think he will give up in time the ground upon which he now supports his course—not the object but his position."

In these anguished days young Isaac was one of the few friends to whom Brownson could turn for sympathetic understanding of his gropings, for Hecker was going through much the same experience. In their discussions before Brownson's fireplace in Chelsea and in the parlor at Brook Farm each stimulated the other in his quest for truth.

Indeed that had been Brownson's primary pursuit for most of the last twenty years, and it was the activity he loved best.

"Truth," he wrote, "is [the mind's] object, and it seeks and accepts it instinctively, as the new-born child seeks the mother's breast . . . Place the mind and truth face to face, with nothing interposed between them, and the truth evidences itself to the mind . . . The assent termed knowledge follows immediately from the joint forces of the intelligible object and the intelligent subject . . . Whenever the truth is immediately present, and reason looks it full in the face, it knows that it is truth without further evidence." This was the idea that Dryden had expressed in *The Hind and the Panther,* the poem in which he defended his Catholic faith.

> *For truth has such a face and such a mien,*
> *As to be lov'd needs only to be seen.*

Brownson's eloquent plea in the January 1844 issue of his *Review* for the restoration of the Church of God in all its unity and catholicity brought him a well-reasoned letter from an anonymous Philadelphian. It struck a solar-plexus blow that made Brownson reel and stagger. It read: "How can you, who so powerfully appeal to the 'fact of eighteen hundred years,' set aside the historical view by which alone you get at that fact? History teaches you . . . that the Church of God is and has been through eighteen centuries. To history I appeal to show what it is . . . and where it has been . . . The inner life of the Church no history can touch—it is a thing of experience and experience only. But the organized life of the one Body has been seen, heard, looked upon, and handled, from the day of the Apostles until now."

Then the writer took Brownson to task for ignoring the continuous functioning of the Church and her organization. "Your theory of development is wrong," he wrote. "Most truly you assert a continuous inspiration. But of what kind? of addition? No; but of living breath, of vocal utterance, of articulate expression of the one, unchangeable, changeless, Eternal Word . . . Go on, Sir, in your outspoken zeal; but beware of speaking without searching further . . . Believe all you do of the Church's life and work; but neglect not her *organization.*"

The nameless correspondent told Brownson what he desperately needed to be told: "Stop looking to a hypothetical future to find a

Church stamped indelibly with the marks of unity, catholicity and apostolicity; open your eyes and you will see it not only in all the other countries of the world but at your very door." In the April issue Brownson with characteristic honesty admitted the gist of the writer's contention and squirmed uncomfortably in trying to explain why he was still outside such a Church.

"We were addressing ourselves to old friends," he said, "to show them that entire submission to the Church . . . demands no surrender of individual freedom of thought or conscience . . . We raised the question of the *Nature and Office of the Church,* stated it to be the paramount question of the day; but we did not undertake to answer it . . . Our real purpose was to show, 1. That, throughout Christendom, there is a strong tendency to return to the unity and catholicity of the Church; 2. That to effect this return, it is necessary to take up the great question of the Church itself; 3. That this question may be taken up and discussed in the freest and fullest manner, in any and all of our professedly Christian communions; 4. That the answer, the germs of which each sect may find in its present faith . . . once obtained, all particular communions will be destroyed, by being absorbed in the Catholic communion."

Then Brownson stated explicitly the two facts which he thought were implied in his previous article: "1. That men have broken away from the Church because they have lost the sense of its profound significance; and, 2. That the recovery of this sense, that is, the full understanding of the true nature and office of the Church, will bring them back to the one Catholic communion, because the moment they come to perceive . . . they must perceive that a Church not one and Catholic, can be no Church at all . . . The Church has never lost its unity and catholicity, for it cannot lose them without ceasing to be the Church of God . . . The reform we demand is never of the institution, but of the individuals. We believe in no Church that can ever need reforming."

What about the correspondent's claim that Brownson was overlooking the Church as an organization? Brownson saw that he could not stop short of recognizing the Church as an organization and he now went all the way. "We do not overlook the Church as an *organization,* for the Church in any other sense, is to us no Church at all. The Church is an organic body . . . under one visible as well as invisible Head, with one common center of life, out from which through communion, flows the life to all its members. We may indeed recognize . . . the grand communion of saints; but this is not what we mean by the Catholic Church. The Catholic Church is a divinely instituted body to prepare us for admission into this glorious company of saints. Like the Gospel net it gathers all, good and bad; for we come into it, not because we are sanctified; but that through its ministries, we may be sanctified. Through its ministries, Christ, who is its head, its life, and its efficacy, works for our redemption from sin, and reconciliation with the Father, and our practical holiness."

The Philadelphian had rendered Brownson a providential service: he pulled him up short, caused him to open his eyes and look around and see the Church which was and had been reconciling sinners to God for eighteen centuries and bore upon her brow the indelible imprint of her divine Founder. It is a pity that the correspondent's name has never come down to us, for he did his work well, and doubtless his name has been written by the recording angel in the Book of Life.

There could be little doubt now as to where Brownson was heading. Letters poured in from his old Transcendentalist friends and from ministers of many denominations seeking to deter him from the fatal step. Some professed to see benefits in disunion: the rivalry between the sects promoted religion, the competition prevented any sect from gaining a preponderance. Irritated at such a line of reasoning, Brownson remarked, "It is as though the Christian Church were a disease in the social body, and, since we cannot expel it altogether, we must prevent the concentration of the virulence on any one point."

On March 11, Brownson wrote to Hecker: "My own feelings and convictions, in spite of my struggles to the contrary, carry me to the Catholic Church, and I foresee plainly that I must sooner or later become a member of it. There is no help for it. I seek, however, to maintain my position for the present."

Why was Brownson seeking to maintain his "position for the present"? Hecker was later to supply the answer: "[Brownson] was occupied in working out that problem philosophically and for the universe. I was looking out for number one . . . He told me once that he was like the general of an army born in rebellion, and his duty was to carry as many back with him to the true standard as he could."

In the April issue Brownson postulated the necessity of a Church as the only means of social reform. Archimedes, the Greek physicist, declared he could lift the world if he were provided with the proper fulcrum: this dynamic law applied likewise to the moral universe, and to secure effective action there must be provided a divinely established fulcrum; the Church of the living God. "Either," he said, "there is already existing the Divine Institution, the Church of God, or there are no means of reform."

The walls of the fortress outside the Church, in which Brownson had taken refuge, were beginning to crumble under the sledge-hammer blows of his own inexorable logic. He was now profoundly convinced that Christ was not only a wise teacher and a far-visioned reformer as he, along with most of the other Transcendentalists, had envisaged Him, but was also truly divine. The Scriptures tell of His choosing Apostles, tutoring them with great care, choosing a leader among them, authorizing and commanding them to teach in His name His life-giving truths to all nations with the assurance that He would be with them all days "even unto the consummation of the world."

Thus did Christ found His Church, the members of which were to be members of His own body, wherein they would be nourished with His divine life. That great institution had been fulfilling her divine mission for nearly fifteen centuries before Protestantism saw the light of day: at her bosom had been fed all the nations of Europe. Brownson looked about him and saw that she was still carrying out her divinely appointed task. Yet, curiously enough, he was outside. Why? Didn't he believe in Christ? Wasn't he concerned for his own salvation? These were the anxious thoughts to which he now gave utterance.

"More and more," Brownson relates, "I was dissatisfied with myself. My position, asserting the Church, and the necessity of communion with her, as the condition of living the life of Christ; and, yet, living aloof from all communions; belonging, in fact, to no Church, struck me . . . as anomalous, nay, as untenable. Was I living the Christian life myself? . . . Suppose I die before I have effected the reunion of Christendom—what will become of my soul?

I am engaged in a good work; but, what if I become, myself, a casta-way? Here is matter for serious thought."

The more Brownson reflected upon his position, the more clearly he perceived how untenable it was. Of what use were all his words pleading for a reunited Christendom? Do not actions speak louder than words? Was he not contradicting his words by his example? These were the thoughts which now gave him no rest.

"How can I," he asked himself, "consistently ask the obedience of others while I refuse my own? Rewards and punishments are personal, and meted out to men as individuals, not as collective bodies. There is, then, but one rational course for me to take, that of going to the Church, and begging her to take charge of me, and do with me what she judges proper. As the Roman Catholic Church is clearly the Church of history, the only Church that can have the slightest historical claim to be regarded as the body of Christ, it is to her I must go, and her teachings, as given through her pastors, that I must accept as authoritative for natural reason."

He is frank enough to reveal that the thought of doing this for one who had been so deeply immersed in Protestantism all his life was not a peasant one. "But," he adds, "to be eternally damned would, after all, be a great deal unpleasanter."

Accordingly, with fear and trembling, yet with firmness of purpose, in the last week of May 1844 Brownson called on Bishop Fenwick of Boston, a Marylander and a Jesuit. The prelate had been reading the *Review* and had noticed that Brownson was approaching the Catholic position, save for his views on the papacy.

"What," asked the bishop, "can be your objections to the pope?"

"I do not object to the pope," Brownson replied. "Some time ago I was foolish enough to say that the problem of the age is Catholicism without papacy; but I no longer entertain that notion. The Church without the pope would be to me no church at all."

"Why then," inquired the bishop, "are you not a Catholic?"

Brownson explained that he would be one except for not wanting to declare Protestants all wrong and without the possibility of being saved.

"God is just," said the bishop, "and you may leave your Protestant friends in His hands. If they break the order He has established, that is no good reason for you to remain where you are and to neglect to make sure of yourself."

The prelate was wise in refusing to win Brownson by watering down dogma. Upon reflection, Brownson admired Fenwick's uncompromising stand, which had the relentless character of his own reasoning, and he decided it was high time to make certain of his own salvation: the logic of God, he regretfully concluded, is inexorable.

Brownson was not slow in making his position amply clear to his readers. In the July *Review* he repudiated his old religious liberalism: "We have demolished hell; scouted the devil; laughed at the fall; reduced the Son of God, first, to a promising Hebrew youth, who was a successful mesmeriser, and, finally, to a mythic personage, created by the creeds and fancies of men; we have, moreover, successively disrobed God himself of His justice, His truth, His sovereignty, His paternity, His providence, at last of His personality, and resolved Him into a blind force, or a mere fate or irresistible necessity. And in all this we have been guilty of no heresy . . . have been, in fact, good, true, faithful, enlightened, liberal Christians, the reformers of the church and the restorers of primitive Christianity!"

In another article "Church Unity and Social Amelioration" in the same issue Brownson sternly confronted his friends with the only two alternatives open to them. "Do, then, take some position: either accept the Son of God, or reject Him; either accept the church as it is, or reject it altogether. For if it has become corrupt, it is a false church, was always a false church, and always must be a false church; and if it be not corrupt, but the true church, then to refuse to accept it is to refuse to submit to God . . . Our logic allows us no alternative between Catholicism and Come-outerism. But we have tried Come-outerism." In New England at this period the so-called "Standing Order," the old Puritan political and religious polity, was breaking up. Those who would not patch up the old order, but who wanted something new, were called "Come-outers."

After a few more visits Fenwick turned Brownson over to his young coadjutor, Bishop Fitzpatrick, Boston born and educated at Montreal and by the Sulpicians at Paris. The instructions started off with a minimum of rapport between the two: the instructor had the impression that his neophyte was "proud and conceited." Hecker, who had consulted the bishop about his own difficulties, throws some light upon the situation. He says that Fitzpatrick had "a native ability far above the ordinary . . . his knowledge did not embrace the intellectual trend of the present age nor take in the signs of impending changes among men outside the Catholic Church."

When Hecker had called upon the bishop he expected to be asked, "What truths were the steppingstones that led you here?" Instead, his mind was probed for the errors it might still contain. Such a mode of procedure was, Hecker thought, especially inappropriate in Brownson's case, "for he was one who had come into possession of the full truth not so much from hatred of error as love of truth." In the account of his conversion, written thirteen years later, Brownson makes, however, the following gracious and magnanimous reference to Bishop Fitzpatrick: "He was my instructor, my confessor, my spiritual director, and my personal friend, for eleven years; my intercourse with him was intimate, cordial, and affectionate, and I owe him more than it is possible for me to owe to any other man. I have met men of more various erudition and higher scientific attainments; I have met men of bolder fancy and more creative imaginations; but I have never met a man of a clearer head, a firmer intellectual grasp, a sounder judgment, or a warmer heart. He taught me my catechism and my theology; and, though I have found men who made a far greater display of theological erudition, I have never met an abler or sounder theologian."

The difficulty Brownson encountered was not in accepting the Church's doctrines—having accepted her authority to teach, he accepted her doctrines without question—but in his instructor's attitude and method. Evincing no interest in the difficult, boulder-strewn path by which Brownson had come to the Church's threshold, Fitzpatrick put his brilliant neophyte through the routine course of instructions and simply ignored the Transcendentalist theories and views as so much highfalutin nonsense. That was a day when the psychology of conversion and techniques of instructing converts were unwritten chapters in the pastoral theology textbooks used in our seminaries.

With his customary vigor Brownson applied himself to the study of Catholic theology: He admired its definiteness and its well-reasoned character and found it meeting the deepest needs of his mind and heart. It did not need the brilliance of an expositor to make it glow with truth and beauty: it reflected the wisdom of the divine mind from which it stemmed. Upon the completion of the course of instruction, Brownson was received into the Church by Bishop Fitzpatrick on October 20, 1844.

When Hecker learned that Brownson had started taking instructions, he took the same step and was received into the Church two months before his friend. Soon afterward his wife Sally and all the children, except Orestes who was away at sea, entered the Church together. When Orestes returned home he was at first so shocked that he went to live with some relatives in Ohio. After a short time, however, he entered the Jesuit college at Cincinnati to complete his interrupted education, and there he was baptized by Bishop Purcell.

Brownson's brother Oran, who had gone West and become a Mormon, returned for a visit in 1851. He and Orestes had long talks about religion. George Parsons Lathrop gives a vivid picture of the scene. "Oran," he wrote, "would put a question, which Orestes would answer with uncompromising, unsparing force. Then Oran, without saying a word, would dart out of the house and walk a long time in the hot sunshine; after which he would return and put another question. The same process was repeated: Oran still making no rejoinder. When this odd dialogue ended, there was no summing up: Oran went away in silence. After nine years, during which the brothers had not met again, Oran wrote to Orestes that he had become a Catholic. From Dublin, Ohio, he had gone to Dublin, Ireland, where he was received into the Church." It is probable that if Orestes Brownson could have seen more of Daniel and his sisters, the same thing would have happened to them.

Commenting in later years on his own conversion, Brownson attributed it to the grace of God. "Faith is not of ourselves, it is the gift of God, and conversion is the work of grace, not of argument or logic." Arthur M. Schlesinger, Jr., professor of history at Harvard, has written a carefully documented life of Brownson. After tracing the long and devious path by which the pilgrim reached the Church's threshold, he concludes: "When Brownson embraced Catholicism, he abandoned not reason, but the pride which exalted individual reason above the accumulated experience of mankind and raised private intuitions above the study of objective reality. He chose the wisdom of the ages as the guide to life in the place of his own unsteady desires, which had thus far always misled him. He believed profoundly in God, in morality and in logic; and he was passionately eager to combine the three in one final whole. If God were more than human illusion, it must refer to absolute truth."

Then he tells how Brownson found his three convictions amply fulfilled in the Catholic Church: "Brownson's reason, his sense of good and evil, his faith in reality and in its ineffable Creator were superbly justified and consoled in Catholic theology. But theology, intellectual awareness of the truth, was not sufficient. Brownson desired to *live* the Christian life—to love God, obey the moral law, and find the truth. He needed grace, and grace came alone through the Church, which was the authoritative expounder of God's word on earth, the only institution with an intrinsic relation to the truth. Catholicism absorbed Brownson's three convictions into a full and rigorous system, which satisfied alike his head and his heart."

In 1872, four years before his death, Brownson recalled the details of his conversion with great vividness, and remarked: "The question with me came not in the shape, What shall I believe? but in this other shape, What shall I do to be saved? . . . I came to the question of the church as a sinner in need of a Savior . . . I never sought the truth; it came to me . . . and I believed as the child believes the father or mother, and for thirty years have never doubted."

II. WARRIOR OF MANY BATTLES

When Brownson's Romeward tendencies had become apparent to his old associates, Thurlow Weed voiced the thought of many of them when he said, "He'll wreck whatever he anchors to; and I hope it's the Roman Catholic Church." That prophecy was never fulfilled, for Brownson had at last found the truth and the whole truth, for which he had been searching so long and so intently. Contrary to the opinion of many, Brownson had not shifted his position and transferred his religious loyalty because of any inherent instability of character, but because of his honest and fearless refusal to cling to a viewpoint or a creed once he discovered it to be erroneous. "To live is to change," said Newman, "and to be perfect is to have changed often." Consistency of viewpoint from youth to old age is usually the mark of unprogressive minds.

The record of Brownson's beliefs, as he worked his way from the gloomy rigorism of Calvinism through the latitudinarianism of Uni-

versalism and the de-Christianized humanitarianism of Unitarianism
to Catholicism, reads like a catalogue of the popular fads, fancies,
and heresies of the day. Back of all that sloughing off, however, was
the relentless drive of an inordinately penetrating mind in passionate
quest of truth. "Without seeing clearly this passionate love of truth
in him," said Hecker, "it is, I think, hardly possible to understand
him."

Thus did the disciple who knew him best penetrate to the heart
of the psychological problem presented by Brownson's myriad
changes of conviction. It is that inexorable ruthless persistent quest
for logical coherence and unalloyed truth which alone provides an
underlying consistency to the vagaries of his earlier life, which puzzled, amused, and irked his friends so much. His shifting antics are
vividly depicted in the *Fable for Critics* by James Russell Lowell,
who failed, however, to discern the purpose behind them:

> *He shifts quite about, then proceeds to expound*
> *That 'tis merely the earth, not himself, that turns round,*
> *And wishes it clearly impressed on your mind*
> *That the weathercock rules and not follows the wind;*
> *Proving first, then as deftly confuting each side,*
> *With no doctrine pleased that's not somewhere denied,*
> *He lays the denier away on the shelf*
> *And then—down beside him lies gravely himself.*

Up to his conversion Brownson had been not only in the main
stream of American Protestantism but also one of its outstanding
leaders. He knew that mind in all its vagaries as did few others:
he was at the peak of his fame and influence. He knew that by embracing the faith of an unfashionable and despised minority, he
would be forfeiting the coveted position he had won by his years of
writing and lecturing. Yet he did not hesitate, once he was convinced of the truth of the Catholic faith. He had, however, to earn
a livelihood to support his large family. To what new field would he
turn? He was already an authority on constitutional theory and he
thought of becoming a lawyer: a profession which would be useful
if he entered politics.

Indeed Harvard would have done well to have hearkened to the
advice of the French philosopher Cousin and have secured Brownson for its chair of philosophy. In the spring of 1838 Charles Sumner

wrote excitedly to Justice Story, then a member of the Harvard Corporation, about "a remarkable conversation" he just had with Cousin in Paris. The philosopher was "very anxious with regard to the professorship at Cambridge" and strongly recommended Brownson, "whom he thinks one of the most remarkable persons of the age, and wishes to be placed where he can pursue philosophy calmly, thinking his labors will redound to the advance of science throughout the globe." It is not likely, however, that the governing board troubled themselves even to look into the qualifications of a man who was holding a job in the customhouse under George Bancroft, and who hadn't had even one year of formal schooling.

Bishop Fitzpatrick told Brownson not to put his light under a bushel and urged him to continue his *Review* in order to give the Catholic faith a hearing among the Transcendentalists, Protestants, and intellectuals, to whom it was but little known. In this way he could disavow his previous erroneous views and bring Catholic principles to bear upon the questions of the day. The idea was indeed laudable, but Brownson, a neophyte in the Church, with no formal training in philosophy or theology, was unprepared for such a formidable task.

Despite his misgivings, he yielded to the bishop's insistence and became, as Daniel Sargent remarks, "a defender of the Catholic faith, its champion in the printed word, two months after his conversion, without even a spiritual retreat in which to collect his thoughts." Under the bishop's direction Brownson began an intensive study of St. Thomas, St. Augustine, and the manuals of scholastic philosophy. Wearing a scapular, and with a crucifix and a statue of the Blessed Virgin on his desk, he worked till sundown, when he arose and recited the Rosary. For some time he also followed the practice of pious meditation according to the rules of Ignatius Loyola.

With his former uncertainties and frustrations washed away, Brownson entered with characteristic vigor and enthusiasm into a new and deeper spiritual life. "Our life," he said, "begins with our birth into the Catholic Church." With the removal of his former tensions, he became relaxed with the peace and joy of a good conscience flooding his soul; his gauntness disappeared and he took on weight. Militantly proud of his faith, he championed it on every occasion with a truculence which dismayed many of his co-religionists. Thus when he was in the office of the publisher of his *Review*, a Mr.

Hoover made a slurring remark about Brownson's new faith. Where-upon Brownson seized him by the coat collar and the seat of his trousers and threw him over a stove into the corner.

That action was typical of the aggressiveness with which he be-gan in the *Review* to champion his faith; he analyzed and refuted errors with devastating logic. He sought to destroy, in Schlesinger's words, "all the strongholds between atheism and Catholicity, where Protestants might seek shelter." His writings echoed not only with the conviction of intense belief and certainty but also with hostility to all who differed from him. Whereas before his conversion he had written with the moderation of an earnest seeker after the truth and the open-mindedness of a man prepared to find it anywhere, he now wrote with the stern intransigence of one who had entered the temple of truth and was intent upon chastising all who stubbornly remained outside. To make the metamorphosis still more complete, he frequently expressed himself in the newly acquired terminology of scholastic philosophy with which his non-Catholic readers were unfamiliar.

Imagine their dismay at the transformation which had taken place in so short a time. "Is this our old friend Brownson," they asked, "shouting at us in such intemperate and savage language? What has become of his moderation and restraint, of his patient understanding of our groping for truth? Does he think that he can browbeat us with logical syllogisms and scathing abuse into his new spiritual house-hold?" "It would be impossible," remarked Rufus Griswold, "to link his former opinions with his present ones, by any connection, either logical or psychological."

In all this Brownson was betraying the excessive and riotous zeal which so often characterizes the new convert. How much of his man-ners and methods is to be attributed to him and how much to Bishop Fitzpatrick, his instructor and the censor of his *Review,* is difficult to decide. Both Isaac Hecker and Brownson's son, Henry, place much of the responsibility upon the bishop.

"He was switched off the main line of his career," wrote Hecker, "by the influence of Bishop Fitzpatrick, who induced him to enter upon the traditional line of controversy against Protestantism at a time when the best minds of New England had long given up belief in the distinctive errors of that heresy . . . Had he held on to the way inside the Church, which he had pursued outside the Church in finding her, he would have carried with him some, and might perhaps have carried with him many, non-Catholic minds of a leading character . . . What Dr. Brownson was best able to do he was not called upon to do enough of." Regardless of where the responsibility may be, it is abundantly clear that the neophyte had been requested to undertake a difficult and delicate task, for which he was not, nor could he be expected to be, adequately prepared.

It is probable that on many issues Brownson considered it his duty to present not his own ideas but the thought of his bishop. Futhermore he was too recent a convert to be sufficiently aware that the full acceptance of the teaching authority of the Church still leaves ample room for differences of opinion in the realm of prudential judgments. "Having experienced the need of authority," he explained in 1862, "having suffered more than we care to repeat for the lack of some infallible teacher, we thought, and could think, only of asserting authority in season and out of season."

Another circumstance that may partly explain the militant tone of much of Brownson's writing at this time was the timid, apologetic attitude of many Catholics who wanted, not controversy, but simply to be left alone. Only a decade previously a wild mob had burned the convent at Charlestown to the ground. Even while Brownson was under instruction in Boston, there occurred in Philadelphia an outburst of mob violence in which several Catholic churches were destroyed and a number of Catholics wounded and killed. In the efforts to bolster the morale of Catholics and to elevate the standards of the Catholic community, Brownson sought, as he says, to encourage "a firm and bold profession of their faith, and an independent and fearless, though quiet, assertion of their rights as Christians, as citizens, as men."

Whatever may have been their effect upon Catholic morale, there is no doubt that his method was not calculated to win converts. Years later, in 1856, in a letter to Father Hewit he acknowledges that his approach was mistaken. "My own conviction," he wrote, "is that our true policy in dealing with the American mind is to study first to ascertain, not its errors, but the truth it still maintains, and to show it that that truth can find its unity and its integrity only in the Catholic Church . . . My own method, I believe, is the worst of all, that of logic."

How true! Yet logic remained, for weal or for woe, the chief instrument which Brownson used in intellectual jousting all his life: it reflected the distinctive quality of his mind and, of course, acquired additional formidableness through constant usage. With all his logic, relentless and inexorable though it was, Brownson never seemed to perceive with sufficient vividness and compelling force that one may crush an opponent with the sledge-hammer blows of logic and leave him still unconvinced, and the more he is overwhelmed, humiliated, and hurt by such tactics the more recalcitrant and obstinate he becomes.

Man is not a mere logic machine, but a creature moved as much— or more—by his heart as by his head. The failure to embody in his writings and lectures this basic psychological insight, so important for all engaged in persuasion and conversion, lies at the heart of both Brownson's failure to win the number of converts which might have been expected from his prodigious intellectual endowments and of his unfortunate facility in stirring enmities through rubbing people the wrong way. One can't escape the conviction that Brownson would have profited from the reading of a book such as Dale Carnegie's *How to Win Friends and Influence People,* with its stress on the role of the feelings in the reactions of people to whatever is presented to them. Simple, elementary, and obvious though this principle may be, it can be ignored with impunity by neither the Fuller Brush salesman nor the philosopher. And Brownson ignored it plenty: it was a tactlessness which exacted a heavy toll throughout his life.

This does not mean, of course, that Brownson did not know in an abstract theoretical sort of way that the emotions exercise great influence upon thought and conduct, nor that he was unaware of Pascal's famous saying, "The heart has its reasons of which reason knows nothing." Indeed in *Charles Elwood* Brownson had written, "As a general rule, would you gain the reason, you must first win the heart." Such was the lip service he gave to this principle, of which, however, he rarely showed any practical recognition. It was more honored in the breach than in the observance.

Unlike Newman, who made St. Ambrose's famous saying, "It is not by dialectics that God was pleased to save His people," the lodestar of his writing apostolate, Brownson clung to the sledge hammer of ruthless logic. It was this unconquerable propensity which caused even such an admirer as Hecker to say of him, "He *defeats* but will never *convince* an opponent."

Of such crucial importance is this point in the understanding of the success and failure which Brownson experienced as a champion of Catholic thought that we think it worth while to present the testimony of an additional witness. Theodore Maynard made an exhaustive study of Brownson and his work, and in his excellent biography he brings out this characteristic of Brownson with unmistakable clarity. He speaks of his "harsh and forbidding" treatment of opponents. Instead of showing these earnest but confused persons that what they were fumbling for was to be found in its fullness in the Catholic Church, Brownson said to them in effect, according to Maynard:

"This is what the Church holds. I will now demonstrate it so clearly that even your thick wits will be able to grasp it. But if you do not accept it to the last iota, you will understand that you are headed straight for hell." This is not a good way to win converts or even dispose people favorably toward the faith.

In spite of Brownson's knock-down-and-drag-out manner of presenting his case, he wielded no small measure of influence among the intellectuals. They recognized the flaming sincerity and the remarkable genius of the plain-spoken warrior who called a spade a spade and scorned all camouflage and compromise. Influenced by his example, William J. Davis and George Leach of Brook Farm, as well as Sophia Ripley, followed him into the fold. Even George Ripley seemed for a while to be nearing it, but then he shied away. Brownson even had a respectable following among European intellectuals. "This man *astonishes* me," Father Glover, a scholarly English Jesuit in Rome remarked in 1845; "He is clear and strong beyond compare; that is the most masterly refutation of Kant I have ever read. I think God has raised him to hunt down and destroy the absurd principles now in vogue in politics, in philosophy, and in religion; but his very greatness makes me fear for him; for unless he be solidly grounded in humility, the success, which so great power applied to teaching the truth assures him, will turn his head, and make him forget he has all from God, and none from himself. May he remember that there have been Origens and Tertullians as well as Augustines."

Newman's conversion, just a year after Brownson's, started a renaissance of Catholicism in England: his followers in the Oxford

Movement viewed with intense interest what seemed like a similar movement in America. "Your name is well known to the students," wrote W. G. Ward from St. Edmund's in 1847, "and they have lately ordered your *Review* to come regularly to them." Six years later the interest in Brownson had become great enough to compel a British edition of the *Review*.

Brownson looked somewhat askance, however, at the Tractarians and all their quibbling about a *via media*. With no established Church, like the Anglican, to mediate between Protestantism and Catholicism in America, men were either for the Church or against it, and Brownson's writings tended to confirm such definite and un-equivalent attitudes. His distaste for what he regarded as the quib-bling methods of the Tractarians became vocal when he attacked their distinguished leader.

While in retirement at Littlemore, John Henry Newman had writ-ten *An Essay on the Development of Christian Doctrine*, which he permitted to be published shortly after his conversion in 1845. "Mod-ern Catholicism," he wrote, "is nothing . . . but the legitimate growth . . . of the doctrine of the early church." This growth was a manifestation of inherent vitality. "An idea," he continued, "grows in the mind by remaining there . . . All great ideas are found, as time goes on, to involve much which was not seen at first to belong to them." Even Christ had told His disciples, "I have yet many things to say to you, but you cannot bear them now."

This point of view infuriated Brownson, who thought it cut at the foundations of the faith once for all delivered to the saints. The Ox-ford scholar did not maintain that anything needed to be added, or could be added, to the original deposit of faith, but only that the complete comprehension of that deposit called for time and the operation of the Holy Spirit. Hence the development was in the *minds* of the believers rather than in the *matter* of the dogma itself. This represented, pointed out Newman, "a real progress of the Church in her own apprehension and understanding of the sacred deposit of faith committed to her charge."

With the belligerent orthodoxy of a new convert, Brownson rushed in to demolish Newman's thesis. "The Church," he declared, "has no natural history, for she is not in the order of nature, but of grace." The Church, he continued, "denies that she has ever added a new article to the primitive creed." Newman had written that "time is necessary for the comprehension and perfection of great ideas." Brownson pounced upon the word "perfection" as implying a development of the doctrine itself, while Newman had used it to indicate a development in the *understanding* of the doctrine. Indeed all that the Oxford scholar was trying to bring out was that the original deposit of divinely revealed truth "is not and cannot be taken in all at once by the human mind."

He did not deny that it had been *implicitly* held by the Church from the moment of its foundation, but maintained that this did not necessarily imply it had been held *explicitly* and with full envisagement of all its far-reaching implications. It is a profound and subtle distinction which was forced upon Newman's mind as he studied the formulation of doctrine in the writings and sermons of the early Greek and Latin Fathers and Doctors and compared such formulations with those of the Church in his own day. For this piece of historical research Newman was equipped as were few scholars in the English-speaking world of his day. A profound master of Latin and Greek, he had read the writings of the Fathers at least three times, as W. G. Ward was to tell Brownson, before setting to his task.

It was this profound research, lasting over many years, which helped mightily in making crystal clear to Newman that the Catholic faith in the nineteenth century was substantially, essentially, and in all its basic dogmas identical with the faith of the Church of the first four centuries. This was the path which led him into the Church and he felt that path would be useful to many other scholarly truth seekers. It was this belief which prompted him to publish the book after his own conversion.

"It is the general pretext of heretics," he says in the book, "that they are but serving and protecting Christianity by their innovations; and it is their charge against what by this time we may surely call the Catholic Church, that her successive definitions of doctrine have but overlaid and obscured it." Hence he undertook the task of accounting historically for these definitions by showing they were simply the drawing out in explicit form of what was already implicitly contained in the original deposit. The work has eminently fulfilled Newman's purpose in writing it, as it has served as a beacon light showing thousands of sincere truth seekers where they can find today, in all its pristine purity and integrity, the faith of Christ, of the Apostles, and of the Fathers.

When Brownson rushed into the attack he was armed with little more than a convert's belligerent zeal and his virtuosity in logic: of patrology he knew virtually nothing, and without Newman's mastery of the classics could never hope to approximate his eminence in this field. With characteristic tactlessness and indelicacy he accused Newman of having written a Protestant book. Back of this headlong assault lay a deep-seated dislike for the whole Oxford school, whom he delighted in calling "ex-Puseyites." He resented their Oxford manner, cultured air, and alleged "insular arrogance."

His son Henry tells us that Orestes "rarely, if ever, reviewed a publication by the converted Puseyites without finding more or less fault with it," and that he always read them with a presumption against them. In the colloquialism of our day, "They had two strikes against them when they came to bat." "Our Tractarian friends," wrote Brownson, "brought up to look upon contemporary Catholics as an ignorant, feeble, cunning, credulous and superstitious set of mortals, far inferior in learning, talent and morals to themselves, and accustomed to regard the scholastics as dealing mainly in vain subtleties and distinctions without a difference, very naturally passed from the study of their jejune Anglican theology to the study of the Fathers, whom they were forced to read through the spectacles of their more famous Anglican divines. They thus not only had not the requisite preparation for studying them, but had views and habits which wholly unfitted them for studying them, with even passable success." This, of course, was grossly untrue, and shows that Brownson was using, though perhaps unwittingly, his famous virtuosity in dialectics chiefly to satisfy his prejudice. It was surely unworthy of him.

Though deeply pained by the unprovoked attack, Newman did not reply. W. G. Ward came to his defense, however, in the *Dublin Review*, protesting against the "extreme injustice and cruelty" of Brownson's assault. Cardinal Wiseman likewise upheld Newman, getting from Newman the reply, "I have not allowed Dr. Brownson's rudeness to annoy me, yet it is a very great satisfaction and comfort to receive such an assurance as you have written to me." Nevertheless Brownson continued intermittently to attack Newman and his book, writing in his *Review* enough articles on this general subject to fill several volumes.

The controversy involving two of the leading converts of the English-speaking world was distressing to most of the American bishops, and some of them sought to divert Brownson from this issue. "I want to beg you," wrote James A. McMaster, a Catholic journalist, reflecting their mind, "to let alone that unfortunate topic, which has done you more hurt, and in more ways than you know of." Brownson's assault on Newman damaged likewise the prestige of the *Review* by making it seem the organ of a particular philosophical school instead of the Catholic Church. For a few years he left "Developmentism" alone, but in 1852 he lost his temper over a work by John Morris, another Oxford convert, and launched a full-scale attack upon the Tractarians, accusing them of intellectual dishonesty and castigating Newman for viewing questions narrowly instead of comprehensively.

At bottom Brownson was infuriated over Newman's assumption that a differently constituted mind might perceive truth through a different form, congeries, or array of evidence and that a whole series of converging probabilities could issue into a certainty. Brownson argued that such a line of reasoning rendered objective certainty impossible, stripped knowledge of its guarantees, and struck at the foundations of religious faith. In this contention he was not entirely without a following.

Newman followed his *Development of Christian Doctrine* with *A Grammar of Assent,* in which he begins with premises acceptable to an agnostic and gradually rises to belief in God and the Catholic religion. Distinctively Baconian, it avoids abstractions and metaphysics, and focuses attention upon the problem of concrete affirmation, its motives in fact and its relation to the personality of the individual. This was a previously unexplored province of apologetics, while the objective reasons for assent had held the spotlight: it might be called the casuistry of belief. To the treatment of his subject Newman brought a deep psychological insight and a subtlety of expression that matched his penetrating analysis.

He stressed *implicit* logic, varied and converging proofs, and an assent that was a vital, distinct, and determined act, instead of a mere mechanical echo of the syllogism. Here the will, which in Brownson and in many other schools of thought was sacrificed to formal intellect, recovers its power, and genius and common sense are justified. This does not mean that pure logic loses its rights, or that truth is merely "that which each man troweth," but that the moral being affords an indispensable premise to arguments bearing on life, and an influence of the pious disposition (*pia credulitas*) in leading to the act of faith is clearly recognized.

To Newman the reason by which men guided themselves was *implicit* rather than *explicit*, but it was reason nonetheless. God reveals Himself in conscience, and apologetics, to be persuasive, should address the individual: real assents, no matter how multiplied, are each single and *sui generis*, so that even a universal creed becomes in this way a private acquisition. The author labored over his treatise for years, writing some portions of it as many as ten times. Its general description of the concrete act of assent has weathered the critical scrutiny of scholars for a century and seems destined to remain the classic in its field. It is one of the most profound and penetrating analyses of the grounds and motives of assent ever written, and provides an unsurpassed picture of the role played by the intellect, will, emotions, and feelings in arriving at the final act of assent in belief.

Lacking Newman's dialectical subtlety and psychological penetration, Brownson found the work incomprehensible. He threw up his hands in despair, unable, as he remarked, to make head or tail of it. Despite the severe attack which he had made on Newman in 1852, which pained the Oxford scholar grievously, Newman extended an extraordinary offer to his scolding American critic toward the end of the following year, when he was appointed rector of the new university in Dublin: an invitation to accept one of the chairs in the university. It shows the remarkable magnanimity of the man and his willingness to recognize the exceptional intellectual endowment of the rambunctious, self-educated "logic-chopper," even though the whole grain of Brownson's mind differed so diametrically from his own.

The subject suggested was geography, but Newman indicated that under that nominal heading Brownson would be free to lecture about a variety of subjects. "Viewed under its different heads, as physical, moral and political," wrote Newman, "it gives scope to a variety of profound philosophical speculations." He concluded with, "You are the first person to whom I have applied." After Brownson still demurred on geography, Newman wrote to reassure him. "It has struck me," he said, "you would not be disinclined to take the chair of Philosophy of Religion, or the evidences of Christianity . . . Would not the subject you mention of *Civilization* come into it, without going into the subjects of theology or metaphysics, which, as I have said, the bishops will reserve for ecclesiastics?"

Lord (then Sir John) Acton, then a young man of twenty, supplemented Newman's invitation with an enthusiastic letter urging Brownson to accept. "You alone," he wrote, "can prepare us for the great controversies by founding among us a school and arming it with the principles of a sound philosophy . . . Your intercourse will be as an infusion of new blood in many places in Dublin, in London, in Paris, and in other places." This appointment for the fall of 1854, which would have made Brownson a member of a faculty embracing Döllinger, Newman, and other great scholars of Europe, was, however, nipped in the bud.

After receiving Newman's invitation Brownson incurred the widespread antagonism of the Irish in this country and abroad. On August 23 Newman had to write him: "I am urged . . . now for the first time, in quarters to which I cannot but listen, to ask you whether it would be inconvenient to you to postpone your visit here, on the ground of some offense which happens to be taken *just now,* in America, and, I believe in Ireland, at something you have lately written." Whereupon Brownson wrote to say it would be advisable for him not merely to postpone the appointment but to decline it definitely. Newman replied that he was not going to announce a definite refusal, for he still hoped that when things had quieted down, Brownson would be able to come. Meanwhile he would not fill the professorship.

It was undoubtedly a grievous disappointment to Brownson, who would have achieved international recognition and enhanced prestige from the appointment. It was all the more trying, as it came at a time when he was thinking of leaving Boston, which the Irish were making too hot for him. The magnanimous action of Newman was not, however, without its effect upon Brownson. In his letter asking Newman to accept his declination of the invitation, Brownson made a complimentary reference to Newman's *Loss and Gain* and adds:

"If I had seen that work at an earlier date, many things which I have written concerning you and your friends, the Oxford converts, would never have been written . . . Forgive me, Reverend Father, whatever injustice I may have done you, and ask them in my name to forgive me also. Believe me, I was moved by no personal considerations, but thought I was only doing my duty."

We have detailed at some length the relations between these two champions of the faith because it brings out striking contrasts in their methods of approach to problems, in their characters, dispositions, and in the whole topography of the thought worlds in which they lived and from which they looked out upon the phantasmagoria of passing events and the objective realities of the external world.

This brings us to the storm Brownson had caused in the summer of 1854, which led to the withdrawal of his appointment. In the role of defender of the Church, Brownson undertook to answer the charges of the Native Americans in their new guise as "Know-Nothings." In the July issue of the *Review* he published an article, "The Native American," in which he commended the spirit of nationality but repudiated the methods of the so-called Nativists. At the same time, however, he rebuked the newcomers for their alleged failure to accept the American nationality and for perpetuating their own foreign manners and customs.

He reminded the Irish, so "sensitive to remarks derogatory to their national characteristics," that they ought to accept the fact that "whether it be for good or for evil, the American nationality is and will be determined by the Anglo-Saxon portion of our population." The refusal of immigrants to conform was "the secret of the native American hostility to foreigners naturalized among us." Conceding that the Native American feeling was to some extent anti-Catholic, he traced this largely to the resistance of the immigrants, largely Irish Catholics, to assimilation—an abuse of American hospitality.

Passing from such generalities, he got into still hotter water. After remarking that the Irish had often been vilely slandered, he went on to discourse about "a miserable rabble . . . a noisy, drinking, and brawling rabble," and then seemed to support the Nativist charge by observing that the Irish, because they never considered the laws of England legitimate, frequently lost their respect for all law. Irish Catholics, clinging to their Irish ways and manners, had created in the American mind the conviction that Catholicism was incompatible with Americanism and were thus doing the Church a disservice. "The more prominent we make the Irish nationality," he wrote, "and the more we identify it with Catholicity, the more do we confirm the prejudices of the American people against our religion."

In all this Brownson meant well, and there was, of course, an element of truth in what he said. In all probability he intended no disparagement of the Irish—later in the article he speaks highly of them—but his presentation was tactless and needlessly offensive. Furthermore his assumption that the type of American to whom the Irish should conform was the *Anglo*-American, betrays a failure to appreciate two significant facts: the type would change as the population changed, and the Irish themselves would help mightily in changing and enriching that type with their own distinctive qualities of mind and heart. With the streams of immigrants from all the countries of Europe already pouring into America, it should have been evident that no one ethnic group would constitute the standard type: he is a replica of all.

His article stirred a hornet's nest. The Irish were infuriated: they considered it uncalled for, disparaging, and insulting. They had suffered persecution for the faith for centuries, and here was a Yankee newcomer lecturing them on what was dangerous for the Church. Even a people less sensitive than the Irish would have been incensed. The warmheartedness which normally characterizes the Irish in friendship and repose was suddenly transformed into a cyclone of indignation and rage which swept across the Atlantic to the homeland.

In reviewing an Irish novel, Brownson had, moreover, commented on "the voice of bombastic orators and ignorant editors, turning even Irish virtue and nobility into ridicule." The "ignorant editors" took up the cudgels at once. "Since Mr. Brownson's conversion to the Catholic faith in 1844," wrote one, "he has been treated with remarkable forbearance by Catholic editors," and they immediately set out to remedy that distressing condition. In July and August at least nine Catholic journals took him to task for insulting honest immigrants and kindling anti-Irish feeling. In most cases the censure was voiced with the unrestrained violence and bitterness typical of the maddened Hibernian. "Hell hath no fury like a woman scorned"— or an Irishman enraged.

So great was the uproar that many Catholics wondered if he could any longer be regarded as the spokesman of the Catholic Church on public issues. Bishops and priests of Irish origin or descent were deeply hurt. Newman was forced to act by the repercussions of the storm in Ireland. Even Brownson's friend, John McCaffrey, the president of Mount St. Mary's College, felt impelled to warn him: "I'm afraid that, touch the Irish as you will, unless you tickle their vanity, you will stir a hornet's nest . . . Their nationality is intense, touchy, suspicious, unreasoning, morbid—as irritable and as easily hurt as a patient with inflammatory rheumatism."

Brownson was aghast at the intensity and extent of the reaction. He was caught between two fires. While trying to defend Catholics against the attacks of the Nativists, he was caught by the fire from his own side—the enraged Irish. The outcome was not happy. "I own," he wrote to F. X. Weninger in September, "I have lost some of my first fervor with regard to a portion of the American Catholic body. They have so misrepresented and denounced me, and are so ready to seize every opportunity to blacken my character, that I do not feel that lively confidence in them that I did . . . [But] I love the Church more and more every day."

The task that the well-intentioned Brownson had assumed was far too delicate for him—and for most others. Accustomed to forthright and even blunt language, Brownson's forte was certainly not the exquisitely fine art of getting across suggestions and corrections, not only without ruffling feelings, but even making the recipients appreciate them. Perhaps St. Patrick or St. Francis of Assisi could have accomplished the difficult task, but Brownson was far from being either one.

During the decade that had elapsed since his conversion Brownson had, however, accomplished much. In a clear, firm, manly tone he had spoken out on virtually every issue of importance, and in general he had reflected Catholic thought faithfully and ably. The issues of the *Review* during this period show that there was scarcely a notable work on philosophy, politics, sociology, literature or religion, which did not come under his skillful analysis and generally competent appraisal. So able and intrepid was his defense of the Catholic faith that the bishops of the United States assembled in Plenary Council at Baltimore in May 1849 took the unprecedented action of sending him a letter of encouragement and approbation, which he proudly carried on the inside cover. Partly as a consequence of this unique recognition, and in spite of the controversial character of much of his writing, the *Review* had a larger circulation than in 1845. In April 1854 Pope Pius IX sent him his apostolic benediction for his work.

In 1854 Bishop Fitzpatrick was in Europe and Brownson's articles were censored by a substitute. Upon the bishop's return, however, Brownson did not resume the practice of submitting his articles. The resulting tension between them, combined with the antagonism now shown toward him by many of the Boston Irish, prompted him in October 1855 to follow Hecker's suggestion that he move with his *Review* to New York. It was not long, however, before Brownson was having difficulties with his new ordinary, Archbishop Hughes. The latter had looked askance at Brownson's articles on the spiritual and temporal power published the previous year, and he had written to Brownson about them.

Despite this fact Brownson published in 1856 his article, "The Mission of America," developing the thesis, later presented at the close of *The American Republic* (1865), that America has a providential destiny "far higher, nobler, and more spiritual" than the "Manifest Destiny" usually spoken of—"the realization . . . of the Christian ideal of society for both the Old World and the New." The implication that a new type of leadership was necessary for the Church in America irked the archbishop, who advised Brownson to stop agitating the question of Americanizing the Church.

During this period Archbishop Hughes had to contend with the nationalistic movements of the various races in his cosmopolitan see, each of whom wanted a German, a French, an Italian, an Irish church for itself: topping all these now was the Americanist movement. As a shepherd of the universal Church, Hughes sought to tone down all these factions and have them realize that they were members not of a national but of a supranational institution. Hence his opposition to Brownson's constant harping on the need of Americanizing was nothing personal, but was necessary to preserve the unity and catholicity of the Church. Brownson felt hurt, however, by the archbishop's attitude and moved to Elizabeth, New Jersey, to be under a different bishop.

In article after article Brownson stressed the importance of distinguishing between Catholic tradition and the tradition of Catholics, and pointed to the danger of confusing "what is of religion and what pertains only to the social life, nationality, or secular habits, customs, and usages of Catholics." He did not hesitate to declare that many Catholics were "not up to the level of the Church," but were "merely men of routine, creatures of the traditions and associations inherited from their ancestors, and which they seldom ever dream of distinguishing from their religion itself."

During the period from 1860 to 1864 his sympathies were increasingly with the European Catholic thinkers whose political and social views were liberal. It seemed to be part of the new apologetic method he was using, namely, stressing his Americanism in the face of what he regarded as reactionary elements in the Church at home and abroad. His theory was that he could thus make Catholicism less objectionable to the majority of his countrymen, while at the same time he would open the eyes of the Catholic immigrants to all their rights and privileges as Americans.

Not content with airing these liberal views, Brownson began to censure Scholastic philosophy as ill-suited to cope with the pressing philosophical problems of the day. In addition, influenced by Gioberti, he began to philosophize in a way that brought upon him the charge of ontologism. Hence it can be seen why his theological, political, and social views were viewed with suspicion in certain quarters. His article, "Rights of the Temporal," was interpreted by some of his critics as minimizing the temporal power of the Church. As a result, his writings on the subject were delated to Rome, but Cardinal Barnabo gave Brownson an opportunity to explain his thought more clearly. When no grounds for censure were found the matter was dropped.

Brownson's real ambition was to make Catholicism a creative and revivifying influence in every field of contemporary thought and activity. He viewed with great sympathy the efforts of certain Catholic European reviews, such as Montalembert's *Le Correspondant* and *The Rambler* with which Newman was associated, to achieve the same objective. Like Newman, Brownson might be called a moderate liberal, but he never for a moment defended religious liberalism. In his article, "Lacordaire and Catholic Progress," he wrote eloquently of the work of Montalembert, Lacordaire, and Ozanam and declared himself their ally.

"How often," he wrote of Lacordaire, "have we heard him traduced, denounced as a radical, a Jacobin, a socialist, concealing the *bonnet rouge* under the friar's hood. Yet he persevered, held fast to his integrity, held fast to his convictions, and continued on in the line of duty marked out for him, unshaken and unruffled, calm and serene . . ." Stirred by Montalembert's description of the Catholic renaissance in France, Brownson said: "Our own country presents a fair and open field for this *renaissance*, for the union of religion with civilization, and that new Catholic development which will restore to the Church the nations she has lost, give her back the leadership of human intelligence, and secure her the willing obedience and love of mankind."

Brownson was one in spirit with all these farseeing scholars and their objectives, and it was one of the great tragedies of that period that they were too often silenced for their errors instead of being given the positive direction they were seeking. In a letter written in 1882 Newman speaks with regret of "what might be called Nihilism in the Catholic body and in its rulers. They forbid, but they do not direct or create." To those words, Brownson could surely say "Amen." He was denounced by the ultraconservatives for his liberal views at this period, while Newman, a more moderate and restrained controversialist was denounced in Rome, and even delated to the Holy See, as "the most formidable agent of Catholic Liberalism in England."

Brownson wrote many articles on the relation of Church and state, a thorny subject at best, as the type of government varies so enormously. In five successive issues of the *Review* Brownson developed the doctrine that obedience to the state is justified only when it means obedience to God. As a corollary to the supremacy of the spiritual over the material, of God over man, he maintained that the Pope had the right—not to depose a prince—but to decide when a prince had forfeited his right by acts of outrageous tyranny. This sounded much like raising in the nineteenth century the long-outmoded academic question of the Pope's deposing power, and raising it at a time when the Know-Nothings were attacking the Church as an alien institution which menaced the rights and liberties of American citizens.

Brownson's articles alarmed many of the bishops, who thought they were doing the Church a serious disservice. As a result, Archbishop Kenrick of Baltimore wrote to Brownson early in 1855, pointing out that his articles were being "brought forward to prove that we profess principles at variance with our civil duties." He suggested that it would be well for the editor "voluntarily" to remove from the cover of his *Review* the letter he had received from them in 1849. "Your own prudence," he wrote again twelve days later, "will dictate the best course to be adopted to meet the effort which is made to convert our letter of encouragement into approval of every sentiment or view which you may express." This was followed by a letter from Bishop O'Connor of Pittsburgh peremptorily requesting that his name be withdrawn. There was nothing for Brownson to do but to remove the letter.

When the issue of slavery came to the fore, Brownson's devotion to the Union prompted him to support Lincoln and the Republican party in 1860: throughout the Civil War he was an ardent and able defender of the Union cause. In 1864 he decided to support General John C. Frémont for the presidency, but when he suddenly withdrew from the campaign, Brownson was left stranded. "My *Review* died of Frémont," he wrote. "I stopped it because I had sacrificed my position, and had no party to fall back upon." In addition, Brownson was now in poor health, his eyesight was failing, and his two sons were recently killed in the war. Disheartened and discouraged, he ended the *Review* with the October 1864 issue.

Brownson planned a series of volumes, with the material to be drawn largely from the *Review*, which would give systematic expression to his thought on important subjects. Only one such volume, *The American Republic* (1865), was brought to completion. He was prevented from completing the others by the numerous articles he was now contributing to the *Catholic World*, the newly established *Ave Maria* at Notre Dame, and the New York *Tablet*, to the latter of which he was a regular contributor.

Having been an editor so long himself, however, he was none too happy over the revisions to which some of his articles were now being subjected. Just before her death in 1872 his wife urged him to revive his own *Review* and this was all that was needed to trigger Brownson's own inclination into action. In the first issue of the *Review* revived in 1873 Brownson declared, "What is most needed in these times . . . is the truth that condemns, point-blank, the spirit of the age, and gives no quarter to its dominant errors." In this conservative tone Brownson carried on the *Review* for three years, but his best work had been done.

After the final number of the *Review* was finished in the autumn of 1875, Brownson left Elizabeth, New Jersey, to live with his son Henry in Detroit. For years he had been suffering from the gout, and toward the last he had such difficulty in holding the pen in his crippled hand that he was obliged to dictate his articles. After moving to Detroit he was able to complete but one article, "The Philosophy of the Supernatural." The extraordinary physical and intellectual energy which had sustained him through so many years of writing and of lecturing waned rapidly.

On Holy Saturday his friend, Father Hennaert, heard his confession and on Easter Sunday he received the Last Sacraments. At dawn the next morning, April 17, 1876, while the prayers for the dying were being said at his bedside, Brownson breathed his last. He was buried from St. Anne's, the first Catholic church he had ever seen—fifty-three years ago. Ten years later his body was transferred to the crypt of the university church at Notre Dame: here it lies in the middle aisle in an atmosphere of tranquillity and peace, in sharp contrast to the storms and tempests which marked his life.

On the marble slab over his tomb has been carved the epitaph: *Hic jacet Orestes A. Brownson qui veram fidem humiliter agnovit, integram vixit vitam calamo linguaque ecclesiam ac patriam fortiter defendit, ac licet morti corpus abierit mentis opera supersunt immortalia ingenii monumenta*—"Here lies Orestes A. Brownson, who came humbly to the recognition of the true faith and devoted his entire life to the valiant defense, by voice and pen, of Church and Country. Although his body has gone down into the dust, the works of his mind stand as everlasting monuments to his genius."

As we gaze each morning upon the university students who walk over the marble slab as they go up to receive Holy Communion, we find ourselves occasionally wondering: To how many of these students does the name Brownson mean anything? Could any name a single book or article he wrote? How many have ever stopped to decipher the inscription over which they walk so nonchalantly? The name which a century ago was on everyone's lips is now rarely heard; the scarred veteran of a hundred intellectual combats has faded from the minds of men. The twenty volumes of Brownson's *Works*, containing the articles that appeared in the *Review*, have long since been out of print. So, too, are the three large volumes, *Early Life, Middle Life*, and *Latter Life* in which his son Henry tells the story of his father's eventful and turbulent career.

Yet his thought lives on in the minds of others. He made important contributions to the cultural and religious life of his day, and each generation is the debtor of the past. The stern, vigorous, relentless logic of his mighty intellect served as a much needed currycomb to scrape away much of flamboyant folly and specious fallacy from the thought of his day. Indeed probably no writer wielded such intellectual influence in so many fields of American life and thought in the thirty-year period from 1840 to 1870; the period when America was coming of age. The perusal of the six thousand letters and documents in the famous Brownson Collection—the chief documentary source of his life and work—in the archives of the University of Notre Dame reveals the amazingly large number of persons, prominent in many fields, who were in correspondence with him.

Like other great thinkers of the past, Brownson lives today through the immortality of influence, and that influence is wholesome and good. A small number of scholars widely scattered throughout the English-speaking world still delight in immersing themselves in the sea of his collected works and find in it endless refreshment and a stimulation rarely encountered elsewhere. Father William J. Bergin, C.S.V., a professor of philosophy and an unusually penetrating thinker, who was closely associated with us for many years, always maintained that there was no discipline more calculated to develop rigorously logical thinking than the daily reading of this inexorable master.

Alvan S. Ryan, associate professor of English at Notre Dame, brought out in 1955 *The Brownson Reader,* containing selections from Brownson's articles in many fields, with helpful notes in each section. Published by P. J. Kenedy and Sons, this book is well suited to give readers an insight into Brownson's logical reasoning and lucidity of expression, and thus enable them to know at first hand the real Brownson.

Writing in the *American Catholic Quarterly* for July 1876, Dr. Corcoran paid the following tribute to Brownson: "His *Review* is a rich mine, which will never lose its value for the student of controversial theology, of Christian philosophy, and Christian politics. His style, based on the best English models, gives an additional charm to all he wrote. He stands out certainly unsurpassed, perhaps unequalled, by any of our countrymen in his masterly handling of the mother tongue. But the beautiful workmanship is as nothing compared to the glorious material which it adorns. It is like the mantle of gold which enwrapped the matchless Olympian Jove of Phidias."

In the *Catholic World* for June 1876 Father Hewit, C.S.P., who knew Brownson well for twenty years gave the following appraisal of his friend: "In his calibre of mind we think Dr. Brownson may be classed with those men whose capacity is only exceeded by a very small number of minds of the highest order of genius. Intellect, reason, imagination, and memory were alike powerful faculties of his mind, and his great weight of brain, with a corresponding nervous and muscular strength, made him capable of the most concentrated, vigorous, and sustained intellectual labor. Within the scope of his genius there was no work, however colossal, which he was not naturally capable of accomplishing. His gift of language, and ability of giving expression to his thoughts and sentiments whether original or borrowed, was even greater than his power of abstraction and conception, and his style has a magnificent Doric beauty seldom surpassed, rarely even equalled."

While paying tribute to Brownson as a valiant champion of the faith, a versatile genius, and especially a master of rigorous and relentless logic, we think the record shows that he suffered badly, as do so many men of genius, from a want of practical prudence. The timing of many of his articles left much to be desired, and he had a curious tactlessness which led him into many unnecessary antagonisms, which did neither him nor his cause any good. Valor is an admirable virtue, but without prudence in its use, it occasions its possessor many needless bruises and wounds. A fair appraisal of Orestes Augustus Brownson, it seems to us, must steer between the Scylla of the adulation that styles him "America's greatest philosopher" and the Charybdis of the depreciation which dismisses him as a wild radical who was constantly shifting his position.

That his intellectual endowments were prodigious few will deny: that the obstacles which hemmed in the adequate development of those talents were enormous is equally clear. That he attained such scholarly eminence in spite of the almost complete lack of formal education—his attendance at school was estimated at only a few months—is a staggering feat. One can scarcely refrain from the fascinating speculation of the eminence he might have achieved if he had had the educational advantages of Newman, and had enjoyed the lifelong association of great scholars who would perhaps have rubbed off many of his angularities, given him a balance, and helped him to concentrate in one field. What a prodigy in philosophy, political science, economics, or theology he might have become!

That he climbed over so many barriers by the sheer force of his mighty intellect is sufficient evidence of his genius, and the influence of his thought upon other minds has enabled him to achieve a longevity rarely granted to those who spread themselves over so many fields. He was a valorous warrior and a formidable thinker and richly deserves a place of honor among the giants of the faith.

ISAAC HECKER
Modern Apostle

I. "ERNEST THE SEEKER"

Prominent among the men who have left the distinctive imprint of their thought and ideals upon the Church in America is Isaac Thomas Hecker. The friend and disciple of Orestes Brownson, Hecker has been in all probability a more potent and abiding influence than his more learned and gifted master. Convert, mystic, missionary, and author, Hecker displayed a rare insight in sensing the need for a more apt and appealing presentation of the Catholic religion to fit the peculiar genius of the American people and to meet its distinctive needs and aspirations. The founder of the Missionary Society of St. Paul the Apostle, our most distinctively American community, Isaac Hecker touches the religious life of our nation at many salient points today: through his spiritual sons he sparks the Church's effort to bring the fullness of divine truth to the millions of our churchless fellow countrymen. Indeed some writers have referred to him as an American Cardinal Newman and to his apostolic labors the great oratorian himself paid tribute.

Born in New York on December 18, 1819, Isaac was the youngest child of John Hecker, a native of Wetzlar, Prussia, and Caroline Freund of Elberfeld, Prussia. John Hecker had emigrated to this country in 1800, while Caroline, who was fourteen years his junior, had come as a babe in the arms of her parents in 1796. John professed no religious faith, while Caroline had been reared a Lutheran, but shortly after her marriage she became a Methodist and remained a fervent member until her death in September 1876.

Mrs. Hecker was a woman of strong character, devout nature, and of a sympathetic and cheerful disposition. From her, Isaac derived his marked individuality, and he was bound to her by the deepest affection. After marriage John Hecker opened a brass foundry which for a time prospered. Isaac had one sister, Elizabeth, and three brothers, John, Henry, and George: the last was slightly less than two years older than Isaac, and between these two there was a singularly strong attachment which remained through life.

The atmosphere of the Hecker home was one of affection and harmony, the difficulties of one becoming the generous concern of all. When in later years John became a High Church Episcopalian and Isaac and George became Catholics, the spirit of family unity and affection remained unaffected. A neighbor once remarked to Mrs. Hecker that she could not be reconciled to her daughter's conversion to Catholicity. Whereupon Mrs. Hecker replied, "I would not change the faith of my sons. They have found peace and joy in the Catholic Church and I would not by a word change their faith if I could."

While the father had marked mechanical ability, he seems to have been rather easygoing and somewhat unstable; the mother's influence was paramount and she assumed the leadership of the home, with the oldest son John managing the business affairs. With kindness but with firmness Mrs. Hecker governed the household, and the children yielded cheerful and unquestioning obedience. Her two youngest sons never smoked. "Mother forbade it," recalled Isaac, "and that was enough for George and me."

She had the knack of rewarding her children with marks of affection and rebuking them with signs of displeasure without resorting to force. "The severest punishment she ever inflicted on me," remarked Isaac, "was once or twice to tell me that she was angry with me; and this so distressed me that I was utterly miserable, sat down on the floor completely overcome and so remained till she after a time relented and restored me to favor."

Like his mother, Isaac was deeply sincere and did things with all his heart: he knew no halfway measures. Energetic and resourceful, Isaac strove never to allow obstacles to stand between him and his goal. He was not always sure of his objective; but once it was fixed clearly in his mind, he showed marked persistence and determination in his struggle to achieve it.

Shortly after the yellow-fever epidemic swept New York in 1822 Isaac came down with confluent smallpox. For a while it looked as if the sickness would prove fatal, and so the mother told him of the danger. "No, Mother," replied the sick child, "I shall not die now. God has a work for me to do in the world and I shall live to do it." His reply was almost identical with that of Cardinal Newman as he lay sick and apparently dying at Leonfort in Sicily. It was only the later years which showed how important was the work which God had in store for both of them. Though Isaac recovered, the disease left his face pock-marked and his eyes weakened, requiring him from the time he was twenty-one to wear glasses.

Isaac loved to visit the clock shop of his grandfather, Engel Freund, next door to his home. Here he would converse in German with the kind and friendly patriarch as he watched him assemble the parts of a clock. Before the old man died Isaac could proudly display a clock he had made; the twelve-year-old boy presented it to the church attended by the family, where it ticked faithfully for forty years until it was accidentally destroyed by fire. A normal, healthy boy, Isaac entered into the games of his playmates, shouting and laughing as loudly as the rest. In later years he was fond of recalling a little verse which he and his companions used to sing as a kind of gathering call:

> *Boys and girls come out to play,*
> *The moon does shine as bright as day;*
> *Come with a whoop, come with a call,*
> *Come with a good will, or don't come at all.*

Isaac attended the public school in Chrystie Street, where, in accordance with the custom then prevailing, the Bible was read daily. On Sunday he went with the family to the Methodist church on Forsyth Street, and was instructed in the fundamental doctrines of that creed, either during the regular services or in Sunday school. As the father's foundry business suffered reverses, Isaac was able to attend school for only about six years before being obliged to go to work to supplement the family income. When about thirteen Isaac got a job with the publisher of a Methodist newspaper, *Christian Advocate and Journal,* and later went to work in a brass foundry.

By this time his two brothers, John and George, had learned the bakery trade and opened their own shop, where Isaac joined them. With a pushcart he delivered the bread to the homes of customers and watched the ovens; then he learned to make yeast, mix the in-

gredients, and knead the dough; before long he had become a skillful baker. As business prospered, the brothers opened additional
shops and branched into the milling business: this was the beginning of one of the outstanding present-day milling concerns, Hecker,
Jones, Jewell Company.

The lot of the worker at this time was not an enviable one: his
workday extended from seven in the morning till six in the evening.
The wages were meager, commonly less than a dollar a day, and
were often paid at irregular intervals and sometimes even in bad
money. While the moneyed classes were living in comfort and luxury, growing richer each year, the laboring class was finding it
increasingly difficult to keep body and soul together. Mingling intimately with the laborers, Isaac was able to understand their difficulties as well as their aspirations.

Sensitive to injustice, he made common cause with those loudly
crying for reform. Something was wrong, he realized, with a system
which ground the toiler down to the status of a beast of burden and
robbed him of nearly all the fruits of his industry. He threw himself
into public questions in the effort to promote the economic and social welfare of the worker. This interest took him into politics and he
joined a radical democratic party called the Equal Rights party; he
participated in park meetings, agitating for the rights of the workers,
thus gaining a firsthand knowledge of politics and its inner workings.

One evening Isaac attended a lecture on social reform and was
greatly stirred by the sincerity, vigor, and force of the speaker,
Orestes A. Brownson. Little could he have realized at that time the
important role this man, to whom he felt so strongly attracted, was
to play in his life. Years later he remarked, "Of all the men I ever
knew, Brownson had the most influence on me."

When did the contact with Brownson begin? In his *Life of Isaac
Hecker*, Father Walter Elliott, C.S.P., puts the year 1834—when
Isaac was only fourteen—as the date of Hecker's meeting with
Brownson. Writers who have followed this biography—the standard
one—have likewise put the date at that early period in the boy's life.
In a painstaking piece of scholarly research, *The Early Years of Isaac
Thomas Hecker*, Father Vincent F. Holden, also a Paulist, has shown
that the date was actually about seven years later. "It is quite ob-
vious," he says, "that before the close of the year 1841, Isaac Hecker
and Orestes Brownson were not on very intimate terms."

He reproduces the first letter known to have passed between the two, which is dated November 14, 1841. Isaac was then a young man of twenty-one, and not a boy of fourteen, as he would have been under the erroneous assumption commonly held. This makes sense, puts the whole relationship in a more credible framework, and relieves one of the difficulty of trying to picture a child of fourteen engaging in serious discussion of social and economic problems with a noted scholar and lecturer sixteen years his senior. It shows too that at the time Isaac was participating in park meetings he was considerably older than he has been hitherto represented.*

In the intellectual giant who stood on the platform that night, and strangely warmed his heart, Isaac had found a kindred soul. Completely and wholeheartedly did he share the lecturer's contention that man's inherent dignity must be recognized and that the groundwork of all lasting social reform is to be found in the moral law and in religion. Following the lecture, Isaac and his brothers met Brownson and discussed with him the possibility of further talks in New York. The upshot of it was that the Hecker brothers were authorized to arrange for future engagements, which they did.

Important as were these lectures for the mental stimulation they gave Isaac, they were even more helpful because of the opportunity they afforded him for personal contact and private discussion with Brownson. During the series of lectures which he gave in the winter of 1842, Brownson made his home for those three weeks with the Heckers: much of this time was spent with Isaac in the discussion of social and political questions in which both were deeply engrossed. As was his wont, Brownson often supported his theories with metaphysical and philosophical arguments, thus opening a

* Father Elliott accepted the year 1834 as the date of Hecker's meeting with Brownson on the basis of an article written by Hecker in the *Catholic World* in 1887—the year before he died—when his health was failing badly. He says Brownson came to New York to lecture "somewhere about 1834" and mentions the general topic. By checking the files of the New York newspapers, Holden was able to determine the exact dates of those lectures, which were delivered not in 1834 but in 1841. It is easy to see how an old man in ill-health, writing from memory of events which took place nearly a half century ago and cushioning his reference with the phrase "somewhere about," could miss by seven years. Dr. Holden's research findings are embodied in his dissertation for the doctorate in history at the Catholic University and his entire study bears the marks of meticulous care and painstaking accuracy, with documentation for every detail. It is published by the Catholic University Press, Washington, D.C., 1939.

whole new and wonderful world to the serious-minded young baker.

At this period Brownson was stressing the importance of social institutions to bring about the needed reforms. He was searching for a religious institution adequate for the task: he rejected Catholicism as exclusive and excessively spiritual, and Protestantism as destructive and exclusively material. This prompted him to look to the Church of the Future and to work for its establishment as the answer to the pressing needs of society. He was emphatic in his insistence that man could not do the job alone. "No man," he said, "can rise above himself or lift himself by his own waistband."

The young Isaac hung upon his words as those of a sage and a prophet: they were the catalyst which quickened Isaac's brooding conviction that he had a work of great importance to do and they were beginning to throw light on the way to do it. There is little doubt that these talks provided Isaac with the most effective schooling he had yet received, and sparked his determination to find the answer to life's deepest questions. After listening to Brownson discuss the great problems of philosophy, Hecker began to be conscious of questionings stirring in his own soul.

"How," he asked, "can I be certain of the objective reality of the operations of my soul?" It was a profound question and a practical one for Hecker, who was deeply mystical by nature and given too much to introspection. As Isaac could not read French but did know German, it is probable that Brownson referred him to the works of some of the German philosophers. He became so engrossed in these that he was later to recall himself "kneading at the dough-trough with Kant's *Critique of Pure Reason* fastened upon the wall" before him.

He also read Fichte and Hegel and took a deep interest in religion. On Sunday morning he would walk three miles to hear Orville Dewey, a popular Unitarian preacher, hold forth in the pulpit of his church. Little by little Isaac began to lose interest in the mundane matters of business and to habituate himself to a life half of thought and half of imagination. He would leave his home alone at night and wander down by the wharves on the East River, musing under the silent stars. "What does God desire of me? What is it He has sent me into the world to do?" These were the questions that came increasingly into the forefront of his consciousness.

This brings us to one of the periods in Hecker's life most difficult to explain. His disinterest in business and his dissatisfaction with life in New York had reached such a crisis in December 1842 that Isaac felt practically compelled to leave home. Why? Until the time of his intimate contact with Brownson, he was not noticeably different from the young men of his own age: in his work and in the circle of his family and friends he had found sufficient outlet for his energies.

Interested in social reform but uncertain as to how to achieve it, he found in Brownson's lectures and conversations a new solution in the form of religion and the Christian philosophy of life. But at this time the problem of social reform becomes obscured by an interior personal conflict which now absorbed all his attention. During the period from 1842 to 1844, when he became a Catholic, this struggle was paramount in his life and at times reached alarming intensity.

On the face of it, the change, decidedly religious in character, was the result of God's action on Hecker's soul, drawing him closer to Himself and away from material things. This, Isaac did not realize and was puzzled and mystified by the new influences in his inner life, which gradually acquired the force of compulsions. He speaks of "an irresistible influence" drawing him from his work and home to "a new life," the precise nature of which remains obscure to him. Though the thought of leaving a home in which he had been so happy and had enjoyed the affection of all brought agony to him, he felt a compulsion to leave, which he could not resist.

The predicament in which he found himself puzzled and bewildered him. His difficulty was further increased by a series of dreams after the summer of 1842, for he felt they were more than dreams in the ordinary sense. Describing these influences, he writes in his diary:

"How can I doubt these things? Say what may be said, still for all, these have to me a reality, a practical good bearing on my life. They are impressive instructors, whose teachings [are] given in such a real manner that they influence me, would I or not. Real pictures of the future, as actual, nay more so, than my present activity. If I should not follow them I am altogether to blame. I cannot have such advisers upon earth; none could impress me so strongly with such peculiar effect, and at the precise time most needed."

Among these dreams there was one which exercised a particularly profound influence upon him and removed the thought of marriage.

"I saw," he wrote, "—I cannot say I dreamed . . . a beautiful, angelic being, and myself standing alongside of her, feeling a most heavenly pure joy. It was as if our bodies were luminous and gave forth a moon-like light which sprung from the joy we experienced . . . It was this picture that has left such an indelible impression on my mind. In my state previous to this vision I should have been married ere this, for there are those I have since seen who would have met the demands of my mind. But now this vision continually hovers over me and prevents me, by its beauty, from accepting any one else; for I am charmed by its influence, and conscious that, should I accept any other, I should lose the life which would be the only one wherein I could say I live."

As a result of several such "visitations" Isaac was more convinced than ever that he must leave his family, business friends, and old associates and forego marriage. When at last he confided these things to the members of his family, they had different ideas about his condition. His mother thought he was undergoing a severe religious change and that he wanted "a giving up of his whole mind to Christ" and then he would be all right. John was of the opinion it was due to too much exercise of mind and advised him to check it. The severe nervous strain affected his health and a physician was called in. He advised employment which would give moderate exercise to his mind and body, urged Isaac to take a greater part in social life and marry as soon as possible. The latter advice only exaggerated his tension, as since the time of his dream he had not merely no desire for marriage but even an aversion to it.

In spite of all the kindness and solicitude of the members of his family, Isaac felt they were unable to give him what he craved most —an understanding heart. In this loneliness of soul, he thought of Brownson, who had given him many hours of his time during the past winter. Brownson came to New York for three lectures early in December 1842, stayed with the Heckers, and thus afforded Isaac a good opportunity to unburden himself. The upshot was that Isaac would visit Brownson in Boston the following week.

The members of the Hecker family were delighted. "He [Isaac] has," wrote John, "since he has become acquainted with you, always thought more of what you said than anyone of the family . . . There is no person I could have selected for him to stay with sooner than yourself." On December 24, 1842, Isaac left to visit Brownson at his home in Chelsea. At this time Brownson was writing articles on government for the *Democratic Review* and every Sunday he preached in Boston, where he attracted a notable audience.

Isaac accompanied him and was impressed not only by the sermons but also by the congregation. "There was more original thinking in that congregation than in all the rest of Boston put together; and that is saying not a little." Despite his many preoccupations, Brownson found time to discuss the problem then perplexing his young friend. Isaac wanted to know particularly whether the feelings, aspirations, gropings of his soul had their counterparts in external reality or if he were merely deluding himself with phantoms. By explaining Leroux's doctrine of the objectivity of reality, the communion of the me and not-me, Brownson showed Hecker that these aspirations were not merely subjective.

Out of the solution of the philosophical problem, however, emerged a practical one. Convinced of the reality of the urgings in his soul, Isaac knew that he would not be satisfied in the environment of his home in New York, though his affections were rooted there. "My destiny, which is not my will," he wrote, "I contemplate as a perpetual sacrifice of past hopes." While it was difficult to make this decision, it was still more agonizing to announce it to his family. In his letter he describes the inner urging: "It lies deeper than myself, and there is not the power in me to control it. I write this not with easiness. It is done in tears, and [I] have opened my mind as I have not done before. How this will end I know not, but cannot but trust God."

Learning of Isaac's disinclination to return home, Brownson suggested that he take up residence at Brook Farm. There he would have an opportunity to study, to meet cultured people, and get better oriented for the new life to which he was now aspiring. With the approval of his family Hecker went in January 1842 to live at Brook Farm. This was an experiment in simple living and high thinking: its members sought to establish a society resting on a foundation free of social wrong, where they could share the pleasures and refinements of the intellectual life. Most of the members were Unitarians, men and women living under the intellectual leadership of William Ellery Channing and Ralph Waldo Emerson.

It was started in April 1841 when George Ripley, his wife, and sixteen other persons took possession of a farmhouse in West Roxbury, about eight miles from Boston. At the time Hecker went there, the community numbered about ninety: Emerson, Alcott, Brownson, and Margaret Fuller were occasional visitors. If a member was unable to pay the entire cost of his living, some four or five dollars a week, he would make up the difference by working. Isaac served as the baker and thus cut down his expenses.

It was a new and much more cultured society than he had been accustomed to, and it helped to open a new world to the earnest twenty-three-year-old young baker from New York. Here Isaac read, studied, and discussed the serious questions in which he was interested with cultured people. Many years later George William Curtis described him from memory: "He had an air of singular refinement and self-reliance, combined with a half-eager inquisitiveness, and upon becoming acquainted with him, I told him that he was Ernest the Seeker, which was the title of a story of mental unrest which William Henry Channing was then publishing in the *Dial* . . . Among the many interesting figures at Brook Farm I recall none more sincerely absorbed than Isaac Hecker in serious questions . . . The whole air of the youth was that of goodness."

Occasionally Isaac would go into Chelsea to spend the weekend with Brownson, accompanying him to Boston on Sunday to hear him preach. At this time Brownson was following the Oxford Movement in England with much interest and the two of them would discuss it. Both thought that this unifying trend would spread to other Churches and thus help realize the ideal: one Church, one faith, one baptism.

Amid all the cultural and social activities of Brook Farm, Isaac still suffered from a sense of haunting loneliness and a restless anxiety to learn what God had in store for him. In the absence of any human comforter he turned, as his diary shows, with increasing frequency to prayer: "It is only in Thee I find communion. O Lord, grant that this may be uninterrupted and that I may drink deeper and deeper in Thy spirit." Confessing that at present "my future is dark before me," he places his trust in God and commits himself to Him.

"Into Thy hands, O Lord," he prayed, "I commit myself and Thou dost with me as seemeth good in Thy sight. But grant, O Lord, Thy Spirit to me, that I may be willing to do Thy will and not strive against it. Give me power that I may walk in Thy direction, and teach me how to pray that I may receive Thy blessing, for without Thee I am worse than nothing. And, oh keep me from sinking into a low sense of Thy power, goodness and willingness to help those that call on Thee in sincerity. Lord give me the sense to feel Thy presence always."

By the middle of March his family thought it was time for him to return. Isaac did not feel that he was ready to leave Brook Farm for good, but, knowing how difficult it would be to explain matters by a letter, he decided to go and remained with his family for two weeks: the visit had a salutary effect upon both parties, and at its end his family was reconciled to his staying at Brook Farm until the summer.

Upon his return Isaac was pleasantly surprised at the warm and hearty welcome he received. Previously he seemed scarcely to be noticed; now he felt himself to be one of them. As a result he took a more lively interest in the life about him. He gave up his job in order that he might devote more time to study. Particularly eager to acquire a reading knowledge of French, he enrolled in a class taught by Mrs. Ripley and began to read the Bible in French as well as in Latin. His interest in philosophy never waned, and he attended Mr. Ripley's lectures on Kant: he also included botany and agriculture in his studies.

During his second sojourn at Brook Farm, Isaac's chief preoccupation was apparently a search for the true Church. On his way back from New York he stopped at Brownson's home and found him engrossed in studying the history and the doctrines of the Catholic Church. This quickened his own interest and prompted him to embark upon a similar investigation. The day after arriving at Brook Farm he wrote in his diary the following prayer for guidance: "Oh Lord! lead me into Thy Holy Church, which I am now seeking for, by the aid, I hope, of Thy Holy Spirit. Wilt Thou lead me in the road by which I may come into Thy fold, even as it seemeth good to Thee."

The very next day, Easter Sunday, he went to the Catholic church at West Roxbury and was deeply impressed by everything: the painting, statuary, Mass, and sermon, all of which produced upon him a quieting effect. Returning home, he wrote in his diary: "There may be objections to having paintings and sculptures in churches; but I confess I never enter a place where there is either but I feel an awe, an invisible influence which strikes me mute. I would sit in silence, covering my head. A sanctified atmosphere seems to fill the place and to penetrate my soul when I enter . . . A loud word, a heavy footstep, makes me shudder, as if an infidel were desecrating the place. I stand speechless in a magical atmosphere that wraps my whole being, scarcely daring to lift my eyes. A perfect stillness comes over my soul. It seems to be soaring on the bosom of clouds."

The more he studied and thought about the Catholic Church, the more he felt himself drawn toward it. This interest was further deepened by a German work written by Möhler, which he had begun to read. Under the date of April 24, he wrote in his diary: "The Catholic Church alone seems to satisfy my wants, my faith, life, soul . . . I may be laboring under a delusion, yet my soul is Catholic; and that faith responds to my soul in its religious aspirations and its longings. I have not wished to make myself Catholic, but that answers on all sides to the wants of my soul. It is so rich, so full. One is in harmony all over . . . My soul is filled! Argue not, come and taste, try and see, heaven will make us all agree! There is no controversy in heaven. To know you must come and try."

Despite such an apparent commitment, Hecker did nothing to translate his thought into action. Two weeks later he listened to Brownson preach, and commented in a letter to his brothers on Brownson's inconsistency. "Once admit," he wrote, "the Roman Church is the true Church, or even nearest the truth, and you are obliged to join it." Yet he himself seemed more inconsistent than Brownson, who was at least preaching Catholic doctrine and thus was acknowledging the Catholic Church to be the true one or the one nearest to the truth. But since Hecker was still caught in that strange inner turmoil and uncertainty as to God's plans for him, in this state he waited, hoping and praying that something would make those plans clear to him. Until he died, he could never join any Church.

Having decided that he was not finding at Brook Farm what he was seeking, he set out on July 11, 1843, for Fruitlands, a farm near the village of Harvard, in Worcester County, Massachusetts. There A. Bronson Alcott, Charles Lane, and a few others had established a community which sought through self-denial to achieve a more spiritual life. Isaac did not find there, however, the spiritual enlightenment and help he had anticipated and left on July 26. After a visit at Brook Farm he returned to his home in New York on August 15.

After eight months' experience with man-made Utopias, Isaac had found that they were unable to provide him with what he was seeking. He had, however, learned much, both from the formal courses of study and from the informal association with refined and cultured people. He had come, as George Ripley remarked, "an amateur, self-perfectionizer, an aesthetic self-seeker, willing to suck the orange of Association dry, and throw away the peel."

While at home Isaac resumed his work at the bakery with his brothers, and managed to keep the strict diet he had followed at Fruitlands, living on grains, fruits and nuts, to which he added un-leavened bread. He was still interested in the three reforms which had engrossed him at the time he first wrote to Brownson: personal reform, with its emphasis upon self-denial, holiness, and union with God; social reform seeking universal brotherhood, equality in society, and its rewards for labor; political reform seeking to establish equality before the state.

Hecker's interest in the Church gradually reasserted itself. "Not having had personal and experimental knowledge of the Protestant denominations," he recalled in later years, "I investigated them all, going from one of them to another—Episcopal, Congregational, Baptist, Methodist, and all—conferring with their ministers, reading their books." From them he was seeking the countersign that would tally with the word which reason and God's grace were now apparently beginning to whisper in his soul.

In his diary he tells of having several visits with the Reverend Benjamin I. Haight, minister of the Episcopal Church of All Saints. At the end of the interviews he wrote, "The Episcopal Church is well, but I cannot join a Church which asks no more of me practically than what I am." On March 20, 1844, Hecker went to see Bishop Hughes of New York, as he was beginning to feel that he had a vocation to the priesthood. The bishop informed him that a candidate for Holy Orders must be a member of the Church for two years and after that time he must present a letter from his pastor testifying to his fitness, character, and ability.

In his diary he records this interview and remarks, "I am not prepared to enter the Roman Catholic Church at present. The Roman Catholic Church is not national with us, hence it does not meet our wants, nor does it fully understand and sympathize with the experience and disposition of our people. It is principally made up of adopted and foreign individuals." These observations are significant, especially in view of his later work. In writing to Brownson about the interview, he said he could not join this Church "at the present time, though probably I may eventually be led to take this path."

At this time Hecker began to read extensively in Dionysius the Areopagite, Johannes Scotus Erigena, Bernard Hugo, Meister Eckhart and Ruald of St. Victor. In April 1844, Hecker decided to study Latin and Greek under George Bradford at Concord, and on his way stopped at Chelsea for a visit with Brownson. They had an earnest discussion, in which they endeavored to find a satisfactory explanation of the Anglican schism. Brownson explained that, while the Anglican communion had much to attract him, he could not enter its fold because he was caught between the horns of a distressing dilemma.

Either Christ's Church is a corporate body, such as the Oxford and the Catholic divines maintain, or it is a federal aggregate body. If the first is true, then no separation is admissible. If the latter is true, then the way is open to private judgment. After his own experiences in religion Brownson abhorred private judgment, knowing it opened a veritable Pandora's box of contradictory opinions and washed out any objective basis for truth. After spending the night with his friend, Isaac went on to Concord, where he secured lodging at the home of Henry Thoreau, who had an excellent knowledge of Greek and Latin.

Here Hecker made a careful study of the *Catechism of the Council of Trent,* a complete exposition of Catholic doctrine, which he had brought with him. While he applied himself to an intensive study of Latin and Greek, he found his real joy in "union with the spirit," praising and magnifying the name of God. In his diary he wrote that he had for months been "groping in darkness, seeking Thee where Thou was not, and found Thee not. But, O Lord, my God, Thou hast found me, leave me not . . . take up Thy dwelling in my heart that I may feel *Thy* love *in* me and Thy enjoyment shall give me pleasure and Thy wisdom shall give me light."

Such outbursts of love and devotion recur frequently in his diary and he seems to have been conscious of God's presence in everything around him. He began to wonder if he should not ignore his studies and give himself up entirely to such contemplation, and he wrote a long letter to Brownson seeking his advice. After reading it, Hecker noticed how subjective it sounded, and kept it for several weeks. Then he enclosed it with another along the same lines.

Upon receiving them, Brownson decided that the time had come to jolt his young friend out of what appeared to him to be daydreams and reveries, and bring him down to earth with a vengeance. He sat down and wrote a reply which marked the turning point in Hecker's life. "It was responsible," says his biographer, Vincent F. Holden, "for directing the course of his life into channels that finally brought him peace and happiness."

Mt. Billingham
June 6, 1844

My dear Isaac,

I thank you for your letter and the frankness with which you speak of your present interior state. You ask for my advice, but I hardly know what advice to give. There is much in your present state to approve, also much which is dangerous. The dreamy luxury of indulging one's thoughts and ranging at ease through the whole spirit-world is so captivating, and when frequently indulged in acquires such power over us, that we cease to be free men. The power to control your thoughts and feelings, and to fix them on what object you choose is of the last necessity, as it is the highest aim of spiritual culture. Be careful that you do not mistake a mental habit into which you have fallen for the guidance of the All-Wise.

Is it not the very sacrifice you are appointed to make to our cause, this spiritual luxury, and to become able to do that which is disagreeable? Where is the sacrifice in following what the natural tendencies and fixed habits of our mind dispose us to? What victory have you acquired, what power to conquer in the struggle for sanctity do you possess when you cannot so far control your thoughts and feelings as to be able to apply yourself to studies which you feel are necessary? Here is your warfare. You have not won the victory till you have become as able to drudge at Latin or Greek as to give up worldly wealth, pleasures, honors or distinctions.

But, my dear Isaac, you cannot gain this victory alone, nor by mere private meditation and prayer. You can obtain it only through the grace of God, and the grace of God only through its appointed channels. You are wrong. You do not begin right. Do you really believe the Gospel? Do you really believe the Holy Catholic Church? If so, you must put yourself under the direction of the Church. I have commenced my preparation for uniting myself with the Catholic Church. I do not as yet belong to the family of Christ. I feel it. I can be an alien no longer, and without the Church I know by my own past experience that I cannot attain to purity and sanctity of life. I need the counsels, the aids, the chastisements and the consolations of the Church. It is the appointed medium of salvation, and how can we hope for any grace except through it? Our first business is to submit to it, that we may receive a maternal blessing. Then we may start fair.

You doubtless feel a repugnance to joining the Church. But we ought not to be ashamed of Christ, and the Church opens a sphere for you; and you especially, you are not to dream your life away. Your devotion must be regulated and directed by the discipline of the Church. You know that there is a large Roman Catholic population in our country, especially in Wisconsin. The bishop of that territory is a German. Now, here is your work, to serve this German population, and you can do it without feeling yourself among foreigners. Here is the cross you are to take up. Your cross is to resist this tendency to mysticism, to sentimental luxury which is really enfeebling your soul, and preventing from attaining to true spiritual blessedness . . .

I want you to come and see our good bishop. He is an excellent man, learned, polite, easy, affable, affectionate and exceedingly warm hearted. I spent two hours with him immediately after parting with you in Washington Street, and a couple of hours yesterday. I like him very much.

I have made up my mind, and I shall enter the Church if she will receive me. There is no use in resisting, you cannot be an Anglican, you must be a Catholic or a mystic. If you enter the Church at all, it must be the Catholic. There is nothing else. So let me beg you, my dear Isaac, to begin by owning the Church and receiving her blessing . . . Forgive me if I have said anything harsh or unkind in this letter, for all is meant in kindness, and be assured of my sincere and earnest affection.

Yours truly,
O. A. BROWNSON

This was the first clear intimation that Brownson had definitely made up his mind to enter the Church. It stirred Isaac deeply. He looked into his own mind and heart and saw that he shared the same convictions and aspirations as Brownson for the fullness of divine truth. "To be consistent with my faith," he wrote in his diary of June 7, "to be true to my convictions to the extent that I always have been would lead me to unite myself to the Church, and that to the Roman Catholic Church. I have sought in all the numerous Protestant sects for that which should satisfy all my wants, and my seeking was all in vain. And having examined the Catholic faith, and finding it to answer all my wants, what but wilfulness on my part can keep me from joining the Church Catholic? This moment I cannot say that I have anything essential against her, and she meets all my wants on every side. Oh, this is the deepest event of my past life. I would have united myself to any one of the Protestant sects if I had found them to be what would have answered the demands of nature, and why should I now hesitate when I find the Catholic Church will? Is not this the self will which revolts against the involuntary will of the soul? I feel there would be no doubt that if I should unite myself with the Church I should pursue my studies with vigor."

The following day he went into Boston to see Brownson, who arranged a meeting for him with Bishop Fenwick. After a brief visit, the bishop introduced him to his coadjutor, Bishop Fitzpatrick, who made an appointment with him for June 10. The bishop had been consecrated only four months and was but seven years older than his young visitor. With great earnestness he listened to Hecker's account of his journey to the Church. Convinced of his sincerity and the action of God upon his soul and moved by his ascetic life, the bishop encouraged the young man to follow the voice of God calling him to the one true Church.

Hecker's long conversation with the bishop removed the last vestige of his indecision, and he made up his mind to enter the Church. Learning that his home was in New York, the bishop gave him a letter of introduction to Bishop John McCloskey so he could be instructed and received there. When Isaac expressed a desire to know more of the religious life which Catholics were expected to live, the bishop suggested a visit to Holy Cross College in Worcester, and gave him a letter of introduction to the president.

Having made his decision, his mind was at rest. "I feel very cheerful and at ease and in perfect peace," he wrote in his diary on June 11, "since I have consented to join the Catholic Church. Never have I felt the quietness, the immovableness and the permanent rest that I now feel . . . I feel centered, deeper than any kind of action can penetrate, feel or reach." On the same day he wrote informing his family of his decision. "It seems to me," he wrote, "the difference between embracing the Roman Catholic Church and any other is the same as between remaining as I am and selling all I have and following Christ."

On June 15 Hecker left Concord with Ralph Waldo Emerson for a visit with Lane and Alcott at Still River. On the way over, Emerson, who had learned from Henry Thoreau of Hecker's intention of becoming a Catholic, tried to bring up the subject "with the plain purpose of dissuading me." With adroitness Hecker steered the conversation away from that subject. On the way back to Concord, Emerson returned to it.

"Mr. Hecker," he began, "I suppose it was the art, the architecture, and so on in the Catholic Church which led you to her?"

"No," Isaac replied, "but it was what caused all that."

Neither the reasoning of Emerson, Alcott, or any of the other Transcendentalists could shake Hecker's determination. Two days later he wrote to his family: "There is a conviction that lies deeper than all thought or speech which moves me with an irresistible influence to take this step, which arguments cannot reach, nor any visible power make falter. Words are powerless against it and inexpressive of it."

Hecker spent a couple of days at Holy Cross College, observing the religious life of the students and faculty. Though not impressed by the scholarship of the faculty, he was loud in his praise of the warmth, friendliness, and learning of the president, Father Mulledy. Upon his return home, Isaac was warmly greeted and, due to the courtesy prevailing among the members, encountered only "the mildest criticism" for his decision to embrace the Catholic faith.

On June 25, 1844, Hecker called on Bishop McCloskey and was immensely impressed by him. The bishop was familiar with Emerson's writings and *Brownson's Quarterly Review* and discussed them with Hecker: with this background he was able all the more easily to understand the currents of thought which had influenced Hecker.

"The bishop," Isaac wrote enthusiastically to Brownson, "pleased me personally more than any Catholic I have met. He is a man of wide information, mild and affectionate in his intercourse, one in whose company I hope to be much benefitted."

The bishop gave him several Catholic books to read. While reading and studying in preparation for his reception, Hecker wrote in his diary: "In all our reasoning we must understand that the criterion of truth is not the individual judgment of our personal reason, but the universal voice of the Catholic Church. Not but that the individual reason is to be trusted in some cases, not that it has not light, for the voice of the Church is based upon the light of reason but it is this: the individual reason is not competent to comprehend the universal truth, hence no individual judgment is the criterion of absolute truth."

After a few meetings Bishop McCloskey perceived that Hecker had read the literature carefully and understood the Church's doctrines; he promised him that at their next meeting he would set the date for Isaac's reception. Cheered with this news, he wrote in his diary: "I have commenced acting. My union with the Catholic Church is my first real true act. And it is no doubt the forerunner of many more—of an active life. Heretofore I did not see or feel within me the grounds upon which I could act with permanence and security. I now do; and on this basis my future life will be built."

At their next meeting the bishop told Hecker that he would receive him on the following Friday, August 2, 1844. On that eventful day in old St. Patrick's Cathedral, Isaac Hecker made his profession of faith in Catholic doctrine and was conditionally baptized by the bishop. On the following day the new convert made a confession of the sins of his entire life, received conditional absolution and then made his first Holy Communion; he thus preceded Brownson by several months.

After years of wandering in strange meadows and far valleys, searching for the truth which could satisfy the demands of his intellect and appease the hunger of his heart, Isaac Hecker had reached his goal. He found the security, certainty, and peace, which he had sought with such patience, persistence and determination, in the one institution founded by Jesus Christ to shelter all the nations of the world. It is the trysting place of all truth, the city seated on the mountain, and the universal home of the human spirit.

Past now were the debilitating indecisions, the agonizing uncertainties, the devious paths which had led him hither and yon: dissipated were the clouds by the warm clear sunshine which flooded his soul like a refreshing rain on a parched and withered landscape. The emptiness and heartache of those years were washed away by the joy and rapture which inundated his whole being. It is no wonder that he broke out in exulting praise: "My soul is clothed in brightness. Its youth is restored. No clouds obscure its lustre. O blessed, ever blessed, unfathomable, divine faith! O blessed faith of Apostles, Martyrs, Confessors and saints . . . Bless me, Virgin Mother of Jesus!"

His brother George, to whom he had always been especially attached, soon afterward became a Catholic. In later years this brother was to prove of great financial help to the struggling little community which Isaac founded. His brother John remained an Episcopalian and his mother continued her membership in the Methodist Church.

The next year Isaac spent in further study and in helping his brothers in their expanding business. His heart was not in the business, however, and the ideal of the religious life loomed up with ever increasing appeal. He yearned for religious life in a community and wanted likewise to help his fellow men. Having become acquainted with some Redemptorists in New York, he admired the simplicity and austerity of their life and the work they did for souls. While he was debating about applying for admission, he learned that several novices were sailing for the Redemptorist novitiate in Belgium the very next day.

He immediately set out for Baltimore to see Father de Held, the provincial of the Redemptorists. After traveling all night, he arrived in breathless haste at the provincial's office at four o'clock the following morning. Father de Held was astonished at the impetuosity of his young visitor but was in sympathy with his errand. He gave Isaac some hot coffee and then asked him to translate from the Latin a page of the *Following of Christ*. After Hecker had done this, he gave him permission to join the congregation.

Back in New York that afternoon, Isaac found that George had already packed his trunk, so he bade a hurried "good-by" to his family and sailed that evening with the two other novices. On board the *Prince Albert*, he got better acquainted with his two companions.

One was Clarence A. Walworth, a convert and the son of the Chancellor of New York; he had been admitted to the Bar, and had practiced law for a short time. The other was James A. McMaster, from Pennsylvania, of Scotch-Irish parentage, also a convert. Though he proved to have no vocation and returned home, he later became a prominent Catholic editor.

When Hecker arrived at St. Trond, Belgium, in September 1845 to begin his novitiate he was twenty-five years and nine months old. He entered with enthusiasm into the exercises of prayer, mortification, spiritual reading, physical exercise, recreation, and meditation which constitute the order of the day in every novitiate. He even took on extra penances, sleeping on boards or on the floor, often for only five hours. In after years, one is glad to learn, he condemned such practices as excessive and injurious to health. On the feast of St. Teresa, October 15, 1846, Hecker and Walworth took their vows and became members of the Congregation of the Most Holy Redeemer.

On the morning of that event Isaac wrote a letter to his mother in which he reviews all his trials and experiences in following the divine guidance since he first quitted business. Previously he had been unable to explain the mysterious force which had driven him from home and altered the whole tenor of his life, much to the mystification of his family and friends: it was not until the day of his vows that he was able to understand what had happened. Because it provides a clear and perhaps the only adequate exposition of the events subsequent to the summer of 1842, it is worth quoting at some length.

St. Trond
October 15, 1846

Dear Mother:

My life for some years past may have seemed strange to you at times, compared with what it was before. Not so much to you, dear Mother, whose own experience gave you an insight into mine. As to other members of the family, I am not surprised that it should have seemed strange, for it has appeared the same to me, and inexplicable up to within a very short period. But now that I am able to explain it, I feel it to be my duty towards you and the other members of the family who bore my conduct with so much confidence and love, to give you this explanation.

The road in which I was led to see and embrace the truth, and to give myself wholly to God and His service, was not the ordinary road; and there are very few who travel in it. I will attempt to explain this road to you. God, in seeing a soul sincerely desirous to embrace the truth and be united to Him as its sovereign good, commences to prepare the soul for this end by infusing into the heart a secret love which consumes its inordinate human affections and pleasures of the senses. This love is secret and hidden in a manner from the knowledge of the individual even while it is at work despoiling his heart of its disorders, and it is this change that he is conscious of, while being ignorant of its cause, which gives him so much inquietude . . .

God having thus freed the soul from its imperfections, gradually infuses into the heart all the Christian virtues and graces . . . He enlightens the soul with His light and pours in upon it, sometimes in torrents, His divine love, in order that the soul may embrace the truth that He gives it in secret knowledge and to be united to Him most intimately. I was at Concord when this happened to me, and this is the cause of my sudden return and entrance into the Holy Catholic Church. I went to Concord, as you know, to study in order to find the truth, but God in His Providence made use of this occasion to infuse it suddenly into my soul.

It is impossible for me to relate in a simple letter all that I would otherwise make known to you, and which, if it be the will of God, I will on some future day. I have written this explanation to you, dear Mother, and to the other members of the family in order to give you and them an insight into the hidden cause of my exterior conduct from some years back, which you all bore with so much love, tenderness, and above all with increasing confidence in the sincerity and rectitude of my intentions . . .

Dear Mother, in half an hour I go to the chapel to consecrate my whole being for ever to God and His service. What peace, what happiness this gives me! To live alone for His love, and to love all for His love, in His love, and with His love!

Your son,

ISAAC

The day after taking their vows, Hecker and Walworth went by stagecoach to the house of studies at Wittem in Dutch Limburg.

Having studied three years in an Episcopal seminary, Walworth went into theology, while Isaac was assigned to the course in humanities. His second year, he began philosophy. But Almighty God and divine love were claiming more and more of his attention. Absorbed in contemplation, he was finding it impossible to pursue formal classes. Finally his superiors excused him from class attendance and left him free to study when his mind was free. After two years at Wittem, he was sent to the Redemptorist house in England to continue his preparation for the priesthood.

During his two student years in Holland and a third in England he was unable to engage in any formal study, but his spiritual life matured and deepened, so that he was an object of edification and inspiration to his fellow students and the faculty. Describing this condition ten years later in Rome, he wrote:

"It seemed to me in looking back at my career before becoming a Catholic that Divine Providence had led me, as it were by the hand, through the different ways of error and made me personally acquainted with the different classes of persons and their wants, of which the people of the United States is composed, in order that after having made known to me the truth, He might employ me the better to point out to them the way to His Church. That, therefore, my vocation was to labor for the conversion of my non-Catholic fellow-countrymen. This work, it seemed to me at first, was to be accomplished by means of acquired science, but now it had been made plain that God would have it done principally by the aid of His grace, and if (I were) left to study at such moments as my mind was free, it would not take a long time for me to acquire sufficient knowledge to be ordained a priest. This plan was adopted."

His experience would seem to have some elements in common with that of the Apostle Paul. It will be recalled that some time after his conversion he retired to the Arabian Desert and there was instructed in the truths of the Christian religion directly by the Holy Spirit. Thus he was able to say, "I give you to understand, brethren, that the Gospel which was preached by me is not of man. For I did not receive it from man, nor was I taught it; but I received it by a revelation of Jesus Christ."

Hecker's third year was spent at the Redemptorist foundation at Clapham, three miles south of London Bridge. Here, under the watchful eye of Father de Held, he pursued his study of theology.

But the vigor of his spiritual life went on unabated, while his desire to become a priest to help in the great work of winning the millions of his fellow Americans for Christ grew ever more intense.

In spite of the apprehensions and misgivings of some who did not understand him, he was recommended for holy orders. On October 23, 1849, the feast of the Most Holy Redeemer, he was ordained by Bishop (later Cardinal) Wiseman in his private chapel in London. After serving as a parish priest and a chaplain in England for one year, he returned to New York on March 19, 1851, as one of a band of Redemptorist missionaries assigned to work in the United States.

Thus had Isaac Hecker, in spite of formidable and seemingly insurmountable obstacles, reached his second goal—the holy priesthood. How he reached it seems inexplicable except through the intervention of Divine Providence. Apparently Almighty God had a mission for him in the New World and had brought him safely through many trials and tribulations and through the dark night of the soul to the scene of his future achievements.

II.   FOUNDS A NEW COMMUNITY

As the *Helvetia,* after fifty-two days on the high seas, sailed into the harbor of New York, its passengers saw a little tugboat coming to meet them. On it stood George and John Hecker and Mr. McMaster, whose cheery greetings were the first welcome the young Redemptorists heard. Father Hecker and his companions went to the Redemptorist house on Third Street and on April 6 they conducted their first mission at St. Joseph's Church: it was, in fact, the first mission of a regular series, carried on by a body of men especially devoted to this vocation, given in the United States.

Shortly after his arrival, Father Hecker received a letter from his old friend, Brownson, greeting him heartily and requesting Isaac to come to see him as soon as possible, "in furtherance of the work in which you and I are engaged . . . I am more indebted to you for having become a Catholic than to any other man under heaven, and while you supposed I was leading you to the Church, it was you who led me there. I owe you a debt of gratitude I can never repay."

The little band of Redemptorist missionaries consisted of Fathers Bernard, Hecker, Hewit, and Walworth. Under the tutelage of Father Bernard, Hecker developed into a clear, forceful, and effective preacher. His tall figure, pale blue eyes, and ruddy brown hair made him an impressive figure in the pulpit: he gradually became so proficient that no man, it is said, surpassed him as a doctrinal and moral instructor, though he never attempted the emotional type of oratory.

Subsequently the band was joined by Fathers Deshon and Baker. The tide of immigration was then at its peak, and the missionaries were engaged almost continuously in their arduous labors throughout the country. For six years Father Hecker labored in this field with signal success; yet he longed to be of more service to his non-Catholic brethren.

With this thought in mind, he wrote *Questions of the Soul:* this shows how the deepest yearnings of man's nature and the hungers of his heart are best satisfied through the sacraments, which Christ instituted to bring man into communion with himself. In some of the chapters he illustrates his points by references to his own experience. Completed in a few months, the book was a great success, running through edition after edition. Even from that stern and impartial critic, Dr. Brownson, it received a highly laudatory review.

This was followed in 1857 with *Aspirations of Nature,* in which the author shows the insufficiency of the unaided reason to satisfy the needs of the intellect, and demonstrates the necessity of a divine revelation to supplement reason; it proves also that the Catholic faith truly embodies divine revelation. Like his first book, this too is especially helpful for non-Catholics, because in establishing the dignity of man's rational nature he refutes the fundamental error of man's total depravity: the gloomy heritage of Calvinism. The book, as its predecessor, was put through the press by his old friend, George Ripley, at that time literary editor of the New York *Tribune,* as Hecker was on a mission abroad. Like its predecessor, this book met with marked success and went through several editions.

In the spring of 1857 it was proposed to establish a new house of the congregation either in New York or in Newark, which would be the headquarters of the American members and where the language in common use would be English: this would enable the community to come into closer contact with the English-speaking people of this country. Though Archbishop Hughes of New York and Bishop Bayley of Newark had spoken of such a foundation to the missionaries, the Redemptorist superiors both in this country and in Rome considered the time inopportune for such a venture.

With a view of proving the great opportunities for the congregation in America and of explaining the situation more clearly than was possible by letters, the Fathers decided to send a representative to the general in Rome.* The choice fell upon Father Hecker and he sailed on August 5, 1857 and arrived at Rome on August 26. He was received by the general of the congregation, who, after discussing two or three times privately with Father Hecker his journey to Rome, concluded his action merited dismissal. However, the general did not acquaint him with this decision until August 30 when the sentence of dismissal was read to Father Hecker in the midst of the General Council.

Speechless with amazement, Father Hecker fell on his knees and pleaded with the general to rescind the sentence. His pleas fell on deaf ears. Finally he arose, went out, and prostrated himself before the Blessed Sacrament. Then he returned to the council, and on his knees again begged the general to re-consider his case. The superior refused, however, declaring that his sense of duty would not allow him to act other than he had done. He added that he was not condemning Father Hecker for any inward sin but for his external conduct.

Why such summary action on the part of the general? The reason cited was that Hecker was guilty of disobedience without the requisite permission. The constitution forbade a member to go to Rome to place a matter before the general without permission from his superiors, except under certain exceptional circumstances which the member in his conscience deemed to justify the journey. In 1855 a general chapter of the congregation undertook to alter this article: it granted such a right only after the subject had received in writing previous permission from the superior general. Such a change could

---

* The presentation of this and subsequent phases of Father Hecker's life differs from the one traditionally given by authors who have followed Elliott's *Life of Hecker*. I am indebted to Father Vincent F. Holden for supplying me with additional information for these years of Father Hecker's life. In his forthcoming biography of the founder of the Paulists to be published by Bruce Publishing Company, Father Holden of the Paulist Fathers will have a much fuller and more accurate account of Father Hecker than has yet appeared. This will be the result of extensive research he has made both here and in Europe.

not become effective, however, until it was approved by the Holy See, where it was still under advisement.

There was another circumstance which led the general to take this drastic action. Because of a serious breach of the rule under discussion but not in any way connected with these American members, the general had sent a circular letter to the American province, in which, referring to this proposed change, he stated: "In the General Chapter of 1855 it was declared that any one would merit expulsion who should go to Rome without the previous permission of the Rector Major [the General]. And I hereby declare any one who shall leave America without permission expelled, *ipso facto*, from the Order."

Father Hecker and his companions knew of this circular letter but were convinced its contents did not apply to them. It had been issued as a consequence of a personal situation; theirs was public and concerned the general welfare of the community. They further contended that since the general did not limit to himself the right to grant permission to undertake such a journey to Rome, the provincial was empowered to grant it. Apparently unwilling to assume the responsibility of deciding these points of canon law, the American provincial declined to give Father Hecker the desired permission. However he stated that if he thought he had the right to grant such a permission, he would do it. Also he gave him a letter stating that he had been a good Redemptorist, and that up to that time his superiors had been fully satisfied with him.

While the question of the right to make the journey was primarily one of canon law, there was also involved a question of policy: would it be better to have the American Fathers act as an English-speaking body with a glorious opportunity for the work of the congregation in the Church in America, or should they forego such an opportunity because of a doubtful directive of the superior general? On this question there was a division of opinion. Undoubtedly Father Hecker was fully convinced that he was acting within his constitutional rights: he had explained the matter completely to his provincial, who gave him a qualified permission to make the journey. With a clear conscience he set out upon his errand: his brother George paid his traveling expenses. In Rome the acceptance of such funds was also charged against him as a violation of his vow of poverty.

Such then is the background necessary to understand the general's peremptory action. There is no doubt he acted with complete purity of intention, fully persuaded that the action, though severe, was necessary to safeguard discipline and obedience. Nothing that is said here is intended to reflect in any way upon the good faith or the motives of the general or his council, and it is edifying to note that Father Hecker made no accusations against them, but explained their action in a favorable manner. Indeed he always retained a sincere and affectionate esteem for the congregation in which he received his religious training and in which he was raised to the priesthood.

Father Hecker appealed to the Propaganda and presented to its prefect, Cardinal Barnabo, testimonial letters from Archbishop Hughes, Bishop Bayley, and others. He at once won the sympathy of the cardinal and of many other influential officials in Rome. He helped his cause by writing an article in *Civiltà Cattolica*, a leading Catholic journal, to show that the American people, the freest in the world, were by no means the most difficult to convert but were ripe for the Catholic faith. He was also instrumental in converting George Loring Brown, an American artist of note, in Rome.

"Our affairs," he wrote his American brethren, "are in the hands of God. I hope no one will feel discouraged, nor fear for me. All that is needed to bring the interests of God to a successful issue is grace, grace, grace; and this is obtained by prayer. And if the American Fathers will only pray and get others to pray, and not let any one have the slightest reason to bring a word against them in our present crisis, God will be with us and help us, and Our Lady will take good care of us. So far no step taken in our past need be regretted. If it were to be done again, it would have my consent. The blow given to me I have endeavored to receive with humility and in view of God. It has not produced any trouble in my soul, nor made me waver in the slightest degree in my confidence in God or my duty toward Him. Let us not be impatient. God is with us, and will lead us if we confide in Him."

After careful consideration of the case, during which both sides were heard, Pope Pius IX dispensed Hecker and his four companions from their vows as Redemptorists, and authorized and encouraged them to form a new congregation devoted to missionary work in the United States under the direction of the hierarchy.

Elated with this happy outcome, Hecker wrote to his American brethren: "I look upon this settlement of our difficulties as the work of Divine Providence, and my prayer is that it may make me humble, modest, and renew my desire to consecrate myself wholly to God's designs." He was favored with a second interview with the Holy Father, who treated him with great kindness and bestowed a special blessing upon the work which the American Fathers would soon be undertaking as a new congregation.

He was happy also to bring back with him a letter from Cardinal Barnabo, written in his capacity as prefect of the Sacred Congregation of the Propagation of the Faith. "To each and every one," it read, "who will read this letter of ours, we declare and testify that the Rev. Isaac Hecker, secular priest, is free from all ecclesiastical censure, and that he is a man most illustrious for his religious zeal and sacerdotal virtues, most active in cultivating the vineyard of the Lord, especially in the United States of North America, and for that reason especially beloved, not only by very many bishops there, but also by the Sacred Congregation of Propaganda.

"We commend him most strongly in the Lord to the American bishops, now that he is leaving Rome for America, and ask that they receive him kindly; that they allow him to celebrate the most holy sacrifice of the Mass; and that they do him all those good offices of charity which they think worthy a man who is truly religious and a great worker for the salvation of souls."

During the seven months of Father Hecker's sojourn in Rome the band of American missionaries was busily engaged in conducting missions throughout the East. Their preaching attracted great crowds and long lines of penitents stretched about their confessionals: they were happy in their work of quickening the spiritual life of the faithful and in bringing sinners to repentance and the sacraments. In the midst of all their strenuous missionary labors they did not forget their spokesman pleading their cause in Rome: he was, of course, frequently in their prayers as well.

When he returned to New York in May 1858, with his mission accomplished with such signal success, they gathered about him to plan the new organization. They proceeded slowly, carefully considering each step until July. On the very eve of the community's birth, Father Walworth withdrew to take charge of a parish in the Albany diocese, but rejoined them in 1861. He remained until 1865, when he left the group for good. Meanwhile the others, Fathers

Hecker, Hewit, Deshon and Baker—all converts—organized by choosing Hecker the superior, and drew up the Rule for the community. This was submitted to Archbishop Hughes and approved by him on July 7, 1858. They chose the Apostle of the Gentiles as patron, and called their society "The Missionary Priests of St. Paul the Apostle," and they are commonly known as the Paulist Fathers.

The Rule is closely patterned after the order of spiritual exercises observed by the Fathers while Redemptorists. Instead of vows, however, the members make a perpetual voluntary agreement, affirming their purpose to promote their sanctification by leading a life in all essential respects similar to that led in all religious orders. In addition to chastity, imposed upon them by the priesthood, they observe poverty and obedience and a daily order of spiritual exercises. While they undertake some parochial work, their chief labor is the conducting of missions, and they pioneered missions for non-Catholics.

The archbishop's approval of their Rule afforded the Fathers a status called for in the decree of the Congregation of Bishops and Regulars. This was confirmed by the permission of the Holy See to the archbishop to establish the Paulist Institute in his diocese, with the consent of his suffragans, which was requested and obtained. Thus was born the community which has long been recognized as the most distinctively American one in the Church: its primary aim, aside from the sanctification of its members, being the conversion of America to the Catholic faith.

For some time the little community had no home; during part of this period Mr. George Hecker, taking his family to the country, placed his entire home at the service of the Fathers and made generous provision for their other wants. In the spring of 1858 arrangements were made for establishing a home and parish on Fifty-ninth Street, just west of Ninth Avenue, the present site of St. Paul's Church and convent, which was then a suburban wilderness. On Trinity Sunday, June 19, 1859, the cornerstone of the new building was laid by Archbishop Hughes. The new house and chapel were completed in November.

On the twenty-seventh of the month, the feast of St. John of the Cross, Father Hecker blessed the new rectory. It is interesting to note that St. John of the Cross was one of Father Hecker's special patrons, and that the founder of the new community was within a few days of his fortieth birthday. On the following Sunday the church was blessed, and the work of the Fathers as parish priests began. They were soon joined by Fathers Tillotson and Young, and Father Walworth returned, so that with this increase in numbers they were able to prosecute their missionary and parish work more vigorously.

The period following Father Hecker's return from Rome was one of eager and intense activity. The contemplative spirit, rapt in visions and communions known only to itself, stands up, shakes itself, and becomes instinct with life, vigor and zeal, wrestling successfully with practical problems of all varieties. The crusading energy of his youthful years as a worker for social reform had again come to the surface, though his contemplative spirit always remained intensely active.

These two different sides of Father Hecker's nature disposed him toward the two main objectives of his life: obedience to the promptings of the Holy Spirit and the conversion of his fellow Americans to that obedience by utilizing all the influences and agencies of modern American life. While recognizing that all men as children of God may have direct communion with the Holy Spirit, he always stressed the need of the Catholic Church, as the representative of God on earth, to guide the individual in the interpretation of his inward communions, impulses, and spiritual experiences. He insisted upon "absolute and unswerving loyalty to the authority of the Church, wherever and however expressed, as God's authority upon earth and for all time."

Few spiritual writers have described the action of the Holy Spirit in the human soul with the penetration and clarity of Father Hecker. Removing what might seem a contradiction between the authority of the interior directions and that of the Church, he writes: "The action of the Holy Spirit embodied visibly in the authority of the Church and the action of the Holy Spirit dwelling invisibly in the soul form one inseparable synthesis; and he who has not a clear conception of this twofold action of the Holy Spirit is in danger of running into one or the other, and sometimes into both, of these extremes, either of which is destructive of the end of the Church. The Holy Spirit, in the external authority of the Church, acts as the infallible interpreter and criterion of divine revelation. The Holy Spirit in the soul acts as the divine Life-giver and Sanctifier. It is of the highest importance that these two distinct offices of the Holy Spirit should not be confounded."

Here is an exposition of the operation of the Holy Spirit embodied in the infallible authority of the Church and of His operation in the soul, that is a model of lucid analysis. He then raises the question as to what one must do in order to favor the operation of the Holy Spirit and secure fidelity to His guidance when received.

"First," he replies, "receive the sacraments, the divinely instituted channels of grace: one will scarcely persevere in living in the state of grace, to say nothing of securing a close union with God, who receives Holy Communion only once or twice a year. Second, practice prayer, above all that highest form of prayer, assisting at Holy Mass; then mental and vocal prayer, the public offices of the Church, and particular devotions according to one's *attrait*. Third, read spiritual books daily—the Bible, Lives of the Saints, *Following of Christ*, etc.

"But in all this bear ever in mind, that the steady impelling force by which one does each of these outward things is the inner and secret prompting of the Holy Ghost, and that perseverance in them is secured by no other aid except the same hidden inspiration. Cherish that above all, therefore, and in every stage of the spiritual life; be most obedient to it, seeking meantime for good counsel wherever it is likely to be had . . . The work of the priesthood is to help to guide the Christian people, understanding that God is always guiding them interiorly . . . The guide of the soul is the Holy Spirit Himself, and the criterion, or test, of possessing that guide is the divine authority of the Church."

These quotations from Father Hecker bring out the point stressed in so much of his writing: fidelity to the guidance of the Holy Spirit who speaks to the conscience in prayer, meditation, spiritual reading and in the reception of the sacraments. But that mystical communion with the Holy Spirit must be supplemented by energetic zealous service to Christ and to the Church—His Mystical Body. While at St. Trond he believed that he received intimations from the Holy Spirit that he had been selected as a special instrument of God to work for the conversion of this country. So deep and strong did this belief become that, during his stay in Rome, it seemed that Providence reached out and set his hand to the task.

The differences between nations should not be allowed, he

thought, to prevent their union and harmonious dwelling together within the one fold of Christ. On the contrary, the distinctive character of each nation, fashioned through long centuries not without the concurrence of God, should be used as the instrument to bring each people into membership in the Mystical Body of Christ.

In this country dwell a people who have prospered in industry and business, who have espoused the new principles of democracy and have made their country a place of refuge for the downtrodden and oppressed. Could such prosperity, trust, and generosity have been achieved without God's blessing? By no means. Under Providence, so Father Hecker firmly believed, these results in secular matters were due to the freedom and independent character of the American people.

Why not, then, use this distinctive character as a drawbridge to lead them over the moat of religious indifference into the mighty castle of Christ the King? Why not so present the Church's credentials and teachings in such a way as to appeal to this distinctive character? Why not show them that the Catholic faith is in accord with the principles of true liberty, with the noble and inspiring affirmations of the Declaration of Independence, and the aspirations of free men? Why not show the American people that their distinctive genius will best be fostered, nourished, and developed by the divine deposit of religious truth, which alone makes men free? This was the deposit entrusted by Christ to His Church, to be given to all men under her infallible teaching authority, which is safeguarded by the operation of the Holy Spirit within her.

Having made that discovery through long years of anguished searching, Father Hecker thought that he had the proper background and experience to enable him to respond to the call of the Holy Spirit within him to undertake the task. This was the conviction which set him on flame to begin now the mission to which he had so long aspired. His first means was his newly founded community. "The controlling thought of my mind for many years," he wrote, "has been that a body of free men who love God with all their might, and yet know how to cling together, could conquer this modern world of ours."

Father Hecker's plan was to have his community minister to the special needs of the people among whom they lived, and to stress in their preaching the special virtues necessary to enable them to meet those needs. "The main purpose of each Paulist," he wrote, "must be the attainment of personal perfection by the practice of those virtues without which it cannot be secured—mortification, self-denial, detachment, and the like. By the use of these means the grace of God makes the soul perfect. The perfect soul is one which is guided instinctively by the indwelling Holy Spirit. To attain to this is the end always to be aimed at in the practice of the virtues just named."

The second end is to labor zealously for the conversion of the country by apostolic work: parish work is always to be done as a means of accomplishing this objective. "Our vocation," he stressed, "is apostolic—conversion of souls to the faith, of sinners to repentance, giving missions, defense of the Christian religion by conferences, lectures, sermons, the pen, the press, and the like works . . . He [the Paulist] must do the work of the Church. The work of the Church, as Church, is to render her note of universality more and more conspicuous." But also "a Paulist is to emphasize individuality; that is, to make individual liberty an essential element in every judgment that touches the life and welfare of the community and that of its members . . . The individuality of a man cannot be too strong or his liberty too great when he is guided by the Spirit of God."

With vigor and enthusiasm Father Hecker plunged into the work of the missions. His tall figure, large head with prominent features, and a long forked beard gave him a distinguished appearance in the pulpit and on the lecture platform. He had developed into a forceful and magnetic speaker, with a gift for humor and apt illustration. In great demand as an exponent of Catholic truth, he was eagerly welcomed by overflow audiences in New York, Boston, Philadelphia, Detroit, St. Louis, Chicago, and other large cities. He would usually begin by dwelling upon the American love of liberty and capacity for free government, and then show how the teachings of the Church fostered that love and strengthened that capacity, how they fitted perfectly into the aspirations of our people.

Father Hecker was among the first to recognize the power of the printed word in shaping the thought and ideals of people: he perceived the tremendous growth of the press in this country, sending newspapers and magazines into virtually every home. He struggled earnestly to harness this new and powerful instrument for the dissemination of Catholic truth. In April 1865 he founded the *Catholic*

World, a monthly magazine, which has rendered such signal service to Church and country for almost a century.

The following year he founded the Catholic Publication Society for the purpose of publishing pamphlets and paper-covered books which would enable Catholics to increase their knowledge of the faith as well as to inform outsiders and help lead them into the fold. In 1870 he started *The Young Catholic,* edited by Mrs. George Hecker. This was designed to prevent young Catholics from straying from their faith by deepening their understanding of it, and by strengthening them to resist the temptations common to adolescents.

The burden of maintaining the Publication Society fell mainly upon his community. At first the publications were given away or else sold at, or below, cost. Collecting the necessary funds was no easy task. With a view of interesting the bishops in this venture, he attended the meeting of the Second Plenary Council of Baltimore in 1866, and personally talked to many of them, as well as publicly speaking on the subject in the sessions. His cause found an eloquent champion in Archbishop Spalding and through the efforts of the two of them the council was persuaded to enact a decree that the bishops "establish branches of this Society in their dioceses . . . [and] shall thereafter appoint a yearly collection for their support, to be taken up in all the principal churches, or shall make other provision for the same purpose according to their best judgment." In addition, the council in its pastoral letter urged the clergy to give their strong support "to the undertaking, which is second to none in importance among the subsidiary aids which the inventions of modern times supply to our ministry for the diffusion of Catholic truth."

Elated over the action of the council, Hecker planned to establish branches throughout the country, thus giving the Church in America the support of a strong body of laymen. While the decree of the council bore witness to the Paulist founder's power over men, the needs of the Church in building churches and schools left dioceses with little money to spare for the Publication Society. The first collections were soon spent and no more came in. Thereupon Mr. George Hecker stepped in with generous support and ultimately was obliged to turn the society into a publishing business.

In 1871 the intrepid Apostle made another effort to further the apostolate of the press. Learning that a New York daily paper, a member of the Associated Press, was for sale at three hundred thousand dollars, he jumped at the prospect of having a daily newspaper to further divine truth. He persuaded numerous men of means to subscribe, with Archbishop McCloskey heading the list. With more than half the amount subscribed, Father Hecker was taken ill; there was no one to take his place and the project had unfortunately to be abandoned.

Nevertheless his zealous and able efforts in behalf of the apostolate of the press aroused Catholics throughout the country to the importance of using the printed word on an ever increasing scale to spread divine truth. His fame in this apostolate spread overseas and brought him in 1869 an autographed letter from Pius IX, commending the efforts of himself and the other Paulist Fathers, and bestowing upon them his blessing. The Paulist Press, which today is disseminating millions of pamphlets and inexpensive books each year, developed from Father Hecker's pioneer Publication Society: its copious products brighten and adorn the vestibule of almost every Catholic church in America, and are instrumental in starting thousands of truth seekers on their way into the Church.

When the Vatican Council was about to open in Rome, Bishop Rosecrans of Columbus, Ohio, being unable to attend, appointed Father Hecker his proxy. Arriving in Rome in November 1869, he found so many prelates were in attendance that proxies were not recognized. Whereupon Archbishop Spalding of Baltimore made the Paulist founder his theologian: this afforded him the privilege of reading all the documents of the council, of knowing all that took place in it, and of participating in the deliberations of the American hierarchy, who met by themselves to consider the interests of the Church in the United States.

After the council had defined the doctrine of papal infallibility as an article *de fide* for the whole Catholic world, Father Hecker wrote: "The definition of the Vatican Council completes and fixes forever the external authority of the Church against the heresies and errors of the last three centuries . . . None but the declared enemies of the Church and misdirected Catholics can fail to see in this the directing influence of the Holy Ghost . . . The definition leaves no longer any doubt in regard to the authority of the Chief of the Church."

Among the benefits flowing from the council's action was one which particularly delighted Father Hecker: the Church could now turn her attention and that of her children more directly to the interior authority of the Holy Spirit in the soul. This, he felt, would give birth to her renewal, and enable her to reconquer her true position in Europe and the whole world. "For we must never forget," he said, "that the immediate means of Christian perfection is the interior direction of the Holy Spirit, while the test of our being directed by the Holy Spirit, and not by our fancies and prejudices, is our filial obedience to the divine external authority of the Church."

While in Rome, Father Hecker had two private audiences with Pius IX, who remembered him and again expressed his deep interest in his great apostolate in America. He also called upon Cardinal Barnabo, who received him with open arms. "The affection and esteem," he said, "which I had for you when you were here before has been increased by your labors since then." The cardinal also spoke highly of the important work which the *Catholic World* was doing.

During his sojourn in the Eternal City, Father Hecker preached one of the sermons of the course given during the octave of the Epiphany in the Church of San Andrea della Valle; later on he preached again on an important occasion, in place of Archbishop Spalding, who had fallen ill. He renewed acquaintance with the many distinguished priests and prelates who had espoused his cause when he was there twelve years before.

Shortly before leaving Rome he had a long and pleasant visit with Cardinal Barnabo. As he was about to bid the cardinal good-by, the prelate said, "You ought to be grateful to God for three reasons: first, He drew you out of heresy; second, He saved you from shipwreck in Rome; third, He has given you talents to do great things for His Church in your country."

Father Hecker was convinced that while he was in Rome he received special illumination from God on the sanctifying action of the Holy Spirit in the soul. He mentioned this several times in later years to Father Walter Elliott. The renewal of old acquaintanceships and friendships in Rome, along with the many words of commendation and encouragement which he received on all sides, had a heartening effect upon the zealous apostle. In a letter to his brother's family just before departure, he wrote:

"I return with new hope and fresher energy for that better future for the Church and humanity which is in store for both in the United States. This is the conviction of all intelligent and hopeful minds in Europe. They look to the other side of the Atlantic not only with great interest, but to catch the light which will solve the problems of Europe. Our course is surely fraught with the interests, hopes, and happiness of the race. I never felt so much like acquitting myself as a Christian and a man. The convictions which have hitherto directed my course have been deepened, confirmed, and strengthened by recent experience here, and I return to my country a better Catholic and more an American than ever."

Leaving Rome early in the spring of 1870, Father Hecker visited various places and shrines in Italy. But the spot that appealed to him most was Assisi. As he walked over the very stones trodden upon daily by the gentle St. Francis, his heart throbbed within him. He was stirred almost to ecstasy when he celebrated Holy Mass at the tomb of the saint, and prayed for his little community back in America.

"It seems," he said, "I could linger weeks and weeks around this holy spot . . . What St. Francis did for his age one might do for one's own. He touched the chords of feeling and of aspiration in the hearts of the men and women of his time, and organized them for action." At that holy shrine he doubtless prayed that the members of his community would be enabled by the Holy Spirit similarly to touch the hearts and minds of the men and women of their day.

Full of hope and enthusiasm, with all his convictions strengthened, he looked forward with eagerness to resuming his work in America. "I see nothing, practically, in which I am engaged, that, were it in my power, I would now wish to alter or abandon. I shall return with the resolution to continue them with more confidence, more zeal and more energy." In this buoyant and exuberant spirit he arrived in New York in June 1870.

With renewed energy and zest Father Hecker plunged into the work of the missions, the press, and the parish: there was so much to be done and there were so few members in his community to do it. But God had other plans for him. Toward the end of 1871 his health began to fail and he suffered from increasing nervous exhaustion and fatigue: nevertheless he continued his preaching, lecturing, and other work through the winter and most of the following spring. In the summer of 1872, however, he suffered a complete nervous breakdown, which greatly curtailed his activity. Upon the advice of physicians he went to Europe in the summer of 1873. "Look upon me as a dead man," he said with tears as he bade the community farewell. "God is trying me severely in soul and body, and I must have the courage to suffer crucifixion."

While he derived some benefit from a journey up the Nile and a visit to the Holy Land, he returned to New York in October 1875 unimproved in health. In February of that year while still in Europe he published his pamphlet, *An Exposition of the Church in View of the Present Needs of the Age:* this presents his estimate of the ills of the day, especially in Europe, and their remedies. Realizing that there was so much to be done, and ardently desiring to do it, Father Hecker suffered acutely from the frustration imposed upon him by broken health. His buoyancy of spirits and his hopeful outlook were severely tried in the furnace of extreme bodily suffering as well as of the most excruciating spiritual trials.

During the last sixteen years of his life, from 1872 to 1888, he was rarely free from pain of body and distress of soul. He offered all these sufferings to the Divine Redeemer, bowed his head in resignation to the divine will, and turned increasingly to prayer, meditation, and spiritual reading. Every day he read or had read to him some parts of the Scriptures in English. "Without the Book of Job," he was wont to say, "I would have broken down completely."

From the Scriptures he would turn to the writings of St. John of the Cross, St. Teresa, Lallemant, St. Catherine of Genoa, and other authors of a mystical character. Next to the Scriptures, however, no work gave him such solace and spiritual nourishment as *Abandonment to Divine Providence,* a small posthumous treatise of Father P. J. Caussade, S.J. It seemed to the stricken Paulist that submission to the divine will is taught in its pages as it had not been done since the time of the Apostles. His little French copy was thumbed all to pieces and he knew much of it by heart. At his suggestion an English version of it was published, and it has since soothed the hearts of many afflicted persons.

"To be shut off from the world," he wrote to a sick friend, "and cut off from human activity—and this is what it means to be sick—gives the soul the best conditions to love God alone, and this is Paradise upon earth. Blessed sickness which detaches the soul from all creatures and unites it to its sovereign Good! . . . We think ourselves necessary, and others try to make us believe the same; there is but little truth and much self-love in this. 'What else do I require of thee,' says our Lord in Thomas à Kempis, 'than that thou shouldst resign thyself wholly to Me.' This is what our Lord is fighting for in our souls."

This was the manner in which he struggled with heroic courage and resignation to bear his own intense suffering of mind and body. Despite all those gallant efforts, however, there is no doubt that the pain of having his lifework torn away from him throbbed incessantly within him: he was like a man whose arms and legs had been crushed and then amputated, the phantoms of which were still aching in every ligament, muscle, and nerve. Though resigned and even cheerful in word, the pallor of his face and the blazing of his eyes betrayed his bodily and mental anguish.

In 1887 a collection of Father Hecker's more important later essays was published in a book, *The Church and the Age:* it was widely acclaimed both in this country and abroad. "The author," said the English Jesuit magazine, *The Month,* "displays remarkable breadth of thought, and the book contains many passages which are not only eloquent as a defense of Catholicity, but which cannot fail to impart instruction to the reflecting reader." His pamphlet, *An Exposition,* was run as the first chapter, and it attracted particularly wide attention.

In it Father Hecker cited a curious enigma which irritated no less than it amazed him: a small minority of anti-Christians was permitted entire control of Italy and France, manifesting in the government of those overwhelmingly Catholic countries a pagan ferocity against everything sacred. Instead of rising up in manly indignation and throwing such persecutors out of office, the Catholic majority manifested merely a "timid listlessness," which they covered with extravagant displays of devotional religion. This made the intrepid apostle's blood boil: he pleaded for more manliness, militancy and intestinal fortitude in defending the rights of God, the Church, and religion.

Heartily applauding Hecker's manly appeal, the great English scholar, Canon William Barry, wrote in the *Dublin Review:* "By nature all those who are born into a system are conservatives; and the patience under assault, which our Catholic brethren on the Continent have often shown, may be as much inherited lethargy as Christian meekness. Enthusiasm can always be checked; it cannot be created under the ribs of death. The Catholic Church has never perished in any country because of a wide-spread zeal to defend or to extend it. On the other hand, respectable routine and dull conformity have been, as they ever will be, the prelude to decay and dissolution. The most dangerous of all experiments is that whereby individual effort is thwarted, sneered out of countenance, and tarred with the brush of heterodoxy."

Similar commendation of the words of Father Hecker came from Archbishop Ireland of St. Paul, a towering figure in the American hierarchy. "We sometimes rely far more upon God," he wrote, "than God desires us to do, and there are occasions when a novena is the refuge of laziness or cowardice. God has endowed us with natural talents, and not one of them shall be, with His permission, enshrouded in a napkin. He will not work a miracle, or supply grace, to make up for our deficiencies. We must work as if all depended on us, and pray as if all depended on God."

When Archbishop McCloskey, who received Isaac into the Church, was made a cardinal in March, 1875, Father Hecker was greatly pleased and wrote him a note of congratulation. Then he added, "This elevation to the cardinalate of an American prelate is a cheering sign that the dignities of the Church are open to men of merit of all nations, and it is to be hoped that every nation will be represented in the College of Cardinals in proportion to its importance, and in that way the Holy See will represent by its advisers the entire world, and render its universality more complete. The Church will be a gainer, and the world too; and I have no doubt that your appointment to this office in the Church will be, from this point of view, popular with the American people."

He felt strongly that the mark of Catholicity would shine forth more luminously if more of the nations were represented in the College of Cardinals: such representation would bring out the universal, international, and supranational character of the institution which Christ founded and refute the common charge that it is dominated in every phase of its life and activity by one nation, whose people constitute but a tiny fraction of its total membership. In this contention Hecker was motivated by no spirit of narrow nationalism but by an unselfish and sincere concern for the welfare of the Church and her continued spread among all peoples.

To this theme he returned in *The Church and the Age*, the occasion being the elevation of Archbishop Gibbons to the cardinalate. In commending that elevation, Father Hecker recalled the words of the Council of Trent, which desired that the Sacred College should be truly representative in its members of the nations of Christendom. He wrote not as a nationalist—for the spirit of nationalism is as divisive as it is explosive—but as an apologist and a missionary; and the trend of events is proving that he did not write entirely in vain.

Father Hecker's health continued to fail and he had frequent attacks of angina pectoris for four or five years before his death. Excruciating as were such seizures, they were less painful than the mental agony and the travail of soul which God permitted him to suffer. During most of this time he was unable even to say Mass. Nevertheless he turned increasingly to God in prayer and contemplation; he would add his humble mite to the sufferings of the Divine Redeemer who would see that they came back in blessings a hundredfold.

"God alone," he wrote, "has been always the whole desire of my heart, and what else can I wish than that His will may be wholly fulfilled in me? Having rooted everything else out of my heart, and cut me off from all things, what other desire can I have than that He who has begun the work should finish it according to His design? It is not important that I should know what that design is: it is enough that I am in His hands, to do with me whatever He pleases."

On February 14, 1888, Father Hecker's beloved brother George died, and his passing was an immense loss to Isaac. "George and I," he once said, "were united in a way no words can describe. Our union was something extremely spiritual." The paroxysms of angina pectoris became more frequent and gradually exhausted his slight reserve of strength. By autumn death's pale flag mantled his face with its grim and unmistakable forebodings.

On December 20, 1888, two days after his sixty-ninth birthday, the last sacraments were administered to the dying priest, who received them in full consciousness. On Saturday morning, December 22, the members of his community gathered at his bedside and recited the prayers for the dying. His last act was to raise his feeble hand and with the sign of the cross to give his blessing, uttering the words in a light whisper. On Wednesday, the feast of St. Stephen, his tired and worn body was laid in the vaults of the old cathedral, amid an immense outpouring of sorrowing people and with the full rites of the Church.

His passing brought tributes from prelates, dignitaries, and men and women in all walks of life. From the oratory in Birmingham the aging Cardinal Newman sent a message of condolence, addressed to Father Hewit, and added: "I have ever felt that there was this sort of unity in our lives—that we had both begun a work of the same kind, he in America and I in England, and I know how zealous he was in promoting it. It is not many months since I received a vigorous and striking proof of it in the book he sent me [*The Church and the Age*]. Now I am left with one friend less, and it remains with me to convey through you my best condolement to all the members of your society." In a subsequent letter the cardinal paid tribute to Father Hecker as "an effective Catholic writer and a benefactor to the Catholic religion, whose name will ever be held in honor by the Catholic Church."

After a careful and prolonged study of his life and work, Canon William Barry wrote in the *Dublin Review*: "No Catholic of our century has drawn more hearts with the cords of Adam than Isaac Hecker. His faith in free-will and the 'brotherhood of man' gave his rugged but earnest speech an eloquence by which the vast crowds that came to hear him were mightily subdued."

An attentive student of Father Hecker's work, Archbishop Ireland penned the following appraisal: "Isaac Thomas Hecker lives today, and with added years he will live more fully than he does today. His influence for good remains, and with a better understanding of his plans and ideals, which is sure to come, his influence will widen and deepen among laymen and priests of the Church in America . . . We shall always distinguish Isaac Thomas Hecker as the ornament, the flower of our American priesthood—the type that we wish to see reproduced among us in widest proportions."

Even before Father Hecker founded the Paulists, Bishop Bayley paid him this singular tribute in a letter to Archbishop Bedini in Rome: "Father Hecker, as you already know, is one of the most distinguished converts of whom our religion can boast in this country, and he has already rendered the greatest service to religion by his writing and by his apostolic activities."

Few men knew the founder of the Paulists better or more intimately than Father Elliott. It was while listening to the Paulist preach in Detroit that Walter Elliott first felt the desire to become a priest, and it brought him precipitately to New York to apply for entrance into the community. He lived with Father Hecker for many years and shared his confidence to an unusual degree. "Few men since the time of the Apostles," he wrote, "have felt a quicker pulse than Isaac Hecker when the name of God was heard, or that of Jesus Christ or the Holy Spirit. Few men have had a nobler pride in the Church of Christ, or felt more one with her honor. Few men have grown into closer kinship with all the family of God, from Mary the great mother and the holy angels down to the simplest Catholic, than Isaac Hecker."

If there is any one trait that stood out more prominently in Father Hecker than any other it was his uncanny genius in sensing the peculiar and distinctive needs of his generation: a hunger for a truly spiritual religion with increased emphasis upon the inner life, sensitivity to the promptings of the Holy Spirit, and a manifestation of the fruits of that sensitivity in a clean, honest, manly, Godlike life. High-minded non-Catholics sometimes shy away from the Church because they see only its emphasis upon organization, external ceremonies, elaborate liturgy, sacraments, hierarchical authority, and ironclad laws. Where, they wonder, is that inner life of secret prayer, that worshiping in spirit and in truth, that quiet communion with the Holy Spirit, which are emphasized so much in the pages of the New Testament?

They are scandalized when they see Catholics acting as if they thought that attendance at liturgical functions served as a substitute for scrupulous observance of the laws of honesty, purity, temperance, charity, and social decorum. Reacting against what they construe to be a theory of salvation by mere routine membership in an organization and mechanical assistance at liturgical functions understood neither in language nor ceremony, they imagine they are attacking a Catholic principle when they assert that "religion is a personal relationship between self and God." They fail to see that the Church uses liturgy and ceremony only as a means of bringing the individual into vital union with God; that she places enormous emphasis upon the interior life of prayer, meditation, and communion with the Holy Spirit; that He actually dwells in the inviolable sanctuary of the individual conscience and whispers His admonitions into its sensitive ear. "If any one love me," said Jesus, "he will keep my word, and my Father will love him, and we will come to him, and will make our abode with him."

It is a tribute to Father Hecker's penetrating discernment of the need of his day—and of ours too—that he stressed so strongly the operation of the Holy Spirit within the devout soul and thus made clear the powerful assistance which the Catholic religion offers the individual in living an upright and holy life. The fruits of that assistance are seen in the legion of saints which has adorned the Church in every age; they have spoken to the world through the persuasive eloquence of holy and Godlike lives. In stressing the doctrine of the indwelling of the Holy Spirit in the individual soul, he was pointing out by implication that the actual fruitfulness of external religion may be measured by the degree of interior union attained.

This is the very lesson which the Church seeks to drive home to her children by recalling to their minds the words of Christ: "It is expedient for you that I go. For if I go not, the Spirit will not come to you; but if I go, I will send Him to you." Commenting upon this striking utterance of our Blessed Lord, Father Joseph McSorley, C.S.P., remarks, "It would be hardly possible to say more plainly that the sacraments, the Church, the crucifixion, even the Incarnation itself, are means to an end. The external, visible, is for the sake of what is internal, invisible."

While the doctrine of the indwelling of the Holy Spirit is, of course, an integral part of our holy faith, it was not commonly treated in English books and sermons in the middle nineteenth century. It was not until 1875 that Cardinal Manning, who considered ignorance of this doctrine to have been a major cause of England's loss of the faith at the time of the Reformation, brought out his epochal work, *The Internal Mission of the Holy Ghost*. This remained the classic English treatise until Pope Leo XIII issued his great encyclical on the Holy Spirit in 1899. That authoritative document stressed the need of cultivating devotion to the Holy Spirit to acquire the habit of responding to the inner promptings of grace; it affirmed the special suitability of this devotion for the needs of the age.

From this it can be seen what a trail-blazing pioneer Father Hecker was in stressing this salutary doctrine in his sermons and writings as especially adapted to minister to the needs of an age, characterized by a staccato pace and boundless activity. How striking it is that this man should have stressed and formulated this doctrine with such precision, balance and symmetry that it dove-

tails beautifully into the subsequent exposition both of Cardinal
Manning and of Leo XIII! How, too, are we to explain his uncanny
perception of the aptness of this devotion to minister to the unique
and distinctive needs of his day? Surely here would seem to be either
the insight of a spiritual genius of a high order or the direct and
immediate guidance of the Holy Spirit. Father Hecker, of course,
would attribute it to the latter; in all probability it was a combina-
tion of the two.

It is because the Paulist founder perceived that the synthesis of
the internal guidance of the Holy Spirit and the external guidance
of a divinely established teaching authority is to be found only in
the Catholic Church that he was aflame with zeal to bring the American people into the fold of Christ. Perceiving the tragic error of
the Reformers in rejecting the living authority of the Church and
embarking upon the fatal and divisive road of subjectivism, Hecker
struggled with quenchless zeal and untiring energy to rescue their
followers from the sterile and unprofitable wilderness into which
they had been led. Herein lies the secret of that remarkable missionary zeal which characterized the founder and still remains as the
distinctive mark of his spiritual sons: they are aflame with a zeal
worthy not only of their founder but also of the great Apostle whose
name they bear.

Hecker loved the Church as the Mystical Body of Christ, the pro-
longation in time and space of the Incarnation. "We might attempt
to describe Hecker's vision of the Church," remarks Father Mc-
Sorley, "by saying that when Christ's earthly life was nearing its end,
God formed in the womb of humanity a Mystical Body for his Son—
a heart to throb with sympathy for the afflicted to the end of time; a
brow to wear the glory of Thabor and the shame of Calvary while
the world should last; feet to tread the mountains of all the world,
carrying the messengers of the good tidings of peace; lips to pro-
nounce the pardon of every truly repentant sinner; hands to stretch
to all nations, bearing gifts for every child of Adam; and fingers to
break the bread of life to every famishing soul."

One other vision or foresight of Hecker's is worth noting in this
final summary: the peculiar consonance of Catholic teaching concerning the freedom of the will and the dignity of the human personality with the affirmations of the Declaration of Independence
and the aspirations of the American people. "Let it once be shown,"

he wrote in 1879, "that the Catholic interpretation of Christianity is consonant with the dictates of human reason, in accordance with man's normal feelings, favorable to the highest conceptions of man's dignity which awakens the uttermost action and devotion of all his powers, and you have opened the door to the American people for the reception of the complete evidence of the claims of the Catholic Church, and prepared the way for the universal acceptance of her divine character."

He felt that Europe, "under the lead of the religious revolution of the sixteenth century, turned its back on Catholicity and entered upon the downward road that ends in death; the republic of the United States, in affirming man's natural rights, started in the eighteenth century with its face to Catholicity, and is in the ascending way of life to God . . . When the nature of the American republic is better understood, and the exposition of Christianity is shaped in the light of its universal principles so as to suit the peculiarities of the American mind, the Catholic Church will not only keep her baptized American children in her fold, but will at the same time remove the prejudices existing in the minds of a large class of non-Catholics, and the dangers apprehended from the influence of republicanism will be turned into fresh evidences of the Church's divine character."

What remarkable prescience he manifested here is evident from the following pronouncements of the American Hierarchy at the Third Plenary Council of Baltimore in 1884: "We can claim to be acquainted both with the laws, institutions and spirit of the Catholic Church; and with the laws, institutions and spirit of our country; and we emphatically declare that there is no antagonism between them. A Catholic finds himself at home in the United States; for the influence of his Church has constantly been exercised in behalf of individual rights and popular liberties. And the right-minded American nowhere finds himself more at home than in the Catholic Church, for nowhere else can he breathe more freely that atmosphere of divine truth, which alone can make him free. We repudiate with equal earnestness the assertion that we need to lay aside any of our devotedness to our Church, to be true Americans; the insinuation that we need to abate any of our love for our country's principles and institutions, to be faithful Catholics."

Because Hecker perceived this harmony so clearly, he was able to make Catholicism not only intelligible but also appealing to Unitarians, Methodists, and Democrats. "How impossible would it not have been," remarks Canon William Barry, "for an alien to enter into their thoughts, or to convince them that by submitting to Catholicism they were not yielding up their native-American privileges and falling back into the worn-out ideas of the Old World? But Isaac Hecker had traveled every step of the journey; from them he had sprung, and their principles had been his principles . . . He could say in the very neighborhood of Emerson, and on the same platform, that only in the Catholic teaching was there adequate justification of the principles on which he had ever acted."

Archbishop Ireland paid an impressive tribute to Hecker for his penetrating vision and insight on this matter. Hecker "looked on America," he said, "as the fairest conquest for divine truth, and he girded himself with arms shaped and tempered to the American pattern. I think that it may be said that the American current, so plain for the last quarter of a century in the flow of Catholic affairs, is, largely at least, to be traced back to Father Hecker and his early co-workers. It used to be said of them in reproach that they were the 'Yankee' Catholic Church; the reproach was their praise . . . His favorite topic in book and lecture was, that the constitution of the United States requires, as its necessary basis, the truths of Catholic teaching regarding man's natural state, as opposed to the errors of Luther and Calvin. The republic, he taught, presupposes the Church's doctrine, and the Church ought to love a polity which is the offspring of her own spirit."

Worthy, too, of recalling was Hecker's perception of the wisdom and necessity of pressing all the instruments of modern invention into the service of the Church, especially the presentation of her credentials to the American people. True to the vision of their founder, the Paulist Fathers are in the vanguard of those who entered on an extensive scale into the apostolate of the press. When radio became available, they founded and operated the first Catholic radio station in America. They have pioneered in the establishment of Catholic information centers, and they conduct a large percentage of those now in operation.

They have sparked the convert apostolate in America through such publications as the *Catholic World, The Missionary, The Epistle,*

Information, the pamphlets and books of the Paulist Press, the releases of The Paulist Feature Service, and *Techniques for Convert-Makers.* The latter is a six-page reprint of timely articles on new developments in the convert apostolate: it reaches each month thousands of priests and religious and renders their efforts at sharing their faith with their churchless friends and neighbors immensely more fruitful. It merits a place on the desk of every priest, religious, and seminarian in the English-speaking world.

Typical too of the vision and foresight of their founder is the action of the Paulists in entering on a large scale into the work of the Newman clubs at secular and tax-supported universities and normal schools. With more Catholics in attendance at such schools than in Catholic institutions of higher learning, such fields of ministry are among the most important in America: here cultured and holy priests come in intimate contact with a large proportion of the future leaders of thought and influence in our country. The good such priests do in correcting misconceptions of the Church and in showing the harmony of her teachings with the findings of modern science is incalculable.

We have sketched a few of the highlights of the work of the Paulists because they are the lengthened shadow of the zealous and farseeing personality of their founder. Such a picture helps us to perceive more clearly the impressive and lasting contributions which Isaac Hecker has made to the Church in America. Though probably not possessing the towering intellect of Brownson—and of the other giants sketched in this work—his achievements far outstrip those of his onetime master, both in extent and in permanence.

Any final judgment of Hecker's genius or any searching comparison between him and other intellectual giants is pointless here. That I leave to scholars and specialists. Whatever be their verdict, there can be no doubt about the uncanny brilliance of his intuitions, which take on the aspect of actual prescience. The supreme pontiff, archbishops, bishops, priests, and scholarly laymen paid tribute to his pioneering achievements in several fields: those who knew him most intimately acclaimed his purity of intention, self-effacing zeal and genuine holiness of life. He was primarily a seer and a sower, and like most such he died before the vision was realized and the harvest was gathered. Posterity, however, has witnessed the fulfillment of most of his dreams and the gathering of a harvest that grows ever larger with the passing years. Secure in his niche among the giants of the faith is the impressive and challenging figure of the truth seeker and the finder, the seer and the sower, the gifted genius and zealous apostle, Isaac Thomas Hecker.

SUGGESTIONS FOR FURTHER READING AND STUDY

I. SAINT PAUL. Of all the works on St. Paul the best by far are the Acts of the Apostles and the Epistles of St. Paul. The former presents much of his life, the latter much of his thought: both should be read with a commentary on Holy Scripture at your side. *A Commentary on the New Testament* by the Catholic Biblical Association of America (W. H. Sadlier, Inc., N.Y.), the *Acts of the Apostles* and the *Epistles of St. Paul,* both by C. J. Callan, O.P., are excellent. Other excellent books on St. Paul are: *Peter and Paul,* Isidore O'Brien, O.F.M.; *St. Paul,* F. Prat, S.J.; *St. Paul, Apostle and Martyr,* Igino Giordani; *Paul of Tarsus,* Msgr. Joseph Holzner.

II. SAINT AUGUSTINE. Begin by reading St. Augustine's *Confessions* and then the excellent selections, *Leaves from St. Augustine,* by Mary H. Allies. Other splendid books are: *St. Augustine,* Karl Adam; *St. Augustine,* G. Papini; *The Wisdom of St. Augustine,* Vernon Bourke.

III. JOHN HENRY NEWMAN. Start with Newman's *The Idea of a University* and his *Apologia pro Vita Sua.* Excellent works on Newman are: *The Life of John Henry Cardinal Newman,* Wilfred Ward; *The English Catholic Revival in the Nineteenth Century,* P. Thureau-Dangin; *Letters and Correspondence of John Henry Newman,* edited by Anne Mozely.

IV. GILBERT K. CHESTERTON. Begin with Chesterton's *St. Francis of Assisi,* then read his *Orthodoxy, The Everlasting Man, St. Thomas Aquinas, The Catholic Church and Conversion,* and *Autobiography.* Maisie Ward's biography, *Gilbert Keith Chesterton,* is a *must* for all who wish to have a thorough and detailed knowledge of his life and the development of his thought.

V. ORESTES A. BROWNSON. Begin with *The Brownson Reader,* selections from the best of Brownson, edited by A. S. Ryan. Then go on to *Orestes A. Brownson,* Arthur M. Schlesinger, Jr.; *Orestes Brownson,* Theodore Maynard; *Granite for God's House,* Doran Whalen; and the three-volume *Life of Orestes A. Brownson* by his son, H. F. Brownson.

VI. ISAAC T. HECKER. Start with Hecker's *The Church and the Age,* then read *Questions of the Soul* and *Aspirations of Nature.* Excellent works on Hecker are *The Early Years of Isaac Thomas Hecker,* Vincent F. Holden, C.S.P.; *Life of Father Hecker,* Walter Elliott, C.S.P.; *Father Hecker and His Friends,* Joseph McSorley, C.S.P.; and a new biography to be published soon by Vincent F. Holden, C.S.P., the last to be the definitive biography of Hecker.

Our gratitude is due to all the authors quoted in this volume and to scores of others who have treated one or other of these six characters. In writing this book we have drawn upon notebooks filled over the years with pencil jottings for classroom and lecture use. In a few places it was not easy to determine whether we had written the gist of a passage or quoted a few sentences verbatim. Every effort has been made to put the latter in quotation marks, but if any such have slipped in inadvertently, we shall see that the slip is corrected in the next printing.

GIANTS OF THE FAITH
by John A. O'Brien

Six outstanding figures in Catholic history — all of them converts — live anew in these absorbing pages. Every Catholic knows about these "Giants of the Faith" — but many wish they knew more. The problem all along has been that most of the books about these great men — and most of their own books as well — have been more for scholars than for the intelligent general reader. Father O'Brien now portrays in his popular style the lives, work and significance of . . .

ST. PAUL. "Apostle of the Gentiles," greatest missionary of all time, inspired author of 14 extraordinary Epistles.

ST. AUGUSTINE. Great penitent, author of *The Confessions of St. Augustine, The City of God* and more than 100 theological works; probably the most influential Christian thinker after St. Paul.

CARDINAL NEWMAN. Leading religious figure in 19th-century England; author of *Apologia Pro Vita Sua* and dozens of other memorable books; brilliant and genuinely original thinker whose influence endures and grows.

G. K. CHESTERTON. Most English Englishman since Dr. Johnson and probably the best loved; master of paradoxical wit; author of scores of books encyclopedic in range.

ORESTES BROWNSON • ISAAC HECKER. Together these men personify America's gigantic contribution to the Church. Brownson was an author, editor, and the